Critical Ac...
Sheila Kit...

'Wonderful Mrs Kitzinger, we owe you much'
The Times

'A woman of remarkable insight'
Leslie Kenton, *Harpers and Queen*

'Sheila Kitzinger has revolutionized childbirth'
Woman's Own

'Sheila Kitzinger is the Earth Mother, or Birth Mother, of the nation. If Britain is now one of the most progressive countries in obstetric practice, it is largely due to her'
Polly Toynbee, *Guardian*

'*Ourselves As Mothers* is the culmination of a lifetime's study of mothering across the world . . .'
Irish Times

'A startling new book'
Herald-Sun, Australia

'*Ourselves As Mothers* is an invaluable contribution to our knowledge of women and society. It is a book that reveals a deep awareness of women's shared experiences across the world'
Parent and Child

'There can be no doubt that her work has enabled women in this country to, at the very least, consider all the options and choices available to them during childbirth . . .'
Jan Moir, *Guardian*

'Sheila Kitzinger is the celebrated high priestess of female sexuality and childbirth'
Cosmopolitan

Also by Sheila Kitzinger

SHEILA KITZINGER

OURSELVES AS MOTHERS

BANTAM BOOKS
TORONTO • NEW YORK • LONDON • SYDNEY • AUCKLAND

OURSELVES AS MOTHERS:
The Universal Experience of Motherhood
A BANTAM BOOK 0 553 40549 7

Originally published in Great Britain by Doubleday,
a division of Transworld Publishers Ltd

PRINTING HISTORY
Doubleday edition published 1992
Bantam Books edition published 1993

Some material in this book previously published in
Women As Mothers published by Fontana 1978.

This book is set in Times

Bantam Books are published by Transworld Publishers Ltd,
61–63 Uxbridge Road, Ealing, London W5 5SA, in
Australia by Transworld Publishers (Australia) Pty Ltd,
15–25 Helles Avenue, Moorebank, NSW 2170, and in
New Zealand by Transworld Publishers (NZ) Ltd,
3 William Pickering Drive, Albany, Auckland.

Printed and bound in Great Britain by
Cox & Wyman Ltd., Reading, Berks.

*With thanks to my five daughters,
who have taught me to be a mother.*

Contents

Introduction

To be a mother is to take on one of the most emotionally and intellectually demanding, exasperating, strenuous, anxiety-arousing and deeply satisfying tasks that any human being can undertake. It is a task that shapes and changes you so that you see yourself, and other people see you, in a different way. It also entails commitment that, in one form or another, lasts for life. Yet it often happens by accident, and merely because everyone expects a woman to bear a child, without an awareness of the consequences of such an overwhelming transmutation. Sociologists and psychologists write about it as 'role change' and 'a significant life event' and psychotherapists discuss it in terms of 'maturation'. It is all these – and more.

When a woman gives birth to her first child it can seem as if there has been an elaborate conspiracy to prevent her realizing this, as if somehow society has cheated her by focusing on having a baby, rather than on her transformation into motherhood. The coming baby is often talked about as if it were merely a possession, a gift or prize, that will be hers and for whom she can plan, arrange a nursery, buy clothes and toys, indulge herself in acquiring objects to enhance and decorate this delightful little creature, which will in turn enhance and decorate her – rather than as a being who is going to take over her life and thoughts and feelings, and change them utterly.

She may go to classes in preparation for birth, read books and magazine articles, do exercises, breathe, relax and meditate, and get in trim for what she is often encouraged to see as a sort of assault course on birth. The challenge of the birth is dominant in her mind. How will she behave? What will 'they' do to her? Will she be able to cope with the pain? It seems like the last and greatest hurdle before she can settle down and enjoy her baby.

For many women birth is an ordeal that leaves them with lowered self-esteem and feeling emotionally and physically battered, just when they need the strength to take on the new challenge of motherhood. Yet even when birth is a satisfying experience, the reality of being a mother makes many women feel that they are completely unprepared. When the congratulation cards have stopped coming, the bouquets have died, and the knitted booties have felted up in the wash, they are left to get on with it, still staggering from the shock.

In these pages I share what I have learned as an anthropologist studying the comparative sociology of birth and motherhood, and explore what motherhood means to women in our own and other cultures. I am fascinated by all that is shared by mothers in different historical periods and social systems, and by how they manage, often in very difficult circumstances, to cope with the demands made on them. We can listen and learn from these women. Their lives have direct relevance to our own, and their voices often speak to us with greater clarity and deeper meaning than all the advice of experts.

In our technological society mothers are often socially isolated and left to get on with mothering as best they can. But we are not alone. There is a great sisterhood out there. This book is a celebration of the diversity, ingenuity, the energy and the courage of mothers.

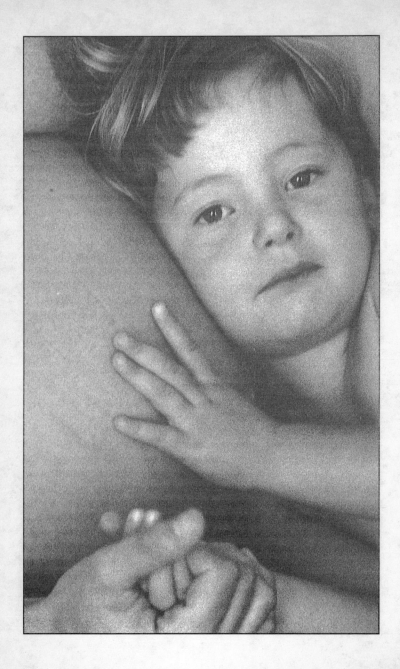

1

Is Anyone Out There Listening?

Birth is a biological process. Powerful physiological forces sweep a woman through the experience, and many things she does feel purely instinctive. Yet birth is also a social act. The way in which those helping her behave, their attitudes towards and beliefs about birth, and the mother's own expectations of what will happen and her ideas about what is taking place inside her body and what she should do – all these things are patterned by culture. Different societies and different historical periods reveal wide variations in the beliefs, values and behaviour surrounding birth.

It is the same with motherhood. Becoming a mother is a biological process; but it is also a social transformation, and one of the most dramatic and far-reaching that a woman may ever experience in her life. In most societies it is valued as a major transition in a woman's role and status, and with the first baby she crosses the bridge into womanhood. She is no longer a girl but a mature woman, and this is independent of her actual age.

In many cultures a woman changes the way she dresses or does her hair in a different way to show that she has obtained the status of motherhood. In most societies she can be identified immediately as a mother because of this different appearance, and she is treated with new respect. Even her name may change, and she becomes 'the mother of John', defined from now on in terms of her children. Her marriage, which until this time was considered provisional and tentative, is sealed by the

1

birth of the baby.

In Arab society, a woman is often called by the name of her first son – never a daughter, for a woman may not even be considered to have the status of mother until she has borne a son.[1] It is the birth of a boy, rather than the biological condition of having had a baby, that is the basis for her change of identity.

In traditional cultures, too, the birth of children, or more specifically of sons, heralds new social power for the woman. This is partly because sons represent an economic investment for the future, and are a source of security and support as their parents get older. It is the mother who nurtures, develops and controls this economic potential. There will be children who can plant, water, weed and harvest the crops, do household tasks, help with the care of younger children, and shepherd the goats and sheep. In Egypt, for example, not only does the birth of the first child cement the marriage, but children represent labour-power almost as soon as they can walk and speak and, 'although the ultimate control over woman's reproductive function and its products rests with men, the actualization of this culturally valued function, and the loyalty which a mother builds in her children are a woman's most significant and durable powerbase.'[2] A woman's power in the extended family peaks when her children marry and she becomes a mother-in-law.

This traditional sequence from bride to mother, mother of a son, to mother of many children, to mother of adult children and mother-in-law is no longer valid in contemporary industrial culture. Yet many older women yearn for it, and when their children fail to marry, or do not produce grandchildren, feel personally deprived, and even humiliated. It is as if they have been denied the final fruits of motherhood, the long-term investment, the justification for all their work and care. Their values are still those of a traditional society, in which female power and status are based on motherhood.

Being a mother is probably more difficult today than it has ever been. The traumas, hazards and challenges of motherhood in a technological culture are radically different from those faced by women in traditional and peasant societies; different, too, from those faced by women in our own historical past, for although these women led arduous lives, there was an unselfconsciousness, a freedom from self-questioning and an inevitability about motherhood that we no longer have in our technological culture.

2

Where children are not required to till the land or to care for their parents in old age, nor to replace others who have died in infancy from malnutrition or disease, fertility is devalued – and with it, motherhood. In industrialized society mothers are treated as an anachronism. But it is still frequently assumed that all women want children, still taken more or less for granted that the deepest fulfilment any woman can experience must be in bearing babies.

The image of motherhood that consists of women with teeming wombs, with babies in their arms and toddlers clinging to their skirts, has been discredited in a world alarmed by the economic and social effects of over-population, an industrial-technological society that has replaced a myriad of working hands with remote-control machinery and electronic wizardry. Yet mothers continue to exist, continue – if over a shorter time-span than previously known, and with conscious limits set on the size of the family – to have babies. They interrupt the smooth operation of businesses and powerful institutions. They are misfits in a culture that is directed to the production of goods and wealth, not people.

When a woman becomes a mother 'welcome to the baby' cards are sent and the new parents congratulated. Yet once the celebrations are over and the novelty has become commonplace, the fact that she has a child and responsibilities as a mother which alter her whole life and her perception of herself, is treated as incidental, or even as something to be ignored or forgotten.

Children are treated as a private indulgence. One consequence of this social attitude is that increasingly women approach birth and the initial tasks of motherhood in a business-like spirit, determined to do it well, but concerned to get back to the situation, in both their working and their private and social lives, that existed before the baby was born. Employers, colleagues, friends, even a partner, often expect this. It is 'returning to normal'.

At the same time there is enormous pressure on her to perform perfectly as a mother. So she reads books about every aspect of birth and child-rearing with the aim of producing and bringing up a secure, emotionally balanced, highly intelligent, creative, well-socialized human being, who can fully justify his or her existence in the world.

This is demanding a great deal of mothers, and because the children then become the object of sustained effort in order to produce exceptional talent and maturity, it can also be very hard on them.

In Western culture childbirth has been removed from the normal life process, the changes and crises that occur as a matter of course in the lives of most women in the world. Instead it is turned into a clinical condition, a pathological event, as if it were like an appendectomy or having an impacted wisdom tooth removed.

In traditional societies pregnancy, birth and breastfeeding are normal states in an adult woman's life. It is abnormal for a married woman prior to menopause to have a year in which she is not either pregnant or lactating. When she breastfeeds for two or three years and conceives within a few months of weaning her child, the intervals during which she is menstruating are short.

In the West, birth and lactation are perceived as abnormal physiological states, which have a negative effect on women's ability to function and which may cause mental unbalance. The charge against a mother who killed her baby reads that she caused the death of her child 'at a time when the balance of her mind was disturbed by reason of not having recovered from the effects of giving birth to a child, or from the effects of lactation'.[3]

Long before conception has taken place, a woman may start to seek the help of experts, not only for her own well-being and satisfaction with this major life experience, but so as to produce the perfect baby. She reads books and magazine articles about pregnancy, birth and babies, and tries to get information on subjects which in a pre-industrial society were handed down from mothers to daughters. She may decide to have 'pre-conceptual care', seek hair analysis to reveal whether or not her body harbours toxic chemicals, put herself and her partner on a special diet in order to produce a super-baby, cut out wine, pain-killers and other drugs that could be harmful, and try to purify her life.

The verbalization which Bernstein and the Newsons perceive as an important part of the middle-class woman's role in relation to her child, and as a primary instrument of child-rearing, is already taking place even before she gets pregnant.[4] She may express her goals about childbirth, the baby, and herself as a mother, and often contrasts these with her own mother's approach. In fact, she is often goal-oriented, and has

4

strong ideas about how pregnancy, birth and motherhood should be.

The Anti-Mother Culture

Western culture is anti-motherhood. It is not only that work-place nurseries are as rare as pearls in oysters, or that, in Britain, family allowances – money supplied by the State which a mother draws herself to help towards the cost of child-rearing – have been pared to the bone, or even that women seeking jobs have to hide the existence of their children like a guilty secret, or say with a nonchalance they rarely feel 'Oh, we have very reliable childcare.' Mothering (and fathering) has to be fitted into the cracks between all the important, solid stuff of social life, such as politics, economics, commerce and industry. Becoming and being a mother is a second-rate activity. When a pregnancy becomes visible, firms often move a woman employee to a back-room job away from public view, so that she cannot tarnish the cosmetic image of the company. This is in significant contrast to what happens in any peasant society. In my own anthropological field-work in Jamaica, for example, the friendliest public greeting that could be given a woman who might possibly be pregnant was: 'You be getting fat!'

Children are no longer needed by the family as its wealth, its unpaid employees, its insurance in old age, and as the outward and visible sign of its status in society. Children intrude on the organization of life in an industrial culture. They cause irritation, disturbance and breakdown in its normal smooth working. Paid work takes place for the most part outside the home, in offices, shops, factories and other large institutions, the functioning of which is disrupted by the presence of children. Children must be cared for, more or less invisibly, in their homes. Today these homes consist of small domestic units, each within the four walls of an apartment or house in which a woman, often isolated from almost all other human contact, struggles on her own to serve the needs of an intermittently visiting male, the father, and of one or more small children under the age of four. She shops, cooks, cleans, clears away, plans and organizes, launders, disposes of waste and rubbish, and manages on behalf of this small group of people who are utterly dependent on her for their survival.

The home is supposed to be a haven of love and good

feelings, and thus it comes as a great disappointment to many women that it proves not to be so for them, for it is a place where the ugliest and most destructive emotions are experienced, where there is disturbing inter-personal conflict, and inside its four walls these raw feelings are concentrated and mixed together as if in a pressure cooker.

A woman wants to be a good mother, and aims at giving herself to her children selflessly, providing them with concentrated attention, generous care, a lively mind quick to offer stimulus of an appropriate kind, perfectly balanced and delicious meals, unlimited time, and love – just as all the magazines and books say. But the constructive play turns into a litter of cardboard boxes all over the kitchen, tacky flour-and-water paste in the coconut matting, and finger-paints on the curtains. The carefully prepared food is rejected with noises of disgust from the older child and is simply expelled from the baby's mouth in a great glob of goo. By late afternoon she still has not finished the jobs she planned on getting out of the way in the morning, there is nothing to eat for the evening meal and the baby has nappy rash because she has not had time to change him often enough. She pushes the protesting children into a buggy and wheels them to the supermarket, where the older one helps by stocking up the basket with all the things she does not want to buy, while the younger one sweeps tins from their shelves. In the end she slaps the baby's hand and gets a long, cool look from an older woman who clearly thinks she is a baby batterer. She hates what she has become and scuttles back home, with both children whining. She gets more food into them and propels them to the bath, where they play happily and look cherubic and adorable. She relaxes for a moment, only to realize that the new game is squeezing the sponge over the edge of the bath and that streams of water are running under the vinyl. She bends to mop it up with the bath towel. She hears a sound at the front door, sweeps back her hair from her face, and in comes her partner saying cheerfully, 'Had a good day, darling?' or worse, 'I'm ravenous. What's for supper?' or worse still, 'I've got a bit of a headache. It's been a rotten day at the office.'

For many women, of course, the scenario is different. They have jobs outside the home, and rather than being trapped in it must perform a juggling act between their paid work and work within the home. They constantly switch their concentration to

6

wherever they judge it is most urgently needed, and struggle to arrange for child care in their absence, and to compensate for this by offering 'quality time' when they are able to be with their children. With nine out of ten British couples, the mother shoulders most of the responsibility for child care and for running the home, even when she has a full-time job.[5]

In this context, in contrast to traditional cultures, when a woman turns into a mother she is treated suddenly as *less*, not more. She tends to be perceived by men, and by other women who are not themselves mothers, as having fewer skills, and reduced competence, intellectual capacity and commitment to the things that matter. Her identity has become that of 'a mother', and it is as if the rest of her – her working skills, her career goals, and all her other interests – have vanished. For many men, women who can be identified as mothers are not part of the 'real' world, only of the restricted world of home. Happy as a woman may be to have a baby, and although she may really enjoy being a mother, she must now pay the price of motherhood: the virtual annihilation of self.

Uncomfortably aware that motherhood is different from how she had expected it to be, a woman may try to follow the advice in magazines and books. The media bombards her with information about how to have a healthy life-style and care for herself, how to look good, have a sharp mind so that she can slot back into the work-place efficiently, be assertive, keep the romance in her relationship with her man, cook gourmet food and produce candle-lit dinners, and at the same time be a perfect mother. The models presented for all this tend to be sexy popstars, dazzling actresses and willowy royals, who are displayed as being mothers who have retained their glamour, snapped back into shape after childbirth, and who combine the two worlds of domestic bliss and public acts without any sign of tension existing between these two roles. These portrayals of model motherhood are interspersed with advice about what to do about a painful episiotomy scar and stress incontinence, how to give night-time feeds with least sleep loss, dealing with postnatal depression, sore nipples, sexual problems and a crying baby, and how to tackle potty-training and weaning without trauma. Anyone who writes articles for these magazines knows the format: whatever the subject, and however grim the information presented, every piece must end positively, for every mother desperately needs a message of hope.

7

But the image of motherhood that is presented is a false one. A woman who catches sight of herself in the mirror sees a very different picture. And the message is clear: she is a failure.

The Experts

Mothering is under critical scrutiny as it has never been before. Open any newspaper and you see that mothers are scapegoats for a wide variety of social ills and developmental difficulties, from juvenile delinquency, obesity, anorexia, personality problems, autism, hyperactivity, and dyslexia and other learning difficulties, through to schizophrenia, teenage promiscuity, adult sexual dysfunction and marital failure, drug addiction and violent crime. It sometimes seems that if mothers weren't inadequate none of these problems would exist.

In a world of experts in which training for occupations is getting more complicated and prolonged, and in which new specializations pop up like mushrooms almost overnight, motherhood stands out as glaringly unspecialized and unprofessional. Mothers are not trained to do their job, and that (it is implied) is why they fail. Train them and society will be improved.

In Sweden there is a nationwide system of education for parenthood, and one Swedish expert has even suggested that a woman should not be *allowed* to bear a child until she has attended the course. Such is our pathetic faith in training. Only give people information and teach them skills and they will be better parents and produce a better quality product.

There are two flaws in this argument, however. There is no evidence whatsoever to suggest that simply acquiring information about the tasks that mothers usually perform actually makes a woman a better mother. On the contrary, intellectualizing about parenthood may make it all rather more difficult. The things that mothers really find themselves doing are not matters only of technique, but are an expression of the sort of people that they are and the relationship that they have with that particular child, and since mothers are usually required to act on the spur of the moment, there is not time to go and consult the books and see what you ought to be doing. Kissing hurt places better, watching a three-year-old dress in agonizingly slow motion, or deciding how to act when the eighteen-month-old wants nothing of the carefully planned protein- and vitamin-rich menu, leaving

8

you scraping watercress soup, liver, yoghurt and honey off the floor, can invoke very powerful feelings. These emotions are valid. Without them, motherhood would be a very frightening thing, and if a woman has the positive ones – triumph, joy, ecstasy and intense love – it is certain that she will also experience the negative ones – fear, anger and depression.

Reading about goals to be attained and techniques used risks superimposing on motherhood a set of gimmicks, and results in a strange dissatisfaction, and even resentment.

Although the study of interaction between parents and children is fascinating, it is not necessary to have read books about it to be an adequate parent. What is important is that experts inform rather than advise us, and allow us to make our own choices. Often experts are unaware of their own biases and, honestly believing that they are being 'objective' and 'scientific', are convinced that they know the answers, and want to impose a style of mothering that is of its essence culture-bound, ephemeral, and that reflects preoccupations that are linked to changing fashions in child-rearing. Mothers may be told that they must never be away from their small children lest they suffer irreparable damage and are left unable to form good relationships; or they are told that they should work outside the home, and that any woman who does not do so will not be interesting and lively enough to be a good mother.

When breastfeeding is seen as the essence of mothering, women are told that the baby who is not breastfed is deprived, and that they must have something wrong with them if they do not want to breastfeed; and when 'gentle birth' is the fashion, they may be warned that to welcome a newborn baby with shouts of joy is to subject the child to a traumatic barrage of noise, or that to cut the umbilical cord before it has stopped pulsating produces a terrible shock to the baby's system which will have an effect long after it has become an adult. Since fashions are constantly changing, there are a great many women who worry that they have inflicted irreversible harm on their babies, and who feel guilty because of things they did during pregnancy, at birth or in the first weeks or months of the baby's life.

Another reason why parents should be wary about the advice given in books on how to prevent children's emotional deprivation, how to ensure that you meet their psychological needs, or how to raise a more intelligent child superior to all the other mismanaged children of unenlightened families, is that experts focus on relatively restricted areas of behaviour. Perhaps fortunately, no single expert is able to pronounce on the hazards and skills, the whole thrilling adventure, of bringing up children, or on the complex relationships that exist within families.

In fact, we do not yet know enough even to be able to say with certainty that certain types of families are bound to produce certain types of children. We certainly cannot assume that bowel and bladder training, for example, or swaddling, or being free to explore in infancy, or carrying an infant around tucked against the mother's body all the time, or sleeping in the mother's bed, serve as blueprints for later adult personality or shape the child's whole future life, although many claims have been made to this effect.

This is partly because it is not just a matter of a mother performing an action, such as breastfeeding a baby, but of how she *feels* about what she does – and whether or not she behaves in an easy, spontaneous, and above all self-assured way may be a good deal more important than the system of child-rearing she adopts.

Even though mothers are targets for advice, and although it sometimes seems as if everyone else must know how to care for a baby better than the mother herself, most mothers in Western society are frighteningly alone.

Social Isolation and Emotional Upheaval

Once the first few weeks of emotional support and assistance after the birth of the baby are over, a woman is left coping with a child more or less unsupported, and holds complete responsibility for this other human being's welfare and development at a time when she has little confidence in herself. Although she may have a partner who often helps when at home, and enjoys bathing or playing with the baby for limited periods, it is invariably she who has the ultimate responsibility. She often finds herself living in an unfamiliar community to which they moved shortly before or after the birth, with nobody to reassure her that she is doing the right thing, that her baby is normal, or that her ambivalent feelings about the baby are those which other mothers share. Socially isolated and immobilized, she is tied to the home in a way in which she has never been before. Many new mothers are deprived of adult company for six to eight hours a day, and unless a woman has the energy, initiative and confidence to go out and seek social contacts, she may be occupied with the tasks of cleaning, washing, bathing and feeding for more than ten hours in the twenty-four.[6] Feeding often takes five hours, and sometimes much longer. Although some babies finish a feed in half an hour, they need at least six of these feeds in the twenty-four, and a good many take twice as long, and many feed every two hours or so for half an hour or more at a time. As a result, the woman's sense of time is affected and, especially if her baby is restless and 'colicky', days and nights unroll in a seemingly endless ribbon of service to the baby, with no respite and no breathing space in which she feels she can catch up.

When she becomes a mother, it is as if a woman must go deep into the bowels of the earth, back to the elemental emotions and the power which makes life possible, losing herself in the darkness. She is like Eurydice in the Underworld. She is pulled away from a world of choices, plans and schedules, where time is kept, spaces cleared, commitments made, and goals attained, to the warm chaos of love, confusion, longing, anger, self-surrender and intense pleasure that mothering entails.

Many magazines and books make passing reference to this. They talk about the disruption of life 'in the first weeks after birth'. Yet for more women than like to admit it this heady confusion, this emotional roller-coaster, the period described by the psychotherapist Donald Winnicott as one of 'primary maternal preoccupation' – the condition that he said was normal in the first six to eight weeks – continues through the first year of a child's life, and sometimes beyond.[7] Women try to hide this fact because they are told that they should slot motherhood invisibly into their lives, and they are ashamed to acknowledge that they have not.

When she is at school, and later when she has a job, a young woman learns to be 'task-oriented, to measure accomplishments in terms of a finished product and to organize it in blocks of time within a specialized division of labour'.[8] But looking after babies and children is not work of this kind. There is no one right way of doing it, and it involves very deep and often disturbing emotions.

Moreover, as a child grows, different qualities are required from the mother, and this means that she can never perfect

11

her techniques, but must be flexible and capable of adapting to a constantly changing situation. In our isolated families the mother is the person who introduces the world to the child, and communicates the cultural heritage, but she is herself often sealed off from participating in the world outside the home, except through television, and in sharing in and creating the culture. As her child grows out of babyhood, one of her primary roles is to be an agent of acculturation. This is one reason why a woman who feels she copes well with a new baby may find herself unable to handle a toddler, why one who enjoys the activity and constant questions of a toddler may have felt terribly inadequate when the same child was still a baby, and why many mothers feel themselves quite unable to handle the problems of adolescence with understanding and remain on an emotionally even keel themselves.

Before their first baby is born many women in Western culture have had the freedom of being able to fill multi-dimensional roles in a range of social settings, experimenting and playing with how they feel in each one. Their jobs, leisure occupations and social contacts all provide opportunities for making choices about what to do, where to go, how to be. But still today with the birth of a baby a woman suddenly finds she is fixed in one role, that of a mother, and there is little choice left to her because of the baby's unremitting demands. This brings for many women a crisis which is similar to that of retirement for men.

The tasks which caring for a baby involve are repetitive. Eyes may get 'sticky', the nose gets 'snuffly', the scalp has 'cradlecap' which has to be treated with ointments, regurgitated milk dribbles down the baby's clean clothing and spurts onto the mother's T-shirt. Nappies must either be scraped of faeces, soaked, washed, rinsed thoroughly, dried, aired and folded, disposed of down the lavatory where they may block the drains, or put in overflowing bins. A woman feels that she is on a treadmill.

Anyone who has ever dragged a stroller over kerbs, up and down steps and in and out of public transport, or breastfed a screaming baby in smelly lavatories or surreptitiously on a park bench or in a public library, will be only too aware that our society is not geared to mothers and children. Women are put through an ordeal, an endurance test of bearing and rearing children.

Guests are expected, and the woman looks at her home, which she and her partner are still furnishing and decorating

12

together, and is appalled at the chaos that she sees. She has had no time to clean up and there are piles of dishes in the sink, a stain on the new carpet, all the bedding smells of milk, the oven is saturated with grease, she forgot to put the bins out to be emptied so there is a pile of rotting refuse by the back door, and thick layers of dust sit over the furniture. She starts to cry and is told that this must be because of her 'unbalanced endocrine system'.

There is little social recognition of all that is actually involved in the fatiguing task of being a new mother, and women are usually forced to explain their post-partum experience entirely in terms of internal psychological states, their hormones, their psyches, and their own inadequate personalities, instead of acknowledging the realities of the situation as they adjust to the enormous occupational and emotional tasks of motherhood.

One in every six women receives psychiatric treatment for emotional disturbance at some time in her life. The high degree of neurosis and sub-clinical depression experienced by women who never even make it to the doctor also points to something about the role of women in modern society which produces emotional dissonance for many, and complete breakdown for some.

The sociologist Ann Oakley estimates that four out of five women go through a miserable period of reactive depression, often dismissed as merely 'the blues', after childbirth; in addition to this, three-quarters are overwhelmed with anxiety when they first take on responsibility for the baby, two-thirds admit to ambivalent feelings about their babies, and a quarter are severely depressed.[9]

The social causes of depression after childbirth are often ignored, perhaps because we feel that there is very little we can do about them: poverty, poor housing, overcrowding, unemployment – all the things that make life especially miserable for mothers at the bottom of the social scale. Yet even for women who are comfortably off depression runs like a thread through the experience of motherhood, often as counterpoint to, and in strange partnership with, the joy that a child brings.

One problem is that industrial culture makes no provision for the passionate closeness that can exist between a mother and her child. It is a passion far removed from the delicacy of lavender water and lace and the image of the mother in a frilled négligé in the lamplight while her baby sleeps contentedly. It is

a fierce tenderness, and with it there are all the most intense emotions that we can ever feel about another human being.

This is the power of the bond that enables babies to be nurtured and children to be reared by mothers in a society that is basically hostile to mothers and children. It is this bond, and the sensitivity to and sharp observation of human behaviour that it engenders, that brings to women the energy and flexibility in changing circumstances, and helps them develop management skills that are also of value in the world of work outside the home. For any woman still struggling through the survival course of life with a baby it may not seem like it, but motherhood is a superb education.

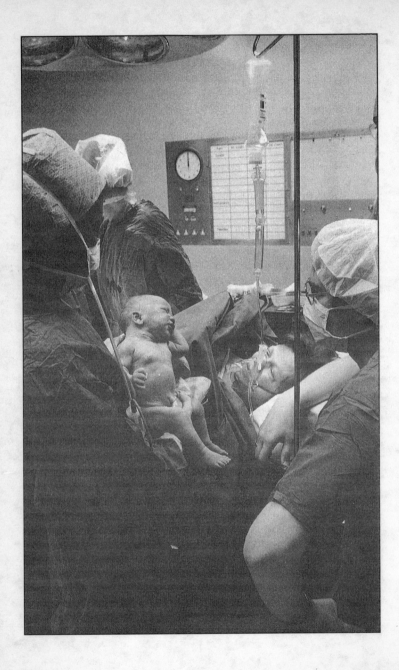

2

Mothers Cut To Shape

Every society regulates the right to motherhood and 'selects' those women who are allowed to become mothers. In most of them, the rule is that a woman has to first belong to a man. This union must be socially approved, and she is handed over by her father to a husband. A Kgatla girl who becomes pregnant before marriage is ostracized, and neighbours may gather outside her house and sing obscene songs. In the past the baby was probably killed at birth. The Xhosa of the South African Transkei do not approve of pre-marital pregnancy, and once a girl is pregnant outside marriage she knows she has no hope of marrying. Even in those cultures which permit the free expression of sex among adolescent boys and girls, as in some East African pastoral tribes, the right to bear a child is strictly controlled, and transgression of the rules may result in severe punishment: the baby and the mother, and sometimes both parents, perhaps being put to death.

The dances and rituals of traditional societies that illustrate the drama of the relationship between the sexes, and which sometimes include representations of sexual intercourse, are not primarily an expression of the power of sex, but of fertility. In these cultures girls learn from an early age that pregnancy is fruition. A Sanskrit poem describes a woman's loveliness as enhanced in pregnancy:

> *The romavali's thick stem supports a pair of*
> *lotuses, her close-set breasts, on which sit*

17

> *bees, the darkening nipples. These*
> *flowers tell of treasures hidden in my darling's belly.*[1]

The songs that are chanted, the drums beating in rhythm, the rocking pelvises and undulating bodies, proclaim birth and renewal, of the crops that grow, the fish, the herds of cattle, and of the wild animals brought in from the hunt, no less than of human babies.

Bonds are Forged by Birth

In many societies, as we have seen, it is when a baby is on the way that the couple's relationship, formerly only half-recognized and provisional, becomes established and really a marriage. The Kgatla of South Africa have a system whereby parents change their names with the birth of the first child, and acquire a new dignity and status. They become known by the child's name, with the prefix *rra* – father, or *mma* – mother.[2] Divorce is often very easy before the first child is born, but once a woman is pregnant it becomes difficult, and involves long drawn-out and bitter disputes between the families.

Among the Mbuti pygmies of Zaïre, after her first menstruation a girl lives temporarily with her future husband in a band consisting of other members of her age-group, in a special *elima* house, where couples are expected to join in enthusiastic lovemaking and sexual experimentation as a preparation for marriage. The girls are able to invite in any boys they fancy, and summon them by whipping them with saplings. What starts as a series of wide-ranging flirtations finishes after a period of one or two months as a serious search for a suitable husband.

When the *elima* festival is over, a boy who has become betrothed goes to the girl's parents for permission to marry her. He sets the seal on the betrothal by proving himself a good hunter, kills an antelope, and offers it to the girl's parents along with other gifts such as a bow and arrows, a machete, or a piece of bark cloth. It is at this stage in the unfolding of the marriage that either the girl goes to live with him or he goes to live in her band. She builds a hut for them and they live in it without further ceremony. But when she becomes pregnant the marriage itself comes into existence. The union is afforded social recognition, and although separation would have been simple and

18

straightforward prior to pregnancy, it is rare once the couple is expecting a baby. Pregnancy provides evidence that the marriage is 'working'.

Although attitudes to conception before marriage vary throughout the world – in some societies pregnancy being welcomed as evidence of fertility, and in others condemned – the important thing everywhere is that the coming child is accepted by a man as his, whether or not he is the biological father.

Many societies have means of giving a child conceived outside marriage a place in the structure, although one who is conceived before the mother has passed through initiation ceremonies and become a recognized adult may be a matter of great shame and disgust.

The most striking example of this is provided by the Kipsigis of Kenya, who believe that bearing a child before a girl has been blessed as a potential mother is the unpardonable sin against the spirits, and contaminates the whole of the community. Such a baby must be born in the bush, where its pollution can harm no one, and be immediately suffocated. It is then thought of as never having lived. The girl goes through a process of ritual purification and, once clean, can later become a mother without further shame. The Christian missions tried to end this infanticide, and adopted the babies. But their mothers, utterly disgraced, then became social outcasts and were never able to marry.

Among the same people it is considered all right for an unmarried girl to become pregnant provided she has been initiated, and this is accepted as happy evidence of fertility by the man who hopes to marry her. He immediately makes the child his own by paying bride-wealth – that is, he makes a gift of cows to the woman's family, and often to certain other of her relatives as well, in exchange for her fertility. He has claimed his rights as a father.

During pregnancy the identity of the father is further emphasized, and publicly proclaimed by ritual. The way he behaves can affect the outcome of the pregnancy. If he commits adultery, for example, the child will get ill. The relationship of a mother to her child is immediately obvious for biological reasons. But that of the father is altogether more vague, so societies everywhere have ways of marking and identifying the father. Many otherwise

19

incomprehensible practices have meaning when seen in this light.

Once pregnancy is confirmed, two social groups, that of the mother and the father, become more firmly linked. It is because these new links are being forged that during pregnancy the expectant mother's mother-in-law really comes into her own, and in most societies with a patrilineal descent system she is the person whose duty it is to give advice, see that the young woman is looking after herself, and make preparations for the coming baby in a culturally appropriate way. In a traditional society she usually tells the pregnant woman about customs designed to ensure a safe path through pregnancy and childbirth. Older women among the Arapesh of New Guinea, for example, tell her to be careful not to eat the bandicoot or she may die in difficult labour, nor frogs, or the labour will be too quick, nor eels, lest the baby be premature. They also remind her not to cut anything in half if she hopes for a boy.

In Guatemala a mother-in-law may warn a pregnant woman that if she spends too long at the lake enjoying herself bathing, gossiping and combing her long black hair, the Lake Goddess will rise up from its depths, and will make her mouth swell up and her teeth fall out.[3] The mother-in-law controls and conducts the pregnancy, and the expectant mother herself is not even supposed to know she is pregnant. The mother-in-law arranges for the midwife to call regularly to 'cure her sickness' and make her periods return, and this fiction is maintained by all. Moreover, if the pregnant woman does not obey her mother-in-law and fulfil her obligations as a good wife and daughter she puts the foetus in peril, and the baby may die. The mother-in-law warns the girl to listen to the midwife, and together they strive to keep her from feeling any violent emotions, and to satisfy any craving she may have. She must not go out of the house when the sun is high, or look at the full moon or the moon in eclipse, or point at the rainbow, or her baby will be malformed; nor must she get caught in a thunderstorm, lest her child have clubfeet.

When a mother-in-law's role is to instruct and guide the pregnant woman in this way she is not merely handing down family and local traditions. Her function is wider and far more significant. She is orchestrating a process of birthing that ensures social continuity for her husband's and son's family. She acts as the ritual agent between past, present and future.

In Western culture we do not acknowledge our need for

plants to sprout, trees to give fruit, animals to bear young, because most of us are so far removed from the soil and farm-yard that we expect these things to happen automatically. The fertility rite incorporated into the drama of the Christian church at the harvest festival has little relevance for most of us. Our food comes prepacked and often precooked, with a guarantee that it is identical to every other package of that kind produced by that particular manufacturer. And as for human fertility, that has become an inconvenience. Childbirth has become a clinical and potentially pathological condition which must take place in a hospital, rather than in the marriage bed over which the rice bestowing fertility on the couple was traditionally strewn on the wedding night.

It is sex rather than motherhood which launches a girl into womanhood. Peasant societies all over the world, on the other hand, stress the first pregnancy and birth as the occasion of attaining adult status. Perhaps in some ways we have lost the balance, as if sexual arousal and fulfilment were the key to being 'grown up', rather than the rights and responsibilities of bringing new life into the world, or for those who do not choose fertility, the ability to accept responsibility for the lives of others.

We tend to think of our own industrialized, urban society as circumscribed by forces outside our personal control, and often idealize simpler societies as allowing greater personal freedom, a more 'natural' way of life, and the spontaneous expression of feeling. Yet there are many areas of human interaction in which the rules and regulations of traditional societies are so pervasive that people do not even notice they are there. Behaviour which breaks the rule is unthinkable.

The nuclear family of a woman, her male partner and their children is found in every society known to us, and this is the form that we tend to think of as 'normal'. To understand the context for this we shall have to look at some of the different forms which marriage takes. 'Polygyny' means that two or more women share one husband. Polygynous marriage used to be practised by the Mormons, and is still the ideal over large parts of Africa. In 'sororal' polygyny the women are sisters, and this is the type that existed among the Hebrews; Jacob worked for seven years to pay the bride price for Rachel, but had to marry Leah, her elder sister, first, and only after that was he allowed to work another seven years before he could marry Rachel.

21

In a polygynous family the women have separate households around a mud-clearing or courtyard, each one cooking meals for her children, with the man sleeping with one woman after another in strict rotation, and the children all playing together in the clearing, but going back at night to sleep in their mother's hut.

'Polyandry', where a woman has more than one husband, is rare, and usually only occurs where people are living close to starvation level. The Marquesan Islanders are polyandrous, and the Todas of Southern India practise fraternal polyandry, with the women marrying brothers. Fraternal polyandry has the advantage that brothers retain the land handed down to them by their father, and pass it down intact to the next generation. But it is difficult to discover who is a baby's father. The Todas solve this problem by having a ceremony in which one of the brothers gives a miniature bow and arrow to his wife during her pregnancy, so claiming fatherhood. In subsequent pregnancies this can be done by one of the other brothers if he decides that he, too, would like to be a father.

When a couple set up home together they can go and live with his parents or hers, or can start a separate home of their own. What is normal for us, making a separate home, is in fact the rarest system; most people live in extended families. That is, they live in a household with their grandparents and parents, and perhaps others as well. Usually the woman goes to her husband's family. This is the pattern in most polygynous societies, and the woman's interests are subordinated to those of the group which she joins as a newcomer, her 'in-laws'. In other societies it is the man who moves into his wife's parents' home, and then he is the outsider who must work for the welfare of the group he has joined, and his authority is limited by the rival authority of his wife's brothers. He never quite 'belongs', and the Dobuans of Melanesia actually call him the 'boundary man'. Going to live with the woman's family tends to occur in matrilineal agricultural economies, where land is owned by women.

In some societies the couple can choose whether to set up home with the husband's or the wife's family. When couples have a choice the society may either be a developed one in which men and women have equal property rights, or, at the other end of the scale, be a simple wandering band of gatherers. In those societies where couples make their own separate home, the pattern is usually one of monogamous marriage, with emphasis on the importance of an individual finding his own way of life and achieving personal success.

The extended family system is one in which it is easier to maintain and hand down tradition than in the type of marriage that produces short-lived households which disintegrate when parents die. Years before that point is reached for many families the household consists of only two people, the father and mother whose children have left home. Extended families, on the other hand, have a kind of immortality.[4]

Nuclear families are usually linked by only one member who is common to both, the person who moves from his or her family of 'orientation' (the one they grew up in) to a new family of 'procreation'. The Western family system is like a long chain of beads, instead of the intricate system of sometimes incredibly geometric patterns which is characteristic of what are often called 'simpler' societies.

Child-rearing practices stem to a large extent from the size of the family. When it is as small and isolated as the modern middle-class family, the child becomes very dependent on its parents. There are no other adults to share responsibility and care. In an extended family, where there are aunts and uncles, cousins, grandparents and others to turn to, the parents' power over their children is modified and checked by the opinions of others. In the modern family, however, the father is usually absent from the house because of his job, so the mother has complete responsibility, and is supposed to control and bring up the child and represent the world to it.

The white middle-class urban family is especially isolated from any other kin, whereas in extended families, blood-ties between parents and children and between brothers and sisters are emphasized. Our own society underplays all this, and emphasizes instead links between people with whom we are in daily contact. In the West we usually have no names for people who in most societies would be considered relatives in one way or another, what anthropologists call 'classificatory kinship terminology'. Although we have aunts and uncles, we do not, for example, have a word for 'my mother's maternal aunt's paternal nephew', whereas in many other societies everybody knows exactly who this is, and there is a special name for him.

23

Some societies put special emphasis on the mother-child bond. They are mother-focused in the sense that the mother has functions central to the kinship system; there is relative equality between the sexes, and women are important economically and ritually. The role taken by many black women in the United States, especially in the deep South, as mothers and wage-earners, if necessary without the support of a male, is often assumed to be the product of a breakdown in the system.[5] Black single mothers rear their children with the help of grandmothers and other female relatives. Yet this is to some degree characteristic of all West African societies. The Ibo of Eastern Nigeria have, for example, a patrilineal system, but the smallest social unit consists not of a man, a woman and their children, but of a woman and her children, which has been described as 'an eating unit'.[6] There is a male head of the polygynous household, but the day-to-day running of the home operates almost independently of him, and women rely on each other for help.

Legitimacy implies the possibility of illegitimacy, and unmarried mothers are at a disadvantage in most societies. Even in those rural communities where illegitimate children are absorbed with little fuss into their mother's parents' families – extra mouths to feed, but later also extra hands in the fields – the bearing of children before marriage is considered unfortunate unless it serves to precipitate the marriage ceremony, offering the bridegroom proof of fertility. Historically, in some societies – farming communities in Scandinavia, for example – evidence of fertility was thought essential before a man married a woman. The Banaro of New Guinea only allow sexual intercourse between husband and wife after she has had a child by a man selected for insemination.[7]

In many parts of the world, including the black ghettos of the United States, black townships in South Africa, and in the West Indies and Latin America, girls bargain for a man with their fertility, and use sex in what is sometimes called 'consensual courtship', either risking the birth of a child, or actually bearing children 'for' a man, in a short-term, often highly unstable relationship, whether or not it involves legal marriage. In these societies birth outside marriage is considered normal, though usually, at least in economic terms, regrettable. More than half of all Americans living below the poverty line are single mothers and their children. Only one third of white

24

single mothers obtain child support payments from the fathers, and the proportion is lower still for black mothers.

In England and Wales, illegitimacy dropped steadily from a peak in the mid-nineteenth century until the 1930s, and then began to climb again. In the USA today the rate is more than 25 per cent, in Britain 21 per cent, and in Sweden 48 per cent. In modern industrialized societies there is much more illegitimacy at the lower end of the socio-economic scale, and children are more likely to be born within eight months of the wedding. People working on the land also have more conceptions outside marriage than do workers in big cities. On the other hand, in Europe there is a general trend for the lines between cohabitation and marriage to be blurred, in contrast to the USA, where single motherhood is more closely associated with poverty and with being black or Hispanic.

Women can have babies over a longer span of their lives today than they could a hundred years ago. Girls start menstruating earlier and the menopause comes later. Their health is better on the whole and they live in better social conditions. But fertility has, in fact, declined. In the United States, for instance, the span of childbearing is now half as long as it was two generations ago. This decline in fertility has implications for the relationship between a couple and between parents and children, and for a woman's image of herself. When she has finished childbearing there is a long period of life in which a woman's maternal role becomes gradually less time-consuming and is no longer central to her view of herself. If we are to respond to this radically changed family development cycle we have to create a new picture of motherhood. It is not just a question of mothering skills being different from those of our mothers and grandmothers, but of motherhood having to adapt itself within a dramatically changed social context. And that means that not only motherhood must change, but fatherhood too.

One problem is that because motherhood is occupying less of a woman's life, the skills which come with experience may never be learned. The problem of the oldest child in a family is well known. This is the child with the feeding and the sleeping and the potty-training problems. This is the one whom parents practise on, and also the one they often become anxious about. When the second baby comes along they are much more relaxed, and confident in themselves as parents.

In small families, children do not get the opportunity to learn parenting skills in caring for younger brothers and sisters, and so start out on parenthood themselves without any idea as to what it is all about. In childbirth classes expectant mothers often say that they have never held a baby in their arms, never even seen a newborn infant, nor had the opportunity of watching a mother look after a small baby. No amount of lessons in child care or practising with a rubber doll in a bathtub in the few weeks before a baby is born can ever make up for this deprivation.

To a large extent, especially before the advent of effective contraceptive techniques and human milk substitutes, woman's biological endowment defined her social roles. Her physiological state, in particular menstruation and the moon rhythm of her life, and childbearing, governed her existence, and her day-to-day activities were plotted according to the things she might or might not do when she had her period, or was pregnant or lactating. The jobs she could do, the illnesses from which she suffered (some mental illnesses, for example, are still explained entirely in terms of a woman's possessing or having lost her uterus, or her passage through the menopause), the manner in which she could worship, the books she could read, the way in which she walked and sat, her speech and forms of language, the games she could play, and the way in which she was educated, were all dictated by what was considered inalienably associated with being female.

Traditionally, woman's most important role has been that of passing on culture through mothering. She not only bears children but is largely responsible for their care while they are babies, and sometimes for much longer. She is the first and most important channel through which the culture is communicated to her baby. She introduces the world to her children and teaches them the basic differences in sex roles, and often does all this quite unconsciously. She begins the socialization of the small child, and in most cultures continues it with the help of a network of mothers and grandmothers.

Mothers tend to identify with their own mothers. They also tend spontaneously to recreate patterns of child care which they may consciously reject, finding themselves, nevertheless, doing things in much the same way as their own mothers did them. Helene Deutsch said, 'In relation to her own child, each woman repeats her own mother-child history'.[8] In a traditional society young mothers are aware that they are sharing in a flow of mothering behaviour similar to that of their own mothers. In my own field work in Jamaica I asked adolescent girls and women having their first babies if they wanted to be 'the same kind of mother' as their own mothers were. Everyone wished to be 'the same' except that some of the schoolgirls said they wanted to 'have a job before getting a baby'. In contrast, Jamaican women who had emigrated to the UK and were having babies in this country wanted to do things differently. They were deliberately adopting patterns of child care which they felt were superior to those of their own childhood, and contrasted 'the old-time way' with techniques they had learned at the clinic or at home economics classes in school.[9]

In our own society we often try to mother in a different way from our own mothers, but still find ourselves behaving as they did. A woman not only acts like her own mother, but may in many ways feel like her too. Perhaps that is why she is sometimes able to appreciate and begin to understand her for the first time. When the first child is born, and after the difficult transition period of learning to be a mother, there is often a reconciliation between mothers and daughters who have previously been locked in conflict with one another.

Women often find it easier to identify with girl babies, but boys are given more general social approval. In many cultures mothers stress the sexual difference between themselves and their sons, and between boys and girls in the family. In the West they comment on the boy's strength, boisterousness, aggression and naughtiness. This is what it is to be a real boy! In peasant societies the size of a baby boy's genitals may be admired, and mothers play with them. In Southern India the Havik Brahmins are much more lenient in their treatment of girls because mothers say that girls have to leave their homes when they marry, so they specially cherish their daughters because they know that sooner or later they must be separated from them. The boys are going to be around all the time, and will bring their brides back to their mother's home.

In all cultures, from the very moment of birth, there is pressure on the mother to define the baby's gender identity very clearly. 'Is it a boy or a girl?' friends ask, as if it were the most important thing about a baby. The next task is naming the child, which will fix its sex unmistakably for everyone to realize. They

27

look into the carrycot – 'He's a real boy!' they say, or 'Isn't she sweet? She's so pretty and feminine!' A mother may choose to dress her baby boy in blue, her girl in pink. In France flowers of the appropriate colour fill the mother's room. There can be no doubt! She talks to her boy and her girl in subtly different ways according to sex, and later is explicit about what little girls do and how they dress and have their hair arranged, as distinct from little boys. She often still chooses dolls and miniature irons and cooking things for the girl and trains and Action Man and footballs for the boy. The result is that a child has a clear and irreversible sense of whether he or she is a boy or a girl by the age of three.[10]

When a mother is the sole person to look after a child, who is completely dependent on her, acute sensitivity to her approval may be the result. She represents love, and if this is withdrawn the child has no one else to love it. We tend to think of this as normal, but in most other societies a child does not need the mother's love so unconditionally. There are others who can love and rear the child. Women in peasant societies are often deeply shocked when they learn that in the West a mother may reject, neglect or batter a child. In traditional societies there are always others watching over the care that a woman gives her baby, helping with chores and sharing responsibility. Even in a social system like that of Jamaica, which has been fragmented by slavery, very few babies find their way to orphanages because there is always a grandmother, sister or cousin to take care of a child if the mother is unable to look after it. Usually it is one of the grandmothers. In a patrilocal society, where the family is reared in or close to the father's parents' home, this is usually the father's mother.

Even in those societies where the young couple make a separate home, if the mother has easy access to her own mother, as is often the case in tightly knit communities, the maternal grandmother may have responsibility for guiding the new mother. This is so in London's East End, for example. Sometimes she actually takes over child care completely. This often happens when a toddler is weaned, and 'goes to granny', in order, the West African expression goes, 'to forget its mother'. In ex-slavery societies the maternal grandmother (or in her absence a maternal aunt) often rears the first-born children of her daughters because they have not yet settled down in stable relationships

28

with men. So, in these societies a middle-aged woman expects to have a second family of small grandchildren to bring up.

When a small child is completely dependent on its mother and care is not shared, the mother's threatened withdrawal of love is often used to control the child's behaviour. Children compete to gain love, and as they grow older are encouraged by the mother, and increasingly by the father, too, to strive for success at school and in the world outside the home in order to gain more approval from their parents, which, it is implied, is 'contingent upon performance. For, although his parents are consciously committed to loving their child regardless, they too have success needs that must be met partly through the child.'[11]

Mothers, nervously suspecting that their child may be falling below standard, and that their offspring are not fat or beautiful enough, have too few teeth, are not consuming as wide a variety of solid foods as the next baby, are not talking, sitting up or walking as soon, or are not potty-trained or reading as early as the child next door, compare their children's performance and compete with other mothers.

It is part of the socialization process for living in an industrialized, capitalist society in which the success ethos is all-important and where individual accomplishment is all. Some children never survive it, since nothing they do can ever live up to their parents' expectations or demands of them. Others succeed, and reinforce this system of child-rearing in their turn when they themselves have children, whom they encourage in the same way.

A parent achieves success through the child, and in a highly competitive society one who has little personal success may have a great incentive to live through the child, and see him or her as an extension of self. A mother who is restricted to the home but who longs to compete in the outside world is particularly likely to express herself through her children. She may try to do this in an inappropriate way, to the child's shame, because, not operating in the larger world in which the child is required to act, her modes and standards of behaviour are outdated and irrelevant. The father is more likely to have an occupation which gives him a sense of achievement outside the home and family unit.

Parenthood is not a static situation, of course. As the family grows and develops, and relationships within it shift, so parenthood itself involves change. It is a process, not merely a role to be adopted. The type of mothering which works well with a newborn baby is unsuitable for a toddler, and that which is right for a toddler is wrong for the adolescent. Mothers need to be capable of continual adaptation to the new challenges which come as their children pass from babyhood into childhood, and then grow up to become new adults. Many excel at one stage of development, but cope badly with other stages.

Societies value and institutionalize different types of mothering, identifying mothering predominantly with enclosure, extension or separation. The traditional Jewish mother emphasizes enclosure to the exclusion of other types of mothering. Perhaps it is because of the Jewish people's history of persecution. Young middle-class parents today are increasingly concerned to experience physical closeness and to feel spontaneous enveloping love for their babies, but many educated women are anxious that they will be unable to feel this unselfconscious enclosing love, and try to acquire it instead through studying books on child-rearing.

In most developing countries parents try to maintain rigid control over their children as if they were extensions of themselves, and it is thought right that children's activities and thinking should be dominated by unchanging parental values. Problems can arise in the parent-child relationship when Arab sons come to the West to study, for example, and are no longer willing to accept parental authority. This type of parenting was typical of that of Victorian middle-class England, when rigid parental values and the ideas that children must be moulded if they are to grow up to be good adults were accepted as normal. It is implicit in Freud's psychoanalytic teaching, since he was reflecting the Viennese world he knew and from which his patients came.

When a mother is unable to experience her child either as enclosed in her love, or as an extension of herself and her own body, and is under pressure to treat the baby as completely separate from birth onwards, both she and the child may suffer emotional deprivation. This must often happen in the upper-class nursery when a nanny takes over the baby from the very early days, and when contact between mother and baby is restricted to the 'mothering time' assigned to the early evenings. It can also occur when there is a rush to make a child as independent as possible as early as possible, so that it will not interfere in the parents' lives. It happens, too, with mothers who cannot trust their feelings – they feel bound to make child-rearing an intellectual exercise rather than a spontaneous relationship. Culturally imposed patterns of child-rearing that deny women the chance to enjoy a marsupial state of interdependence with a baby tend to turn mothering into the difficult task of taming a wild creature, of humanizing the inhuman, and often lead to a battle of wills between the parents and the growing child.

It is when motherhood is at its most spontaneous that it best serves as the channel of the cultural process. It is the first agency of acculturation to which each new individual is introduced. For many it remains throughout life by far the most effective.

It starts with the way the mother feeds her baby. I do not mean by this only the difference between breast and bottle, but the mood in which she feeds. Some mothers relax, forget time and enjoy talking to and watching the baby during feeds. Others are tense, watch the clock and treat the baby a bit like a car which has to be filled with petrol, jiggling it up and down when it stops for a few seconds or starts to play. In the way that the mother presents milk to her baby and responds to the child's need for nourishment, she is presenting her sense of what life is all about. It is the baby's first introduction to the value system of the society into which it is born.

This is only the beginning. Our mental images of motherhood tend to be linked with the initial stages of that relationship. The image of maternity is personified in the enveloping, protecting, encircling arms of the mother. We forget that the mother is also the person who encourages her child to go away from her to explore, but who is waiting ready to safeguard and guide when the need arises. We may forget, too, that the mother has to enable her adolescent child to leave her completely and become a separate personality, a confident man or woman able to enjoy satisfying adult relationships. Motherhood is not just about babies and small children. It is about relationships with grown-up children, too.

3

The Empty Womb

Bring forth and multiply, and replenish the earth. Oh Sun, Moon! Oh Ponomosor! May this woman bear twelve sons and twelve daughters![1]

You son of a clear-eyed mother, you far-sighted one, how you will see game one day, you who have strong arms and legs, you strong-limbed one, how surely you will shoot, plunder the Herreros, and bring your mother their fat cattle to eat, you child of a strong-thighed father, how you will subdue strong oxen between your thighs one day. You who have a mighty penis, how many and what mighty children you will beget![2]

O Son, you will have a warrior's name and be a leader of men. And your sons and your sons' sons will remember you long after you have slipped into the darkness.[3]

For thousands of years and all over the world fertility has been sought and barrenness shunned. How else could a man provide for himself in his old age? How else could his name be carried on? How could the flocks be tended, the earth tilled, or battles fought? The home was, or aimed at being, an economic unit in which more hands meant not only that food had to be shared out further, but also lighter work, and each child started to contribute to the household economy as soon as it could hold a tool or care for others smaller than itself. A woman's pride was in her fertility, the fruits of her womb. 'These,' said the Roman matron, 'are my jewels.'

So great was the emphasis on fertility that in certain African tribes (the Dahomey, for example) an impotent husband urged his wife to sleep with a friend or relative, or, if a wife could not bear children, another woman was brought in to bear them 'to his name'. In some societies barrenness or impotence are sufficient grounds for divorce. In Tikopia, a small island in the Western Pacific, couples may separate on grounds of childlessness without any formal annulment of the marriage. In the Sudan the Nuer bride does not even go to her husband's home until the first baby is weaned: there is no point in the relationship continuing unless the child survives.

Even when families are already large, other children may be adopted. Among the Innuit, women often give babies away as births take place in quick succession, but they also adopt babies, and have as many adopted children as biological ones. This is an important way of linking families together, and those who are united through giving or adopting a baby offer support to each other in times of hunger and hardship, sharing food and providing other practical help. It is also a practice that links the past with the future, since babies are not only named after dead relatives, but are thought of as inheriting their spirits and personalities.

Traditionally, prospective parents always depended on the good wishes and correct actions of the whole society. They depended also on the spirits who represented the tribe, and linked present with past and future, and the natural with the supernatural world. Human beings alive and dead and supernatural beings were all ritually united in promoting fertility. Fertility was not just a personal, private matter, but involved the cosmos.

In most of these societies maternal and infant mortality were high. Where life was hard, as among the Innuit, and wherever there was barely enough to eat during some seasons of the year or after periods of drought, as in large parts of Africa, only those supremely fit would survive to childbearing age. The others died in childhood, or occasionally survived but remained barren. Disease also picked off young people in their prime: malaria, smallpox, measles, tuberculosis, leprosy and venereal diseases. Of 80 women studied in one South African tribe, the Kgatla,

34

in the years 1929–35, there were 206 babies born alive, and 21 miscarriages or stillbirths (9 per cent). Of the 206 babies born, 57 did not survive to maturity (28 per cent). Three out of every 100 died within two months of birth, 8 died later, but while they were still being suckled, and 16 died later in childhood.[4]

In Europe, too, there were periods when death was an everyday fact of life in almost every family. It has been estimated that between 1348 and 1350 a quarter of the population of Europe died from plague. Boccaccio described the plague in Italy as killing 40,000 in Genoa, 60,000 in Naples and 96,000 in Florence.[5]

Even at the onset of the twentieth century, almost half the children of English working-class mothers died before they reached their third birthday. And in many peasant societies infant mortality remains high as the century draws to its close.

Birth Control

Yet with all the emphasis on fertility, the charms, prayers and rites, parents have often been aware that they have too many mouths to feed, and that the children they have brought into the world, although a long-term investment and security for their old age, are at present a liability. Even though they might anger the gods and 'go against nature' by putting a curb on fertility, sometimes it is an urgent necessity. So societies evolved ways of limiting the number of children a woman bore, sometimes effectively, but often involving magic practices, potions and signs which could have had little practical result.

Egyptian papyri describe three contraceptive pastes – a kind of glue, a mixture of honey and sodium carbonate, and crocodile dung – which were inserted into the vagina to provide a spermicidal barrier over the cervix, or neck of the uterus. Papyri of 1550 BC tell how to make lint tampons soaked in honey and fermented acacia leaves. This was probably a good method; lactic acid, which would be produced from the fermentation, is still used in spermicides today. Both male and female sterilization was also known, but was rarely used.

The Talmud permitted Jewish women to use contraceptives. A cotton tampon was used, and an oral contraceptive, consisting of, among other things, pounded crocuses. A woman who did not want to conceive might also try jumping around after intercourse, in a vain attempt to dislodge the semen.

The Greeks may have invented the intra-uterine device, since a hollow lead tube filled with mutton fat was sometimes inserted into the cervix to hold it open. A vinegar douche was also used by women in ancient Greece. Aristotle advised smearing the cervix and vagina with oil. Dioscorides's *Herbal*, written in the first or second century after Christ, recommends eating the fruit of the 'Chaste tree', whatever that may be, and pounding willow leaves and taking them in water. He also advised using pessaries made from pepper, herbs, sicklewort and peppermint juice, mixing the whole lot with honey and sticking this mixture over the cervix.[6] Soranus believed that a woman could avoid conception if she did not have an orgasm, and that she could make matters surer if she leaped around, sneezed, drank a cold liquid and wiped out her vagina after intercourse. But he also recommended wool tampons soaked in oil, honey, resin and the juice of the balsam tree. One possible ingredient was pomegranate pulp, which, like other acid fruits, would have had a spermicidal action. When I was working in Latin America I discovered that peasant women in Colombia today sometimes use a hollowed-out half orange as a cervical cap.

Islamic authorities recommend withdrawal, pessaries made of cabbage, pitch, ox-gall and elephant dung in various mixtures, and oral contraceptive potions, and the physician Rhases went into great detail about how to procure abortion by a method of curettage. He also added, rather hopefully, 'Joking, too, is useful'.[7]

In the Middle Ages midwives were experts on birth control and abortion, and just as women would go to them for a love potion, a charm to prevent a baby from falling ill or simple herbal medicines, so they sought their help to prevent conception or to get rid of an unwanted pregnancy. The Catholic Church saw this as a powerful threat to its authority, and in 1484 a Papal Bull was issued which stated: 'By their sorceries and by their incantations, charms and conjurations, they suffocate, extinguish and cause to perish the births of women . . . so that men beget not nor women conceive.'[8]

Most of the information that comes down to us about contraception in the Renaissance and in both France and England in the seventeenth and eighteenth centuries concerns the lives of courtiers and men of letters, and so it is difficult to get any idea of how peasant families lived, or what they used to avoid unwanted births. We know that complete breastfeeding, that is, without the addition of any solid foods or other milk, and with feeds given every two or three hours, makes it unlikely that a woman will ovulate, and every peasant woman breastfed as a matter of course. In contemporary peasant communities prolonged lactation, for two or three years or even longer, is used deliberately to reduce fertility, and is especially effective because there is often a rule that complete intercourse should not take place while a mother is still breastfeeding her child. The Koran specifically praises those women who breastfeed for two years and avoid intercourse during this time.

Throughout pre-industrial Europe, marriage was delayed until years after women had reached reproductive maturity, and there were religious sanctions against illegitimacy. In the middle of the sixteenth century the average age at marriage was a woman's middle or late twenties. By the end of the seventeenth century it was nearer thirty.[9]

The condom – made from the caecum of a sheep – was widely used in the seventeenth and eighteenth centuries by the middle and upper classes, and many verses were written praising its use. One ballad described a woman who amassed a fortune by collecting used condoms, laundering and re-selling them. Casanova referred to the condom as 'the English overcoat'. There are seventeenth-century references to vaginal sponges and contraceptive potions, too. Ben Jonson asked, 'Have you those excellent recipes, Madame, to keep yourselves from bearing children?', and the lady replied, 'How should we maintain our beauty else? Many births of a woman make her old, as many crops make the earth barren.'[10]

When the vulcanization of rubber was invented in 1843, for the first time a safe contraceptive device could be mass-produced, and this heralded a revolution in birth control. The very first Family Planning Clinic was established in Holland in 1882, and also acted as an infant welfare centre, although the only technique it advised in the early days was a soap pessary. Later it developed the diaphragm, which became known as 'the Dutch cap'. But where effective contraceptives were unknown women still could only try the older methods.

In the Columbus Medical Journal of 1883 a doctor wrote about 'the abuses of carbolic acid', which was used as a contraceptive douche, and described 'the little dark closets' where married women kept 'bottles of ergot, cotton root, savin, oil of tansy, etc.

to produce as they call it "accidental miscarriage"'.[11] It was not until 1927 that Marie Stopes first went on the road with a mobile birth control clinic in England, parking her caravan outside the Bethnal Green public library, and later journeying into the rural areas of England and Wales. Birth control then became a public issue of major importance, and the use of mechanical contraceptives that were fairly efficient spread widely.

Even where parents have wanted 'a full quiver' and where fertility has been greatly valued, in situations of dire poverty, or of famine, infanticide has always been practised. Babies have been 'accidentally' lain on in bed or, as I discovered when tracing my own paternal ancestors among Scottish crofters, records tell of babies who were 'dropped on the head' and died shortly after birth.

Infanticide was practised in ancient Rome, where an excess of children was considered inconvenient. In other societies abnormal babies or those who do not conform to a certain standard are drowned, buried, stifled or exposed, and in parts of Africa one of twins has traditionally always been killed.

The great migrations that have occurred throughout African history and prehistory have necessitated some method of controlling births, since it is difficult to take pregnant women and small babies on long, exhausting journeys into the interior. The Zulu people have regularly moved towards the Zambezi at times of economic and political crisis, and later have flowed back towards the south of the continent again. When I was in South Africa a Zulu chief who is also a senior witchdoctor explained to me the ceremony of 'stopping the wombs of the women'. The use of contraception was a political, not a personal decision. The Elders met and discussed the situation, and before further action could be taken had to offer sacrifices and prayers seeking forgiveness from the ancestors. Small pebbles were then collected from a special sacred river and in the ceremony one was slipped into the uterus of each woman of childbearing age. It has been known for some time that Arab traders who did not want their camels to become pregnant during long treks across the Sahara used stones in this way, so providing the first evidence of the utilization of intra-uterine devices, but this Zulu practice is a unique example of it being used for many centuries in human beings, and as a matter of tribal policy.

Those working in the epidemiology of fertility control attribute the dramatic drop in the birth-rate among those African tribes which went on these long migrations to starvation. It appears that it was also a deliberate consequence of sophisticated population policies, the result not of chance but of planning.

In all societies, throughout history, mothers have not merely been women with fertile wombs. They have also worried about controlling inappropriate fertility, and about spacing their babies.

Western Attitudes to Infertility

In Western culture there is a common assumption that every woman has a right to a child. To deny that right is to take away her freedom. Coupled with this, there is a sense that a woman who has never had a baby must be emotionally unfulfilled and is therefore less than a woman. If she cannot help it, she is to be pitied, as if she suffers a handicap. But if she is childless by choice, she is seen as selfish and hard. Women are under great social pressure to bear children.

Whereas in Jamaica a childless woman is scorned as a 'mule', in Egypt either commiserated with, as barren by the will of God, possessed by an evil spirit or a victim of the evil eye,[12] and in rural Japan avoided because her contagious infertility may affect other women and farm animals,[13] the emphasis in Western culture is on a woman's *right* to have a child and on her supposed inability to be emotionally fulfilled if she fails to become a mother. Any woman in the West who has an infertility problem is expected to seek medical help and to undergo prolonged investigations and treatments. In the hope of having a child women submit themselves to fertility drugs, *in vitro* fertilization (IVF), and lengthy periods in hospital, and may in the last resort turn to surrogate motherhood.

Although the 'rented womb' is the subject of much public debate, the 'test tube baby' has been more or less accepted as a medical miracle, a custom-made child available to any couple who desperately want to be parents. The truth is very different.

Infertility is often a side-effect of medical intervention in the first place. One of the most common causes is pelvic inflammatory disease, and that is often the result of the intra-uterine device, the use of which doubles the risk of infertility. Janice Smale, who gave birth to quads after *in vitro* fertilization, had been sterilized by doctors at the age of twenty-one because she was 'under stress'. The infertility specialist who managed her quad pregnancy, justified his action by saying that she was 'under stress' because she could not have a baby. Thus the same rationale was offered for two diametrically opposed kinds of medical intervention in her life, the second in an attempt to correct the harm that had been caused by the first. Whether she has been less 'under stress' as the mother of four babies, we do not know.

With *in vitro* fertilization, as with adoption, women are allowed to enter the programme only after screening to see if, in the opinion of the doctors who control IVF, they *deserve* to be mothers. Psychologists are sometimes employed to do this screening, but doctors' own impressions and gut feelings often suffice. Women must show they have a genuine desire to have a baby and are prepared to stick at it through all the investigations and treatments. They must also be emotionally well-balanced, and any previous psychiatric illness rules them out. They must be physically healthy and fall within a certain age-group, since chances of success are reduced as women grow older. Some specialists will not accept any women over thirty-five. A woman aged thirty-eight came to me in distress after an appointment with an infertility specialist who dismissed her outright and told her that her ova must be 'old and defective'. Applicants must also be in a long-term stable relationship with a man. Single women, lesbians, and, for some IVF specialists, women who are not legally married, are barred from the programme. One consultant, for instance, 'insists that his patients must have been in a stable relationship for at least three years, women must be aged under 40 and men under 50, and they must have no children living in their home. If necessary women must agree to lose weight before treatment begins. He will not treat the couple if either partner has any physical, psychological or psychosexual problem. He will not treat single women, and only allows three attempts at IVF.'[14]

Photographs appeared in the press showing one of the best-known pioneer infertility specialists beaming paternalistically, surrounded by all 'his' babies. The accompanying text was a story about the heartbreak that has been healed by this great man, how he has 'given' women babies they never thought they would have, and filled their empty arms. For the media know that this is a human interest story with never-failing appeal.

Yet IVF is not altruism. Medical specialists working in IVF

clinics do not do so out of sheer idealism and selflessness. In the USA, Europe and Australia reproductive technology is a way of building a medical career, and one that is a great deal more glamorous and high-powered than mere 'baby-catching'. There is no doubt that doctors working in IVF feel genuine emotions of hope, disappointment, anxiety and pleasure which may reflect those of their women patients. But when a doctor rushes in to a woman who is discovered to be pregnant at last and hugs her in excitement, it is *his* success, *his* triumph.

In the USA IVF is a mushrooming business. On one East Coast university campus I listened as a lawyer tried to interest a fellow academic in a new and highly promising business venture – an IVF clinic. Linked with the name of a prestigious university, the idea was that the company could milk the skills of colleagues who would act as consultants and also be shareholders in it.

The process of diagnosis and treatment, including drugs to produce super-ovulation and repeated attempts to get a fertilized ovum to implant, is a lengthy one. During all this time women and their partners may be subjected to extreme stress. The faint hope of a pregnancy becomes a woman's overriding concern. Even so, the chances of the couple ever getting a baby are low. A survey by the American Fertility Society reveals that in a two-year period 165 clinics reported an average success rate of 11 per cent. This rate ranged from 4 per cent to 38 per cent. It was a very expensive undertaking for the couples concerned, who had to pay up to $7,000 for each attempt.[15] In one study of women having fertility treatment, half of them rated their infertility problem as the most upsetting experience they had ever had in their lives.[16] There are accounts of women who keep on trying to have a successful pregnancy for as long as ten years, stopping only when they run out of money, become seriously ill, or their husband dies.

Pergonal, the drug usually employed to stimulate super-ovulation, causes headaches, exhaustion and depression. But women are prepared to suffer anything in order to get a baby. One woman on a cocktail of three drugs said, 'I felt like screaming all the time. I was shaking like I had Parkinson's disease.' Every month that conception does not occur the woman grieves over a pregnancy that did not start. Women are usually not told how low the success rate is, and may be offered misleading statistics. Even a pregnancy lasting only a few days may be included among

41

the successes, or the number of babies born may be divided by the number of women in the programme, so that if one in ten achieves a pregnancy with sextuplets, it is reported as a 60 per cent success rate.

In vitro fertilization brings with it the risk of multiple births, since it is normal practice to introduce three embryos into the uterus in the hope that one will survive. Some gynaecologists are of the opinion that if a woman super-ovulates and produces an extraordinarily large number of ripe ova, the attempt should be made to fertilize all of them and to get each one to implant, and as a result they have been introducing as many as nine fertilized ova. Because pregnancy with more than one or two foetuses is a severe strain on the mother's system, and there is no chance that she could deliver nine live babies, they then practise 'selective reduction', aborting the superfluous embryos.[17] Ever since *in vitro* fertilization was introduced in the late seventies, triplet, quad, quin, and even sextuplet pregnancies have been on the increase. Although a pregnancy with this number of foetuses may be chalked up as an IVF success, the chances of the woman having even a single live baby in her arms are much reduced. Even when the babies are born alive, once the *brouhaha* is over following a multiple birth, the woman who has carried her pregnancy successfully is left having to cope with an instant family, often crammed in a small house or apartment and facing poverty. Most of these babies are born pre-term and are of very low birthweight, and the delivery is often complicated. They may also suffer long-term physical or mental handicaps.

One American woman delivered seven babies, one of whom died immediately. The remaining six were handicapped. Then, one after another, four of these died. An English woman delivered sextuplets, of whom only one survived. Another conceived quads, of whom one died after twenty minutes and one developed hydrocephalus and lived five months. The remaining two were in intensive care until they were eight months old, and now, nearly three, still have to be tube-fed. The boy has cerebral palsy and hydrocephalus, cannot walk, and is both visually and aurally handicapped. The girl is hearing-disabled too. Their mother says, 'We do not get any let-up at all. I have completely given up my life for them. I have to cope no matter what it does to me or to my marriage.' Her husband states flatly, 'It has ruined our lives.'[18] And it comes as no surprise to hear that a woman with handicapped triplets says that she often never gets to bed all night.[19]

An Australian woman who gave birth to IVF quads decided by the time her babies were three months old that she would have to give all but one away, because she simply could not cope, and started adoption procedures. She said she was suffering 'unendurable' stress.[20]

Soon after the introduction of IVF, lawyers and gynaecologists in the USA started to become brokers for commercial surrogacy. They select those who may enter the programme, initiate and control the contracts, direct the medical procedures, and financially exploit infertility. One of the most famous of these lawyer-brokers, Noel P. Keane, published a book in 1981 called *The Surrogate Mother* – subtitled *Noel, You're On To Something Really Big*. In these commercial arrangements the purchasing male is the key figure. The contract requires delivery of the baby to the man, and the woman is referred to as either the 'wife' of the father or the 'potential stepmother'. In Britain commercial surrogacy is illegal, and surrogacy is permitted only if it is controlled by the medical profession. Either way, between lawyers and gynaecologists, the women who want babies and the women who are prepared to bear them are not those who control the surrogacy arrangements. This is in marked contrast to the kind of surrogacy that is traditional among the Ibo of West Africa, where a woman who is barren may pay the bride-wealth for another woman, after which the other woman's children become her own. The biological mother remains in a kinship relationship with her children, as a kind of aunt, and the two women are linked in sisterhood.

Doctor Richard Levine, who runs an IVF service in Kentucky, described his work on a nationally televised news show: 'I make babies,' he announced. And the surrogate mother interviewed on the same programme said: 'I think of myself as a human incubator.'

In our technological culture it is not only surrogate mothers who are seen as incubators. *In vitro* fertilization offers clues as to how gynaecologists perceive the women in their care. Pregnant women are treated as incubators, and it is doctors, rather than women, who 'make babies'. Daniela Roher, an anthropologist who has made a special study of surrogate motherhood in the USA, believes that 'surrogate mother arrangements represent an extension and reinforcement of men's claim on women's

43

sexuality and reproductive powers'.[21] A surrogate mother is paid for a service rendered to a man, rather than for the baby. It is similar to prostitution. If the surrogate mother has not conceived after six months she is removed from the programme, and another surrogate produced for the purchasing man. If she has a miscarriage, she usually gets nothing. Doctors dictate whether she should have amniocentesis or other investigations during pregnancy, and if the results show that the foetus is handicapped, she is required to have an abortion. If at the end of her pregnancy the obstetrician decides that the birth should be by Caesarean section, the surrogate has to submit to that decision, too. She is entirely under the control of men, who draw up and make the contract and who control the progress of the pregnancy and the delivery of the baby. As Daniela Roher says, 'This primal act of creativity turns out to be yet another reiteration of dependency on men.'[22]

The new reproductive technologies seem to offer women more choice. But they make it very hard for any woman to say 'I don't want a baby' or 'I've decided I've had enough of the treatment.' In contemporary Western culture, as in traditional societies, women are under pressure to marry and produce babies. Reproductive technology serves to sustain that old order. In the end, a baby conceived in a Petri dish on the lab bench is a product not of the breath-taking new technology, but of the dream that a woman meets a man, falls in love, marries, and the couple go on to have babies and live happily ever after. That dream is itself part of a social system, as rigidly controlling in Western as in traditional societies, whereby a woman is valued only to the extent that men affirm her worth and she is at their service.

4

Ways In Which Men See Women: Pure and Polluted

Men see women as a paradox in most cultures. She is both feared and sought after. She is dangerous and unclean. Yet she is also revered as a mother. When she is not a mother she is either just a thing to be used for male sexual satisfaction – a 'tart' or 'crumpet' to be consumed, a body to be photographed, legs spread wide and vulva exposed – and is despised for this; or she represents the forces of darkness, of animal nature, which draw noble men away from the spiritual, threatening to pollute and to emasculate them. St Paul's highly negative view of women as tempters of men is not really very different from the theme running through many Eastern philosophies as well as Persian and Greek ethical writings. These ideas were not introduced by Christianity, but grew out of a long tradition in which the world was seen as divided into opposites: black and white, evil and good, flesh and spirit, the profane and the sacred. Women ensnared men and tempted them to desert their lofty goals. This theme recurs throughout Greek mythology. In a similar way the myth of the 'toothed vagina' that traps and threatens to mutilate the hero appears in the stories of many traditional cultures.

The early Christian church developed this theme in no half-hearted way. St Jerome warned that women were the gateway to the devil. St Thomas Aquinas called them 'defective, ill-formed males', John Damascene castigated them as 'the outpost of hell', 'sick she-asses' and 'hideous tapeworms', and Pope Gregory the

45

Great stated that they had two uses only, prostitution and motherhood.

Yet men idealize women too, seeing them as the source of creativity and love, the embodiment of charity and self-sacrifice. In this chapter I want to look at men's ideas about women as mothers and non-mothers, and the contrasts between them. Perhaps this may suggest some of the reasons for the unattractiveness of birth control, or failures in its use, in those cultures where children are born not only to support their parents in their old age, or even to carry on the lineage, but because without them a woman is nothing.

Women as mothers have been put on an altar for so long and in so many different cultures that there is a tremendous gulf between men's (and women's) own perceptions of the ideal mother and the real women who try to live up to this impossible ideal. Looking more closely at this split in the way women are perceived by men in three traditional societies may help us to see some of the stresses inherent in being a mother. So what is it really like to be an Indian Hindu or Orthodox Jewish mother, or a peasant mother in a Mediterranean society?

Mothers in India

In India a woman is considered a subordinate, spiritually inferior and handicapped person. Her salvation can be found only through unquestioning obedience to her husband, whatever his character and however he treats her. A wife must worship her husband as a god. She must revere him even though he is evil, and she can sacrifice or make a vow only through him as her religious intermediary. In her are incarnate the unbridled forces of earthly existence, the passions of the flesh, attachment to possessions and occupation with the petty things of this world. When she snares a man she drains his capacity to achieve ascetic contemplation and spiritual purity. Indian myths abound in stories of women who have misled ascetics and even gods, and who have ensured that they never escaped from the bondage of sexual desire. She is an agent of pollution by the very fact that she menstruates. She lives in isolation for four days each month, so reminding everyone in the household of her inferior status and her carnal bondage.

As a mother, however, she is revered throughout Indian culture. Her power and influence over her children is reinforced by her complete control over what goes on in the home, and by the traditional withdrawal of the father from any interest in domestic activities. Richard Lannoy, in his analysis of Indian society, emphasizes particularly the love between mother and son.[1] This has been stressed ever since the joint family systems of late Vedic times, and still operates in the modern middle-class nuclear family. Lannoy explores the ambivalence and duality of a woman's role as wife, and therefore sexual being, and as the mother who is venerated. On the one hand 'she seduces her husband away from his work and his spiritual duties' and with her insatiable lust lures him to gratify his desires, makes seminal thrift impossible, and weakens him both psychologically and physically. On the other hand, she is idealized and 'raised to the level of a goddess in the home'.

When urban Hindus were asked to rate the strength of their emotional ties with other members of their families, the vast majority said that the greatest emotional intensity existed in the mother-son relationship; the husband-wife relationship came much lower on the list.[2]

Only as a mother can a woman gain power in her household. It is especially with the birth of her first son that she attains status. Adult men often wax eloquent about their mothers, using religious imagery to describe their purity, wisdom and self-sacrifice:

> *It seems to me that if God is love, He should be conceived of as a Mother and not Father . . . There was a time in my youth when I made myself sick with love of God . . . I . . . concentrated on the face of my mother, believing that if God was, he must be a supreme image of my mother's disinterested love.*[3]

A Hindu child grows up in an environment bristling with inconsistencies and contradictions: an ascetic, punitive, authoritarian paternalism contrasts with indulgent, permissive and tolerant attitudes on the part of the mother. Babies are cared for in a relaxed and flexible way, but the tenderness and indulgence go side by side with an insistence on cleanliness from a very early age, and there is always the threat of parental rejection if the child fails to obey. All this must be very confusing for the child.

Children's learning takes place through direct observation and participation in the extended household. Little instruction is given, and when it is it tends to be conflicting, since the many adults around may direct the child in different and contradictory ways. The small child is merely a 'passive observer of the busy courtyard life',[4] and never has the experience of accepting individual responsibility for anything.

The code of child-rearing puts great emphasis on the warmth and intensity of feeling between mother and child. But whatever the Hindu child-rearing ideal, it is only high caste Hindus who live in the conditions in which it is realistically possible to cherish a child. One out of every ten Indian babies dies in infancy, and endemic diseases such as malaria, dysentery and smallpox take their toll of health as well as life. This means not only that children are more or less taken for granted, but that the doctrine of rebirth gives meaning to and justification for the high death rate. No child is unique: each is part of the great stream of life flowing through the universe.

In the Indian family there is a basic ambivalence which reflects 'the human dilemma caused by the environment in which, for example, climatic conditions are extreme and which cause great suffering to babies, from prickly heat and other rashes, the pervading cloying dampness of the monsoon season, mud, insects, flies, rodents, dust, and in the winter, piercing cold. Jackals cry in the night or adults in the close-packed family quarrel loudly and disturb the child's sleep. As seasons change, storms build up or scorching desert winds blow, the child's routines must change without warning, and the boy or girl grows up to anticipate all change as painful and to feel that no actions of theirs can have effect on the conditions of existence or reduce human vulnerability to the raw forces of nature.'[5] The mother is the mediator between the child and the environment, but can never protect the baby from it completely.

When a baby is born the mother and child are isolated in an inner room in a state of ritual impurity for several days, during which time the baby's horoscope is prepared. The house is purified, but the woman does not go back to all her household and other tasks for another thirty-four days. The baby is fed on demand, and is never left to cry, as this is thought to make it weak. Breastfeeding continues for two years or more, and weaning is gradual. The baby is in flesh-to-flesh contact with its mother's body, astride her back or that of another woman, until able to run around independently, and in some rural areas

49

is carried like this under the mother's sari. A baby is never left alone, and when the mother is working is either bound to her body or laid down close to her.

The Hindu ideal emphasizes the symbiotic interdependence of mother and baby. In practice, extreme poverty, and maternal malnutrition or even starvation, all limit the loving care which can be given to a baby. Impoverished mothers find that their milk dries up because they are under-nourished themselves, or they have to work so hard carrying fuel, cooking, cleaning and working in the fields that the baby must wait before it is attended to.

Bowel and bladder training is relaxed, in striking contrast to the taboos relating to pollution and the 'washing mania' which the adult Hindu observes. Perhaps this is so because at this stage the baby is seen as an extension of the mother's own body, but so far without spiritual and ritual responsibility. Because the baby is close to her own body the mother becomes aware very early on of the exact point at which to pick the baby up and hold it out so that it can empty its bowels. Then she wipes up after it and washes it. At about two the toddler is taught to go out into the yard to squat down, and begins to learn the strict regulations regarding faecal pollution, and at five the child goes to the fields with a pot of water, or, in the middle-class household, uses the lavatory. Mothers begin to teach their child from about the age of two that the right hand is 'clean', and that he should wipe his bottom only with the left, which is 'dirty'. At the same time the child is taught about the permanent and collective pollution of the low caste, so that values relating to personal hygiene and to temporary, individual defilement are immediately associated also with status in the social system and with a wider system of values.

From the point of view of Western technological culture, the Indian baby remains a baby for a long time. Mother and baby sleep together for the first four or five years. Everything possible is done for the small child, who is fed by hand, bathed and dressed. The mother makes little attempt to mould her child's behaviour, apart from the gentle, reiterated and consistent emphasis on the clear distinction between the clean and the unclean, the sacred and the polluted. There are few rewards for good behaviour, but a casual slap or scolding for behaviour which is considered bad or polluting.

50

There are always older children and adults around on whom the small child can depend for help, so there is no need to learn to be self-reliant and, since the whole extended family lives and works together, no need to compete with anyone else. Everyone assumes that the child will conform to the rhythms and life-style of the family.

Mothers have special problems in disciplining and controlling the growing boy. They themselves are under the control of men, and must obey their husbands without question, and children soon learn this. A rebellious little boy exploits this situation and becomes very demanding. A boy does not come under his father's direct control until he is five, and from three to about seven he often takes advantage of his mother's subordinate position in the family, resisting her authority and running away to a place which is not under her control and where she is not herself allowed. He whines, cajoles and pleads until he gets what he wants, and quickly learns that a temper tantrum is an effective way of controlling the behaviour of adults. The mother scolds her naughty child and tells him that he will be outcast, or an 'Untouchable'. She threatens ghosts or witches, and says that Kali, the goddess of destruction (who represents the dark side of the mother image), will come and punish him. If this is ineffective she may lock him in a dark room.

But however a small boy exploits his mother, in later life she is looked back on with something approaching veneration. The great Vedic purification sacrifice, the Soma, embodies the adult's conceptualization of motherhood. To be 'born into divine existence',[6] the suppliant must first return to the womb and become himself a foetus. He must once again become dependent on his mother, the ground of his being. The Soma sacrifice crystallizes ideas about the relationship of men to their mothers and also of men to society. The human body is 'the lotus of nine doors',[7] always vulnerable to pollution from outside and inside. A balance must be found between different parts of the body, and between different parts of society.

Traditional attitudes are changing rapidly in the Indian middle class. Women are often taking on jobs outside the home. In the towns the nuclear family has largely replaced the extended family system, removing some of the old stresses, but introducing new ones. Whereas in the joint family there is an unbroken chain of uniformity, and young people learn exactly what to do by

51

copying their elders, once such a system has collapsed education comes from outside the family. This is accompanied by increased individuality and a striving for freedom and independence. It is often women who agitate to break away from the joint family and who persuade their husbands to leave. But all this entails great psychological adjustment to be able to function alone, in a relatively isolated husband and wife unit, without the support of the family. It is probably hardest of all on mothers, and because there are no other women to help with mothering the maternal role is intensified.

But women in India dare not, as yet, claim equality with men, and competition for jobs is for most of them out of the question. Nor do they demonstrate what Lannoy rather quaintly calls 'masculine traits of behaviour which are familiar in their counterparts in Anglo-Saxon countries'.[8] He claims that they do not *need* to seek success outside the home, because they have power inside it. Much the same was said of Victorian wives and mothers when the suffragette movement was started by brave women who refused to be satisfied with the patriarchal attitudes of the men who controlled their lives.

The Jewish Ideal

The powerful, enveloping and sometimes suffocating love of the Jewish mother for her children is a theme often explored in modern novels. The traditional Jewish family has been called 'a walled garden',[9] the basic unit of the Congregation of Israel, the home its temple, the father a priest, the children acolytes, and each meal a holy communion. Nearly every Jewish ritual concerns the family, and almost every family gathering has its own ritual. The patriarchal principle is embodied in the person of Abraham, and the overriding obligation of the father is to instruct his wife and children. The first commandment is 'thou shalt be fruitful and multiply'. It is the father's responsibility to reinforce the family's unbreakable links back into history, 'the rocks whence you were hewn, and the hole and the pit whence you were digged'.[10]

In ancient Hebrew culture a wife's most important task was to produce male heirs. Her status as a woman depended on her ability to do this. A man could divorce a barren woman, and as his wife aged he might take another wife. Still today among the strictest orthodox Jews women are second-rate members of the congregation, and whereas there are great celebrations on the birth of a son, the birth of a daughter is marked hardly at all. The Talmud teaches that a father should 'look on the birth of a daughter as a blessing from the Lord'. But the morning prayer of the devout Jew is 'Blessed art Thou, O Lord our God, King of the universe, who hast not made me a woman.'

Rav Eliezer ben Hyrcanus was tackled on a point of scholarship by a clever woman, but became impatient, and protested, 'A woman has no learning except about the spindle. Let the words of the Torah be consumed in fire, but let them not be transmitted to a woman.'[11]

A woman's body is like a vessel, the orifices of which must be kept closed, but from which polluting matter seeps during menstruation. 'And if a woman has an issue, and the issue in her flesh be blood, she shall be in her impurity seven days.'[12]

If a man shall lie with a woman having her sickness, and he shall uncover her nakedness – he hath made naked her foundation, she hath uncovered the fountain of her blood – both of them shall be cut off from among their people.[13]

Even if the blood should leave a stain 'no bigger than a mustard seed' the woman is unclean, so the seven days were extended by the rabbis to twelve for safety. The *Baraita de Niddah* stated that the breath of a menstruating woman was poisonous, her glance was harmful, and she polluted the air around her. 'She was regarded as the ultimate in corruption, a walking, reeking, suppurating pestilence.'[14] It was not uncommon for women to consult the rabbi for his advice on whether stains on their underclothing made them impure, and to visit him clutching the stained garments for him to examine, which he did with the impersonality of a doctor making a careful clinical examination.

The Laws of the Shulchan Aruch state that a woman must be responsible for taking precautions so that her husband does not touch her by mistake when she is in this defiled state. In Orthodox homes the double bed is unknown, and has been much criticized by rabbis as a symbol of depravity. When her period is over and there is no possibility of the slightest stain a purification ceremony takes place. She has a ritual bath and must immerse herself three times in moving water, either in the special *miqvah* bath or in a river or the sea. A husband and wife should have intercourse on the night after her immersion, which tends to correspond to the time of ovulation and therefore to be her most fertile period. If after ten years there is no baby, even if the couple have been using birth control to avoid pregnancy, they are considered by the ultra-Orthodox to be living in sin. The use of the condom is considered sinful. It is like the sin of Onan ('wasting' semen by not ejaculating it into a woman). Birth control is acceptable only if the *woman* assumes responsibility, so the contraceptive pill complies with doctrine. Even so, if after ten years there is no baby, the ultra-Orthodox often suspect that a couple must be living in sin.

The Talmud lays down the duties of a wife as being to serve her husband, including washing his face and pouring his drink into the glass, so that he does not have to do these things for himself. Maimonides added many other services which he had picked up from observing behaviour in the Moslem cultures in which he lived and to which he gave his whole-hearted approval. One duty he emphasized was that a woman should breastfeed her babies.

Both parents must ensure that their children are properly educated. But for girls, this means only that they have to learn how to be housewives so that they can marry well, whereas boys must be educated to be wise and govern their women and family. For boys, there is emphasis on academic excellence and on the scholarship which makes for a good rabbi. There is only one Jewish lullaby in the English language, and it embodies the ideal of education for boys as part of the serious business of life:

> O, hush thee my darling, sleep soundly my son
> Sleep soundly and sweetly till day has begun;
> For under the bed of good children at night,
> There lies till the morning, a kid snowy white.
> We'll send it to market to buy sechora [supplies],
> While my little lad goes to study Torah.
> Sleep soundly at night, learn Torah by day,
> Then thou'll be a rabbi 'ere I've gone grey,
> But I'll give thee tomorrow ripe nuts and a toy,
> If thou'll sleep as I bid thee, my own little boy.[15]

Parents borrow and save so that a son can go to university and become 'my son, the Doctor', who by virtue of his education and of the new social world he has entered has different friends, interests and beliefs. The problem then is that he may become a source of disappointment and perplexity, of mingled pride and despair. Chaim Bermant defines the special quality of *naches* which a Jewish parent hopes to get from children – 'a mixture of gratification, pride, joy, thankfulness, a sense of beatitude, the feeling that God is smiling down assentingly' – and says that 'if a parent says reproachfully, "I only want you to be happy", he means "all I want from you is *naches*", and *naches* is best gained if the child does what his parent would have done had he been in the child's place.'[16]

So, in Orthodox Judaism, though academic education is suitable for boys, daughters should become wives and mothers. For it is only in motherhood that a woman fulfils herself and that the inherited taint of female sexuality is overcome.

The Orthodox Jewish woman's province is the home, of which she is in charge and with which she is identified. A rabbi commented, 'I never called my wife "my wife". I called her "my home".'[17] Her primary task is to create 'peace in the house' and a stable family life. The difficulty is that, as families have become smaller, a mother's energy, determination and concern for her children's welfare is concentrated on fewer and fewer children, and this can produce a stifling 'smother love' as they grow up and try to break away from her enveloping pride in them.

Mothers have always had an important ritual function in the Jewish home, but now they have even greater ritual responsibility. As the demands of modern non-Jewish life reduce opportunities for living according to Jewish faith in the world outside, a mother's role in making her home the centre of Jewish culture has become more important. Often household members find it too complicated to bother with kosher dietary regulations away from home, but rely on the mother to observe kosher within it. So, in the modern world the Jewish mother has a unique ritual role. She is there to see that traditions and ceremonies are carried on, that customs are upheld, and that Judaism is taught to her children through correct ritual, such as the Sabbath lighting of the candles. As a result she is the individual on whom the transmission of the culture exclusively depends. It is she, rather than the father, who becomes the embodiment of Jewishness to her children. The basic handicap of having been born a woman is thus transcended, and she represents the historical link of every Jew with the past.

The Mediterranean Ideal

For the Greek peasant woman, too, motherhood is fulfilment, and redemption from the sin of having been born a woman. Women are considered weak and sensual creatures who must fight a constant battle against the innate spiritual disadvantages of having been born female. They must also be forever on their guard to maintain their chastity and to defend themselves against male sexuality. Virtue lies in 'shame' and it is said, 'Better to lose your eye than your reputation.' When God ordered the universe He gave man intellect, but left women unreasonable, emotional, predisposed to quarrelling and making trouble in the village, talkative and silly. 'Men are intelligent,' they say, 'but women are gossips.' They are all 'Eves'.[18]

Menstruation is evidence of female impurity, and a woman in this condition must refrain from engaging in ritual activities such as making the Christmas sausages, baking bread for the liturgy or cooking remembrance food, lighting the church candles, kneeling in front of icons or lighting the sanctuary lamp. The word used, 'to take', is that used about plant grafting too; if a woman does these things, the act will not 'take'. It is pointless, for the grace cannot flow. Men, however, are 'pure', and this makes them more responsible and able to relate to God effectively. The bipolar contrasts between masculinity and femininity have been listed in this way:[19]

Man	Woman
Adam	Eve
Superior	Inferior
Right	Left
Closer to God	Closer to the Devil
Intelligent	Unintelligent, 'stupid'
Strong-minded	Credulous
Cool-headed, brave	Fearful
Reliable	Unreliable
Strong	Weak
Responsible	Irresponsible

Yet a woman has an additional quality – modesty – and this saves her from all her negative qualities. A woman's honour is her family's most precious possession.

> *A mother who is thought to have lost her virginity before marriage or, afterwards, to have been guilty of adultery, or even an apparent inclination towards it, infects her children with the taint of her dishonour, and however closely these children may conform to right ways of behaviour, they cannot retrieve the reputation of their family.*[20]

If a young woman does not preserve her virginity she is dishonoured and faces possible death, or marriage to a widower or a man of ill repute.[21]

Men's shame is rather different; it is not sexual shame, but shame at failure to fulfil the role of a man. For a woman, however, shame is the one means of salvation, and without it she possesses mere animal nature. All the men of the family must protect their wives and children from shame, for their own honour is based on their ability to safeguard their dependants from shame. This is what it is to be a real man.

It is this sense of shame which links each woman with the transgression of Eve. But it can also uplift her from being merely a weak woman, so that she can fulfil the highest role possible for a woman – that of wife and mother. Marriage 'makes possible for woman the transcendence of her nature which is a part of her social and metaphysical heritage. For it is then that a woman has a home of her own and it is through the home that she expresses herself. To the married woman alone is given the charter to . . . tame and conquer those elements by which society is threatened.'[22]

A mother's task is to tame the wayward and unruly natures of her children. By expressing herself in the lives of her children and grandchildren she finds fulfilment through them, and in particular through the honour of her sons and grandsons. A peasant woman said of her grandson: 'I am now as far as little Christos. We live as far as little Christos',[23] which is all the more significant because she ignored his younger sister, Tassoula.

The mother 'holds the house together', and her proper sphere of activity is the home. It is not only her practical work, cooking

and cleaning, baking bread and making cheese, caring for the goats and hens, carrying the water and looking after the children, which is important, but also the way in which she makes the house a sanctuary from the cares of the outside world, and this is partly due to her careful observation of the correct ritual actions. She must keep religious fasts, attend church regularly, as a representative of the house, observe memorial services, make remembrance food, and count the strands in the home-made candles which commemorate the dead from both her own and her husband's families. She is the link with both past and future.

She is closer to her children than their father is. He 'threw them out of his belly', but they came from her womb. Since her husband is occupied throughout the daylight hours outside the home, she is solely responsible for child care, and small children see little of their fathers except on feast days.

The Greek peasant woman, like the traditional Jewish woman, is identified with the house, and the Greek word for 'wife' is interchangeable with that of 'house'. If a woman is long away from her home it is a kind of 'spiritual infidelity'. 'Without the housewife,' the villagers say, 'the house cannot function.'[24] In the house a woman expresses her creativity, and the home is the justification of womanhood. The order and pattern of the sacred world is reflected in the order, generous hospitality, love and peace of the home, and she is the guardian of this household shrine. There must be food in plenty for all who come, and a warm welcome. The home represents the sacred world in microcosm, and the mother is its priestess.

In the three societies at which we have looked in this chapter a woman has little value until she becomes a mother. She has *uterine potential*, and only justifies her existence when she marries and bears children. If women in societies like these are expected to limit their families so that a curb can be put on the population explosion, something else has to take the place of uterine worth, and cultures must change so that women are valued for qualities which can be realized other than through childbearing and rearing.

Traditionally the ideal of motherhood has enriched society. It has embodied concepts of tenderness, compassion, generosity, selflessness, love, harmony and creativity in the face of other more aggressive and self-assertive, quintessentially 'male' qualities such as courage, power, fighting spirit, justice and technical achievement. But we live on the verge of the twenty-first century. In passing through this cultural revolution qualities traditionally associated with motherhood have to find expression in fulfilment other than maternity, and men need to discover these qualities within themselves, too.

The danger is that as the motherhood ideal is toppled from its pedestal, and as fewer women decide to have babies, a society comes to over-value aggression, go-getting career achievement, the exercise of power, shows of strength and overt hostility, and to underestimate the 'feminine' qualities which seem less rational, and are therefore suspect. Perhaps we have to rediscover just those values which motherhood has traditionally represented, and to find them not only in the biological figure of the woman as mother, but in all of us.

5

Experimenting With Motherhood

The issue of 'the family' is a perennial topic of discussion in the press and on radio and TV. The protagonists are ready to hand, those who claim that the family is in its death throes and are shocked, aghast or delighted by this, versus those who claim that the family is as solid as a rock, and that the changes that we see around us – families without fathers, extended families consisting of parents with any number of ex-partners as well as the present ones, and families in which the children are not genetically related to either parent, for example – are evidence of how the family adapts to changed social circumstances.

Like just about everything else in social life, motherhood has been experimented with to fit prevailing fashions and fads, and often subordinated to a religious or philosophical ideal which has forced it to change in a radical way.

Motherhood in an American Utopia

One of the oddest small-scale experiments took place in the 'Oneida Community', the brain-child of an American religious visionary, John Humphrey Noyes, in the mid-nineteenth century. Like Moral Rearmament, peer-group criticism in public was a basic part of this experiment, and every member was subjected to criticism from all the others in meetings held regularly for that purpose. The Perfectionists, as they called themselves, based their organization on communism and on what later became known as 'free love', although Noyes warned

61

his followers against falling in love and 'the temptation to make a separate hobby out of it. One should share all things in common,' he announced sternly, 'and avoid attaching oneself to individuals.' This allowed for free 'circulation' and exchange of 'magnetic influences'. Sexual intercourse was the most intimate and powerful way of 'laying on of hands', and should not be restricted to one partner only. Girls were initiated into sex when they were about thirteen, often by Noyes himself.

In 1848 he introduced a system of 'male continence' or coitus reservatus. Instead of wasting his seed, a man retained it. Ejaculation was harmful to health. Not surprisingly, this proved an effective means of birth control. In 1869 a 'stirpiculture experiment' was started which the Perfectionists hoped would ultimately transform American society and the world. Anyone had a right to refuse to have intercourse with anyone else, but only those chosen by Noyes had a right to breed. Even when a couple were expecting a baby they were not supposed to be specially attached to one another, but had to give way to other members of the Community and not become 'sticky'. The young women of the Community submitted themselves to their masters with these words:

> We have no rights or personal feelings in regard to child-bearing which shall in the least degree oppose or embarrass him in his choice of scientific combinations . . . We will, if necessary . . . cheerfully resign all desire to become mothers, if for any reason Mr Noyes deems us unfit material for propagation. Above all we offer ourselves 'living sacrifices' to God and true Communism.[1]

In practice, since Noyes believed in the inheritance of acquired characteristics, particularly from the father, who he thought had a greater genetic influence than the mother, and because he wished to 'draw the fellowship upwards', it was often older, highly honoured, 'spiritually minded' men who inseminated the women, and it was rumoured that many of the children were fathered by Noyes himself.

It proved very difficult for younger couples to separate as they were supposed to when a baby was on the way, and a visitor to the Community describes a painful incident in which a young man was publicly 'criticized' for being attached to the woman who was bearing his child. He was instructed by Noyes that another man should have intercourse with her. Because there were so many incidents like this it was decided that a couple could live together before and for a short time immediately after a birth, but that then they must part.[2]

Mothers cared for their babies until they were nine months old, and at night till they were eighteen months old. After this time the 'stirps' (the babies) only visited their mothers twice a week, and both mothers and children were publicly criticized if they showed signs of being bonded with each other.

Love between mother and child was not the only suspect attachment. Children who had close friends were also criticized and separated. No one was supposed to 'stick' to anyone else; there was to be no possessiveness of any kind, just commitment to the Community, and exclusiveness from the world outside. Pierrpont Noyes, the son of the founder, wrote of his childhood:

> We Community children lived in a little world bounded on all sides by isolation. We believed that outside those walls were philistine hordes who persisted in religious errors and social formulas under which they sinned and suffered. When I was a child the world 'outside' was a world of taboo.[3]

Children were weaned at about two years, and then were cared for by male and female nurses in the nursery. Mothers had no rights to their children. They were the offspring of the Community.

The comments of one rather perplexed visitor foreshadow some of the observations made much later by René Spitz and John Bowlby about the effects on children of the lack of a one-to-one relationship with an adult:[4]

> The children I saw were plump, and looked sound; but they seemed to me a little subdued and desolate, as though they missed the exclusive love and care of a father and mother. This, however, may have been only my fancy; though I should grieve to see in the eyes of my own little ones an expression which I thought I saw in the Oneida children, difficult to describe – perhaps I might say a lack of buoyancy, or confidence and gladness. A man or woman may not find it so difficult to be part of a great machine, but I suspect it is harder for a little child.[5]

We are never told what the mothers felt about having to part with their children.

Communist China

Some of the most dramatic changes in the role of the mother have occurred in Communist China. Since 1949 the Marriage Law has been the basis of family organization, replacing the system of feudal marriage. It proclaims equality of husband and wife and the duty of each to rear the children. Men are not permitted to apply for divorce during a woman's pregnancy or within a year after she has given birth. In fact, from the 1950s on, divorce has been difficult for all couples with young children.

On marrying, as in the past, a woman often goes to live with her husband in his parents' household, or the grandmother and grandfather come to live with them, so that her relationship with her mother-in-law is central to her life, and affects the way she brings up her children. Delia Davin, a specialist on women in China, says that the tensions between these two women form the subject of much recently published fiction, and fill the columns of problem pages in newspapers.[6] Whereas in the past the mother-in-law was the superior authority in the house, and supervised her daughter-in-law's work, the younger woman now often goes out to work and the older one has to perform all the menial tasks previously done by the younger. Some mothers-in-law escape from this into work outside the home, in which case chores within the home are shared. Others refuse to do housework or to care for children, or will only cook for their son, refusing to feed his wife. Problems like these may be referred to the cadre of village women responsible for supervising the revolution at local level. Often the solution is for the grandfather to take on child care, while both women go out to work.

In the countryside families still live, eat and work together. Peasant women have for a long time been accustomed to helping with the harvest, and babies and small children were left behind in the care of an older woman or one whose feet had been bound and was therefore incapable of doing agricultural work. Communal childminding on a regular basis was an extension of this system.

Traditionally men withdrew from their children from about the age of six years old, in case the children became too intimate and unruly with them. The father was an authoritarian figure while the mother was in league with her children, particularly with her sons. She used her husband's isolation from them to form bonds of affection, acting as the interpreter of their father's behaviour, negotiating to get them off punishments, and serving as intermediary. Girls were 'far more experienced than their brothers at shaping opinions, sensing changes in attitude',[7] evaluating personal advantage and disadvantage. This traditional family system meant that women were already well equipped to function effectively in modern China.

In the cities, members of the nuclear family are usually separated during the day, but meet after work, having picked up the baby from the crèche. Couples still rely a good deal on the help of grandparents even though the man shares the housework, laundry and child care, and though there are many work-place crèches. Women invite a mother or mother-in-law to come and live with them when a baby is born. The fact that both the man and the woman are working outside the home strengthens family ties and cements the bonds between a couple and their parents. Even when there are good nursery facilities it helps to have a grandparent who can take the child to and from the crèche and who can cope with school holidays, or if the child is ill. Far from causing disintegration of the family, the Communist Revolution in many ways reinforced it.

The one-child-per-family policy set up in 1981 has contributed to this by transforming a child into a rare and valued member of the family, and one in whom is invested all hope for the future. There are laws prohibiting early marriage, and special incentives, such as preferential housing, medical benefits, educational opportunities, employment openings, cash bonuses, child care, the provision of top-quality seeds for sowing and financial credit, for couples with only one child, while those who have two or more children may be fined or lose their jobs. As one woman said, 'You only have one baby, one childbirth, so it's more important for us than it was for our mothers.'[8]

A baby boy is precious. Traditionally sons have always been welcome in the Chinese family because they will work the land and look after their parents in old age. Daughters, on the other hand, must move away, and will be caring for their parents-in-law when they are old. The birth of a daughter can therefore be a catastrophe, especially when the one-child family is public policy. So amniocentesis is often used to test the gender of unborn babies, and many female foetuses are selectively aborted. Sometimes women go through the whole pregnancy and are then expected to kill a newborn baby girl. One result is that males now form over half the Chinese population, and in another two decades more than forty million men in their twenties will be unable to find wives, because the young women simply will not exist. Mothers will be in scarce supply.

The Israeli Kibbutz

The other great modern experiment in motherhood has been the kibbutz. The ideal which led to the creation of the Israeli kibbutz had little to do with motherhood, but rather with building a new nation in an ancient land. The kibbutz ideal concentrated on the nature of the relationship between the whole community and its young, the hope for the future. The kibbutz started as an alternative to conventional family life, with a highly diffuse and unemotional form of multiple mothering, although nowadays the relationship of parents and children has assumed central importance.

In the beginning, children were cared for by trained personnel (*metapels*) who worked within the communal 'children's houses', thus releasing mothers for productive work. This was in part a reaction to the traditional female role in ghetto life in which a woman's whole life was devoted to her husband and children. It was considered that the woman pioneer, or *chalitzah*, had to be really free and equal with men, and this could only be so if she were liberated from the tasks of motherhood and shared guard-duty with the men, drove tractors, built houses and dug roads alongside them. In practice, few women took on heavy agricultural labour to the extent that men did. Nevertheless, the ideal of gender equality was there. And it was a practical necessity to utilize all available man- and womanpower towards the common goals of establishing and maintaining the kibbutz. No one could concentrate on private interests. The kibbutzim were a result of the radical rethinking of gender roles as well as community goals.

In the early years of the kibbutzim children were cared for in an institutional rather than a personal way, and the *metapels* in the children's houses changed as a child moved up from one house to another. But mothers often felt guilty about not caring for their children as their own mothers had done. Some couples left the kibbutz when a second or third child was born because a mother wanted to look after her own baby, even though the first time round she had taken it for granted that the baby would be cared for by the *metapels*.

Babies in kibbutzim are normally breastfed, and when I was in Israel I visited one kibbutz where flags are hoisted, the colour of which indicates to a woman working in the field or elsewhere that her baby needs feeding. Six months is considered quite long enough for this, however, and mothers do not expect, and may not be allowed to breastfeed their babies longer. This may be because the *metapelet* has ample time to concentrate on feeding the babies with solid food, whereas the mother tends to hurry feeds, or at least to feed with one eye on the clock, because she has to get back to work. It is not a situation which favours happy breastfeeding. Bottle-fed babies are usually weaned to a cup at four months. It is part of a system in which the baby is urged forward away from infantile dependence and towards working for the communal goals of the kibbutz. This emphasis on independence may also be the reason why I saw babies as young as six weeks placed in high barred cots on a flat, white surface, with space around them on all sides, rather than nestled in cradles or carriers, as small babies are in many other societies.

The pattern in many kibbutzim is for the parents to spend two hours a day (often between the hours of 5 and 7 pm) with their children, while the rest of the time the children are cared for within the communal children's or babies' houses. Originally they all slept in dormitories and did not return to their parents' home at night, but in some kibbutzim children now sleep in their parents' homes. Longer periods are spent with them on the Sabbath. Nowadays the scene in the kibbutz on a Saturday has been described to me as 'like a family convention', not surprising when you remember that there are four generations of families in some of the older kibbutzim, from the age of seventy-five or so down to the newborn baby. In fact, the kibbutz is, perhaps more than any other society today, based on the family. This can make it difficult for those who are childless, and who face a peculiar kind of loneliness in these daily periods and during the Sabbath, when the whole community is joined in what is in effect a celebration of the family.

Because the time spent with children is devoted entirely to them, it tends to be 'quality time'. Parents and children do things together and enjoy each other in a way which it is difficult for many parents in Western culture to do, because there is never space in their lives for it, and which is almost impossible for any mother with small children underfoot all day, while she struggles to do housework and cooking. In the kibbutz a mother is less apt to be a tired, irritable woman who hopes that the children will not interrupt her work. She is more like a fairy godmother who belongs to the child for a limited period of time, and who during that time is generous with attention, admiration, gifts and with demonstrations of love.

In Western society fathers who return from work late in the evening to see the children only when they are bathed and ready for bed, or who only see them at weekends, sometimes fill this role. Women often resent their male partners when they are forced to live most of the time like a single parent, and have to be the sole disciplinarian, educator and source of love. But in the kibbutz both parents can concentrate exclusively on their children and lavish affection on them during their limited times with them. As Chaim Bermant says:

> *The whole ritual is vaguely reminiscent of the practice of nannies bringing the children downstairs from the nursery to have tea with papa and mamma . . . In the kibbutz one's parents become a species of grandparents or Dutch uncles – smiling, indulgent, generous. Discipline, instruction, chastisement are received elsewhere; the sacred hours are for love and affection, for fun and games, for being spoiled. And indeed every home will have its games' cupboard for the occasion as well as a store of sweets and biscuits and an endless supply of drinks. The parents are entirely at the disposal of their children.[9]*

People do not call on each other during these special hours, and there is a pause in all social activities.

Children are the centre of the social life of a kibbutz. The whole community revolves around them, the symbol of the future which can redeem the sufferings of the Jewish past, and the focus of all festivals, both the traditional ones such as Chanukah, Purim and the festival of the First Fruit, and the newer ones which have developed out of the life of the kibbutzim, such as the sheep-shearing festival. In a discussion about motherhood I was struck by the number of times men and women referred to 'our' children, not as the children of a certain pair of parents, but as the children of the whole kibbutz. When children are successful in some venture – passing examinations, or winning travel scholarships or a place in an orchestra – it is not only the proud parents who are glad; the triumph is one for the whole community. When a young person dies in battle in the outbreaks of conflict between Arab and Jew, the whole kibbutz mourns because they have lost a son, and the young people grieve for a dead brother. Both because of the crises engendered by the political situation and because the kibbutz is a large family, the system has restored to its members of all ages the experience of death as a normal life crisis, of facing bereavement and mourning together, which for most of us no longer exists, and has not existed within Western society since the nineteenth century.

The pull of the nuclear family and its interests undermines the identity of the kibbutz. In some kibbutzim communal dining halls, symbolic of common interests, are less and less used and, in place of the great gathering together after work to talk through all that has happened during the day, people carry off triple-deck saucepans full of food to their own quarters, using the dining room like a Chinese take-away.

But, however the kibbutz changes, the children remain its reason for existence. It is a child-focused society, and the qualities of the good parent are those called upon in every adult. It has institutionalized responsible parenthood, and stemming from it, the love and loyalty of siblings as the main bonds welding individuals together in a new social unit. In spite of the children's houses, or perhaps because of them, in a strange way the kibbutz may have rediscovered motherhood.

Men have often dissected motherhood and tried to remould it to their own design, or even to eradicate it, in the service of a passionate religious or social ideal or in the pursuit of power. Sir Thomas More, Rousseau and Freud are just three in a long line of philosophers who have tried to remodel motherhood. A school to train women for motherhood was set up by Napoleon to serve as the moral spearhead of his new society, and motherhood was an important basis for the Aryan master race of which Hitler dreamed. It is as if all the anger that boys have ever felt towards their mothers is expressed in the ways that adult men pronounce

70

on how mothers ought to behave. When they make political decisions that have the effect of further oppressing women, that penalize single mothers, for example, and mothers who go out to work, maybe they are seeking to reinforce their image of the ideal mother, the kind of mother that no child has ever had.

The advantage of seeing mothering from a cross-cultural vantage point is that an observer quickly realizes that instead of one ideal of mothering there are many possible permutations of the motherhood role. No one of these is universally right; each is the product of experience in a specific culture and is finely adjusted to the value system of that society. What works in one would probably not work in another.

If we are concerned about the kind of society in which we live, we ought to think about the role of women as mothers within it. A new Jerusalem cannot be built only by altering schools, laws, economic systems and public institutions. Its foundations lie in the quality of interaction in the family from its very beginnings, and in all the different permutations of the family that exist – dual parent families with a man and a woman, dual parent families with lesbian mothers, single parent families, large extended families, nuclear families living in common or sharing certain aspects of their lives together, families in which the children are adopted or fostered, and other families in which they are not the genetic offspring of the mother or the father. All these different forms of the family are viable.

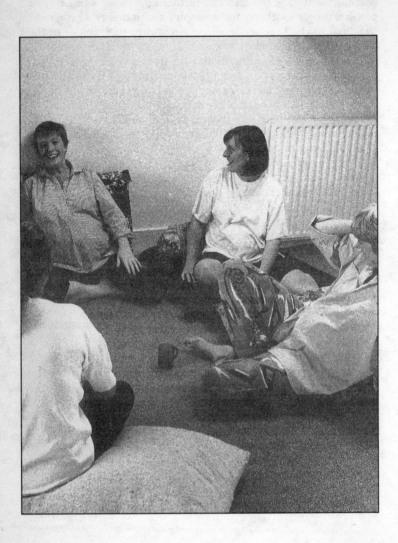

6

With Child

Pregnancy is a ritual state in most traditional cultures. The expectant mother is in a special ritual relationship with society, which includes the father of the child, both their kin groups, the past in the persons of the ancestors, and the cosmic environment represented by the gods. She must tread very carefully.

In Sumatra, for example, the pregnant woman's mother and the baby's father's mother perform rituals to announce the coming baby. These start in the fifth month of pregnancy and serve to link the two families more closely. The woman's mother takes a gift of rice cake to the man's mother, and gives her a present of money. Next month the man's mother returns the call, taking rice to the woman's mother, and later rice cakes to the pregnant woman. In the seventh month the man's mother takes rice, spices, soap, talcum powder and a new sarong to the mother-to-be, and is accompanied by a specialist in Islamic lore who makes a salad of fruit and burns incense so as to invite the souls of the ancestors and other spirits to eat it.[1]

The ceremonies of pregnancy thus have an important integrative function. But more than this, they link present with past, the human with the divine, earth with heaven.

Birth is significant not only because of its effect on a marriage and on the immediate family, but also because it occurs at the linkage point of the generations. Above and beyond its *emotional* significance for all the individuals involved it has *spiritual* significance – and perhaps childbirth derives at least part of its personal emotional significance from this deeper meaning.

Where ancestor veneration is at the root of a religion the

ancestors are intimately involved with conception and pregnancy. The Mossi of West Africa pray to their ancestors to grant them large families; these prayers are made at earth shrines where there are landmarks such as trees, mountains, rocks or rivers. The priests of the shrines intercede for the people, and when this is done correctly the spirits of the ancestors pass into the wombs of women and are born as children.[2]

A pregnant woman is usually considered to be in ritual danger. She is thought of as being exposed to risk because she is in an 'in-between' state, not yet a mother and yet no longer a virgin or simply a bride. She has left one status behind but has not yet been accepted into another. So she is in a marginal state of existence. The French use an adjective, *'liminaire'* – 'of the threshold' – to describe the rituals which help her through this difficult process. These rituals also enable others to protect themselves, in turn, from the dangers she presents, for there is very often the additional element of contagion. As she is passing through this transitional phase of identity she is perceived as a threat to those around her, and especially to men. The unborn baby is in ritual danger, too. It has as yet no place in the social system; no one even knows what sex it will be, what it will be like, or whether it will survive. So it, too, is in a marginal state and treated not only as at risk itself, but as vaguely threatening.

The Lele of Central Africa believe that the child in the womb is vulnerable, just as its mother is constantly in danger. But this baby can also do a lot of damage. The expectant Lele mother avoids going near sick people, who might be harmed by her baby, nor should she go near grain growing in the fields, since her unborn baby may take it and cause a poor harvest. If she speaks to those who are reaping or brewing beer she can affect the quality of their products unless she first makes a ritual gesture of goodwill to cancel the threat. The unborn child has 'jaws agape', they say, and is continually snatching at food because it is so hungry. Food is spoiled; plants will not grow; the smith's iron cannot be worked; the milk goes bad. And the baby's father is at special risk in his hunting and if he goes into battle.[3]

In pregnancy, prohibitions and instructions frequently have the force of taboo, a term derived from a Polynesian word which means 'forbidden'. This concept exists in one form or another all over the world. It is *touda* among the Central African Ila, *bwanga* among the Bemba of the same area, and *haram* in Arab countries.

Neglect of a taboo results in some dreadful change affecting the person who flouts it, a change which can contaminate other people too, so that the offender becomes a danger to others. The consequences of breaking a taboo are quite different from human punishment, for the result is automatic punishment from spiritual forces or gods.

Concepts of taboo operate around a core idea of pollution and cleanliness. Pollution has been described as 'matter out of place'.[4] In many cultures the human body is seen as a vessel which must not be contaminated. Its exits and entrances must normally be kept closed. All body products, matter issuing from the interior of the body, whether blood, pus, saliva, semen, faeces, urine or nasal mucus – even breath and body heat – must not be allowed to invade other people's body boundaries. For some societies, including those within Judaeo-Christian and Hindu traditions, the essence of all these forms of pollution is expressed in the mixing of the male and female principles represented by semen and menstrual blood.

Not only should a menstruating woman keep away from men and all important activities (in some agricultural communities it is still thought that if she churns butter or cures bacon, for example, the butter will go sour and the bacon bad), but in some cultures anybody in an especially vulnerable condition must be careful to avoid a menstruating or pregnant woman. If the expectant Guatemalan mother stares at a baby, an animal or even a plant, her 'hot', 'strong' blood will make it die.[5] Above all, a pregnant woman's body is dangerous to men. If life is to be orderly, male and female principles must remain separate from each other.

Taboos can be very powerful. In the Andaman Islands a name is given to the baby before birth, and from that moment on until it is born and is several weeks old, no one may speak the name of the mother or father. They can say only 'the father of' or 'the mother of' and name the child. The parents also abstain from eating certain foods lest they become ill or the baby dies. It is significant that the Andamanese observe identical taboos when mourning the dead. They never use the name of the dead person, and the relatives must not eat pork or turtle. The parents of the child being born, like the person who has died, have an abnormal ritual status and are thus in danger.

In my anthropological fieldwork in Jamaica I recorded a wide range of rules which guide the pregnant woman and regulate her daily life. If she follows them, she feels she is doing all she can to have a safe birth and a live, healthy baby, in much the same way that women in the West who attend their antenatal clinics with regularity feel that, even though they dislike going, they are doing the best they can for their babies. A pregnant Jamaican woman must not step over a donkey's tethering rope because then the baby may stay inside, nor should she put corks in bottles because this may lead to a difficult labour in which she cannot 'open up'. She must not see a corpse in case her blood becomes chilled and the baby inside her turns cold and dies, for in pregnancy the blood is hot, and ritual separation must be kept between categories of objects which are 'hot' and others which are 'cold'. Pregnant women must drink slowly because too much water drowns the baby. They must not make too much preparation ahead of time or the child may be stillborn. This belief is not so different from the English superstition that if a pregnant woman buys a pram before the birth her baby may not survive.

A pregnant Jamaican woman must not drink soursop juice or she will have great pain in labour; she should avoid drinking out of bottles or coconuts because that makes the baby cross-eyed, and if she walks over soapy water when someone is scrubbing the floor she may get stomach-ache. She must not lift her arms above her head or the baby's neck will stretch, and then when she lowers her arms again and it returns to its normal position it is scorched, so that the baby is born with a birthmark on its neck. She must not eat coconuts or the baby will grow too quickly. If she sees anything shocking or ugly, or is upset about something, the baby may be marked. If she notices a person with an amputated leg, for example, her baby may be born like that, or if she wrings a chicken's neck and feels sorry for the bird, the baby may look like a chicken.

Pregnant Jamaican women are vulnerable to the activities of the spirits of the dead, the duppies. When women suffer from eclampsia (fits), it is thought to be spirit possession. In Hindu India it is also believed that eclampsia is spirit possession, and that spirits seeking reincarnation wander abroad and may inhabit the bodies of pregnant women.

There are other things that pregnant Jamaican women should be careful to do if they want an easy labour and a healthy baby. They should drink 'bitters' in the form of bush teas; this is to keep the blood from becoming overheated and so endangering the child. The expectant mother eats callalu, which is like spinach, to make her blood 'rich', and okra, which has a very slippery interior, so that the baby slips out easily.

Sexual intercourse during pregnancy is encouraged in some societies in order to 'feed the womb' or 'nourish the baby', while in others it is forbidden. For the Hopi of Northern Arizona it is important for intercourse to continue throughout pregnancy so that the baby grows and the birth is easy. One Hopi explained that it was like irrigating a crop.[6] Among the Mbuti of Zaïre, intercourse is taboo during pregnancy because it takes away a man's strength, just as it does before a hunt.[7] The Mbuti depend on hunting for food, so prohibition of intercourse before birth and before going out on a hunt stresses the importance of these two activities. For these hunters and gatherers the forest is not just an environment but a living thing, natural and supernatural, which they depend on, obey and love, and of which they are also in awe.

In many traditional cultures care is given to the psychological state of the mother. Any emotional disturbance is believed to affect the baby. The Tonawanda Seneca, a native American people, say that distress experienced by a pregnant woman can make her baby nervous, and her unhappiness will make the baby inside her unhappy, too.[8] In Egyptian peasant culture it is thought that a woman is likely to have a miscarriage or stillbirth if her husband upsets her. 'The child may be born burned out from the distress because he gets burned from sadness and this affects the child because he eats from the blood of his mother.'[9] Research into the effects of extreme or prolonged stress on pregnancy, and the release of hormones into the maternal bloodstream stimulated by strong emotional arousal, suggests that this traditional wisdom may not be so far off the mark.

As soon as she is pregnant a woman who was until then a low-status newcomer to her husband's family takes on a new status, and with this bonds of affection may be created. In Korea it is the mother-in-law's task to start the training of the child's character while it is still in the uterus. To this end she should show warmth to her daughter-in-law and do everything she can to make her happy, to surround her with beautiful things, and to serve delicately prepared dishes.[10]

In present-day Japan traditional rites of pregnancy are usually maintained alongside antenatal clinic visits typical of an industrialized society. During the fifth month a public announcement of pregnancy is made at the ceremony of the *obi-iwai*, when the pregnant woman wraps around her the *hara-obi*, a long cotton sash which has been bought at a shrine. This act is performed on a special day, a dog day, since the dog is the symbol of an easy birth. The doctor may give advice on how this binding should be done, and may even sign the *obi* with a character of congratulations. The *obi* is often a gift from the woman's parents, who arrive at the young couple's home with a tray of rice cakes to share around, and there is a celebratory meal. The modern Japanese woman can even wear the *obi* with a leotard, since one firm manufactures leotards with a built-in *obi* in the form of a support band under the abdomen. Several weeks before the expected date of delivery the woman may go back to her parents' home and give birth in a hospital nearby, remaining there until the baby is at least a month old.[11]

Whilst pregnancy in most societies is considered a ritual condition, and one which links the woman and the coming baby both to the earth and to the gods, it is not treated as an illness. Peasant women continue their normal activities and work hard in the fields and at domestic tasks such as chopping wood, drawing water from the well and scrubbing and cleaning at least until their contractions start, and usually during most of labour. In fact, it is often thought that if a woman does not keep physically active the birth will be hard. In Thailand she continues to carry water and pound rice so that the womb will be 'loose'. Pregnant Keneba women of the Gambia carry loads of clay or salt weighing up to forty pounds on their heads. They also pound grain, cook, wash, clean, draw water from wells sometimes sixty feet deep, gather firewood, collect edible leaves and snails, look after hens and goats, extract salt a mile from the village, dig clay for pottery, make soap, beat the earth floors of huts that are being built, and work on rice farms up to eight miles from their village.[12] Throughout the world activities of this kind are considered suitable for pregnancy, provided the woman is careful to observe the important taboos which guard her own health and that of the baby.

Becoming a Mother in the West

Western culture lacks ritual celebrating the unfolding process of pregnancy, drawing together the future parents and the families in glad preparation for the birth of the baby, and linking this one baby's birth with universal powers. Instead, the pregnant woman becomes a 'patient' in the same way that anyone who is ill or who suffers a handicap becomes the object of medical attention. The recording and monitoring of pregnancy is taken over by professionals who are not themselves part of the community in which the mother lives, and family and friends are powerless to affect it one way or another. Although pregnancy in a traditional society may have been a time in which alarming warnings were given to the expectant mother about what she must and must not do, our own society has made the journey through pregnancy equally or even more anxiety-arousing by making its progress one of continuous obstetric investigation, assessment and intervention.

However many times doctors may tell their pregnant patients that pregnancy is not an illness, we know that it is *treated* as if it is. And in our northern industrial culture each woman, instead of being in *ritual* and spiritual danger, is at *statistical* risk. Whereas spiritual danger can be handled traditionally by ceremonies that call on the ancestors and the power of nature, there is no way of avoiding statistical risk.

Once a baby is on the way, a woman is taken over by a medical system that treats her concerns as trivial, and that expects her to hand herself over to its care without asking too many questions or disrupting the smooth running of the institution. Any woman who was hoping for negotiation and discussion with her care-givers is likely to be frustrated the very first time she attends an antenatal clinic. Most clinics function as if they were designed to arouse anxiety in the women attending them. Women say 'everything was rushed', 'it was just like a conveyor belt', 'the doctor was so busy I didn't like to bother him', 'I went in with a lot of questions, but when they had finished doing all the examinations I couldn't remember one of them', 'I wanted to ask a whole host of things, but lying with my bottom half bare and my legs up in stirrups I just couldn't', and 'I don't think they are interested in anything except my uterus.'

The undermining and systematic disorientation of women who are becoming mothers starts with antenatal care. Psychologists sometimes focus only on the period after birth, the so-called 'bonding time', and on the emotional work that must be done then in order to nurture a baby. Yet everything that happens once the baby is born is the outcome of all that has gone before.

In technologically orientated cultures, antenatal care might be designed specifically to degrade women and mould them into dependent, compliant patients. The expectant mother is frequently treated as the passive object of management. She is fed into the medical system and her progress through it from point to point is carefully controlled, any wishes or preferences of her own invalidated by autocratic and paternalistic medical obstetric management. Even in those countries where there is a consumer movement, and where women are beginning to voice their concerns about degrading treatment, the power imbalance between doctors and patients means that women have very little say in the kind of care they receive, and are often fobbed off with 'the doctor knows best' or are subjected to emotional blackmail with the threat that they are harming their babies. Antenatal clinics are often a long distance from where those they are intended to serve actually live or work. When a woman does not make it to a clinic appointment that entails going on two different buses and waiting around for two hours before she is seen, she is classed as a 'defaulter'. It is seen as her personal failure rather than the failure of society to provide for the needs of mothers. The clinic is often terribly over-crowded, with the atmosphere of a badly managed cattle market. Facilities for child care may not exist, playthings are rarely provided, and there is nothing to do there except wait. Each time a woman attends she sees different, anonymous faces, for there is no continuity of care. She is probably given conflicting information and advice, and goes away from each clinic appointment bewildered, anxious or depressed. She sees the obstetrician for perhaps one or two minutes, and the contact with him (for it is usually a man) consists of a brief laying on of hands as she is given a pelvic examination. It is as if she has become merely an ambulant pelvis. In some countries women have a screen drawn in front of their faces, or, as in Japan, are required to hold their case notes in front of them so that there is no possibility of human contact or of the doctor ever recognizing the woman whose abdomen he is palpating or whose vagina his hand is investigating. There is no opportunity for asking questions, for voicing anxieties or for any discussion. A woman is merely at the receiving end of care.

The women who are most at risk, those from deprived socio-economic backgrounds and immigrant women trying to learn a new language and adapt to an alien culture, are those least likely to get the care they need. It is often assumed that it is only middle-class women who are dissatisfied with the system of maternity care to which they are exposed during pregnancy. Yet there is ample evidence now that women generally experience antenatal care as largely irrelevant to their own concerns about the pregnancy, and that the message they are given by the factory-farm kind of processes to which they must often submit in clinics is that they are faulty machines at constant risk of break-down, which can only be kept in running order if under the careful surveillance of the senior mechanic.[13]

For many women, especially those pregnant for the first time at the age of twenty-eight or older, and so classed as 'elderly primigravidae', pregnancy is like walking across a minefield of hidden dangers. Too much weight gain and medical brows are furrowed; too little and doctors are concerned about placental malfunction. In a study I made of women's subjective experiences of induction of labour it transpired that women were told they were being induced because they had put on too much or had not gained enough weight, and 'normal' weight gain was defined so narrowly by some obstetricians that only a small proportion of women could hope to qualify for a labour that was not started artificially.[14] Blood-pressure must stay within carefully defined limits. Yet no studies have been done to determine if there are any socially created stresses in the life of a pregnant woman today which may make it likely that she will become hypertensive. Women often believe that just going to the hospital makes their blood-pressure go up. Some comment that their blood-pressure is lower when they are examined in the surgery of a general practitioner whom they know well, and lower still when the midwife visits the home and checks their blood-pressure in familiar surroundings. Although a steep rise in blood-pressure is dangerous, hypertension is used far too indiscriminately as the great argument for induction, and also as a reason for going into hospital for the birth. One midwife remarked that she had been told by an obstetrician, about a woman who wanted to give birth at home, 'That's all right. Just string her along, and in the last week or so I'll tell her her blood-pressure is up and she must come into hospital.'

Abdominal girth, position of the foetus, haemoglobin counts and other blood tests, urine tests for sugar and protein, other tests of blood or urine for oestriol production from the placenta, pelvic assessment, abdominal and vaginal examinations, sonar scans and perhaps an amniocentesis to detect whether or not the foetus has a chromosome abnormality or spina bifida or microcephaly or . . . There seems to be no end to the fascinating investigations which can be made. Used with discretion when there is an indication of the need for them, some of these tests are of value. Used wholesale, just because the apparatus is there, or the team is doing research, with inadequate explanation, and without reference to the woman as a person, they cause confusion and distress. One result is that the majority of expectant mothers have little confidence that they are capable of giving birth to a live healthy baby without medical help. They no longer trust their own bodies. This is a direct consequence of the management of childbirth by obstetricians.

The medical system in our technological culture has its own rituals of pregnancy designed to guard the mother and foetus from harm. The ceremonial of the antenatal clinic serves as a rite of passage, symbolically registering the significance of the transition to birth. It centres on the foetus and its development to viability. The mother is relevant only in so far as she is the container for the foetus. Pregnancy is turned into a medical process in which the foetus is monitored, and its growth recorded and supervised. The woman who is bearing the child takes second place. In fact, she is an inconvenient obstacle to inspection of the foetus.

The first ceremony consists of the formal medical acknowledgement of pregnancy, and the transformation of a woman into a 'patient'. The doctor confirms that she is pregnant, fills in forms that register this, makes arrangements for the medical management of the pregnancy and books her into a hospital. She usually knew she was pregnant before this visit, but only now is the pregnancy legitimized.

There follow clinic visits, at first every month, then every two weeks, and finally each week. A woman who does not attend these regularly becomes a 'defaulter'. She is perceived as failing in her duty to the foetus, rather like a soldier who becomes a deserter.

At each visit routine screening of the foetus is carried out. Some of this provides a fairly accurate record of growth and development, but some is highly inaccurate. Tests that enable doctors to monitor the foetus with some accuracy include systematic assessment of the height of the fundus (the top of the uterus), listening to the baby's heart, and, if it is done serially, the measurement of bone growth and observation of foetal movements with ultrasound.

Tests that produce inaccurate results include use of the ultrasound scan in the first half of pregnancy to predict placenta praevia (the placenta lying in front of the baby's head), an observation that is useful only at the end of pregnancy, routine weighing of the mother, and the regular taking of blood to measure the level of haemoglobin. Many women have a low-lying placenta at sixteen weeks, which is the usual time when a routine scan is done. As the uterus enlarges the placenta rises higher, and diagnosis of possible placenta praevia on the basis of a low-lying placenta is likely to be false. It has been known since the 1960s that there is very little relation between a woman's weight gain and the baby's weight at different phases of pregnancy and at birth, but women are still being weighed regularly.[15]

The idea behind blood tests is to ensure that a woman's haemoglobin level stays high, and to prescribe iron if it is not. Haemoglobin levels normally drop during pregnancy because there is more blood circulating in the body, so it becomes diluted. The trouble is that if a woman who does not really need it has supplementary iron her red blood cells may get so large that they cannot filter through the placenta or pass through the fine blood vessels in the baby's body. Research in the seventies revealed that high haemoglobin levels reduce the baby's growth and increase the risk of having an underweight baby.[16]

Vaginal examination is for some obstetricians another routine practice which is not only useless but can be dangerous, because it leads to infection.[17] The scenario goes something like this: 'Just pop up on the couch, young woman, and we'll have a look.' (In Britain pregnant women are always being instructed to 'pop'.) A gloved hand slips inside and then emerges with a slurp and squelch like that of a rubber boot stuck in a swamp. Thus a woman is ritually dispossessed of her body in pregnancy: the doctors have taken charge. It represents a symbolic assertion that they know more about her body than she can herself; the foetus is *their* responsibility, and only theirs.

Any screening procedure, even one most likely to produce information useful to doctors, can be employed ritually. It cannot be taken for granted that because a test involves modern technology it has a scientific basis, nor that it is being used appropriately, nor that it produces information that is really necessary. A now standard procedure when a woman seeks home birth in Britain, for example, is that the GP sends her to the hospital for a one-off scan, at whatever-stage of pregnancy she happens to be when it becomes clear to the doctor that she intends to have a home birth. A single scan is very unlikely to give any useful information that cannot be derived more simply from other tests and by abdominal palpation from a hands-on midwife. But the compulsory hospital visit and ultrasound scan is obligatory because it is a powerful symbol of medical authority.

Medical technology, intervention, drugs, all the paraphernalia of the modern hospital are used as elements in a ritual performance, as a talisman in the face of risk, charms against danger. When I was in Jamaica, peasant women often poured large quantities of antiseptic into their babies' bath water. This was not only unnecessary but brought the babies out in rashes. The antiseptic was being used ritually, for Jamaican mothers have always used washing blue in their babies' bath water in order to keep away the duppies, the spirits of the dead. Ultrasound and biophysical tests are often employed in the same way in modern hospitals.

Grateful as most women are for antenatal care, even awed by the advanced technology, it is not difficult to understand how a woman can feel that she is merely a vessel for a foetus, and that her body is a barrier to easy access, to the probing of all those rubber-gloved fingers and the gleaming equipment, and even – ridiculous, but we are talking about feelings – that if she were not around the pregnancy could progress with more efficiency. Her experience of care is often one of being 'processed through a clinic, "herded" with other women holding their little bottles of urine', with no one of whom they can ask questions in an unhurried atmosphere or discuss things that are on their minds. Sometimes the system works efficiently: 'We all smoothly slid through the machine . . . One is only a number on a card. I saw a different doctor at most visits.' Sometimes the machine creaks and comes to a standstill: 'Waiting time was anything up to three hours, and was usually at least an hour and a half.' Often the procedures cause acute anxiety 'There was a muddle over dates because too many doctors were involved and skimmed through the notes, and I got very worried' . . . 'The obstetrician stood between me and the scan and said, "Strange". When I asked what was the matter he said, "Nothing. Nothing", so I presumed the foetus had the wrong number of arms and legs.'[18]

Each woman who receives antenatal care in a large modern hospital is at risk of no longer feeling herself the creator, the 'I' who in her unique way makes her unique baby. In terms of human values that is a loss which it is difficult, if not impossible, to estimate. The effect of this is to disempower women just at the point in their lives when they need to be most strong and to have the self-confidence to take on the challenge of motherhood.

Pregnancy in our society can be a very lonely time, too. A woman may turn for support and understanding to her partner. Yet he is often less able to give help than normally because he feels, too, that other people are in control of the pregnancy, and he has neither the knowledge nor the confidence with which to support her. He may say, 'Well, they're the experts, aren't they? You've got to rely on them.' He is also going through an often difficult process of transformation. He may be anxious about losing his freedom, about being weighed down by the extra financial responsibilities, and anxious for his partner, even fearing that she may die. Their relationship is changing too. The couple started off as Jane and Bill and now have to become 'Mummy and Daddy'. The future grandparents may be hundreds of miles away. Even if they live nearby they have no defined roles, and may worry about interfering. Many pregnant women want to show that they can be independent, that they can cope with pregnancy without seeking help from their mothers, so there is often this added emotional barrier to seeking help.

Childbirth Classes: Woman to Woman

There is one striking exception to the pathologizing of pregnancy and to the social isolation experienced by women in technological culture. It is in its own way a ritual process, yet one that is centred on the woman and her needs, on the whole transition to parent, instead of on the demands of the medical system. This is the child-birth education class run by independent childbirth organizations, such as the International Childbirth Education Association in the USA and the Active Birth Movement and the National Childbirth Trust in Britain. These organizations began to come into being in the fifties, first in Britain and then in the USA and in other European countries, set up by women who were themselves mothers and who resisted the increasing medicalization of birth. They sought to provide emotional support and friendship in pregnancy, information about non-pharmacological ways of handling pain, and preparation for childbirth in small, friendly groups.

In the former USSR and communist countries of Eastern Europe, however, birth education was initiated by, and remained firmly under the control of health professionals. When it was introduced in the 1960s in the USSR, attendance at antenatal classes was made compulsory from the thirty-second week of pregnancy. Most Russian obstetricians are women, but there is still heavy emphasis on their role as birth technicians and as employees of the state, rather than on their understanding of birth as women and mothers themselves. In the psychoprophylaxis classes of the sixties they had to follow the rules laid down by a central authority: 'Women must be . . . immunized to labour pain. Physicians must normalize and reorganize the minds of women poisoned by . . . erroneous ideas.' The language is authoritarian and didactic. The objectives of birth education are 'to teach the pregnant woman proper conduct during labour so that she may follow instructions properly'. 'By understanding all the medical measures conducted in the institution the pregnant woman will be disciplined.' 'The physician should emotionally emphasize motherhood's high social virtues confirmed in the Soviet Union by the establishment of Government awards – orders and medals – and honorary titles to mothers of many children.'[19] Russian psychoprophylaxis stressed *control* over the mother and her correct behaviour as a patient. There has now been a political revolution. But revolution in women's health care has yet to come.

Wherever birth education is not under the control of women themselves, but is promoted or imposed by large, hierarchical institutions, it is dogmatic, authoritarian, inflexible, and even punitive towards women who do not conform. Women are told, 'Here is what will happen to you' . . . They are taught to relax, so as not to be a nuisance. They are supposed to lie in bed tidily under the sheet, to be quiet so as not to frighten other women or interfere with the smooth running of the labour and delivery room, to breathe in order to suppress the desire to scream out in pain. What this adds up to is that the woman is taught to control herself so that she can be more effectively controlled by those caring for her.

Because Western childbirth groups were lay organizations,

were not subordinate to the medical hierarchy, and gave woman-to-woman support, childbirth education with them developed along very different lines. Even so, it was not enough for them to state that they wanted to help women. To justify what they were doing at first they appealed to eugenics. In Britain, the Natural Childbirth Association, established in 1956 – out of which grew the National Childbirth Trust – promised in its newsletter that babies born without drugs 'are better babies . . . and we urgently need in Britain a race of good-quality men and women.'[20] Following the Second World War there was great concern about what was forecast as the depopulation of the West and a striving to build a new society in which healthy citizens could realize their full potential. The Association 'promoted motherhood as women's ultimate duty and fulfilment, and promised that natural birth contributed to family harmony and therefore reinforced the foundations of society'.[21]

In spite of this attempt to appeal to belief in traditional family values, one effect of the amateur status of these groups was that doctors and midwives found them threatening, and often ridiculed the women who worked in them and those who attended the classes. As a result a primary concern of antenatal teachers in the sixties was to avoid antagonizing the medical profession. 'We should do nothing to sap a woman's confidence in the place she is to be delivered, or encourage her to discuss the use of drugs with her doctor when she would soon be out of her depth.'[22] Approval by those doctors and midwives who praised the self-control and co-operativeness of women who had attended NCT classes was eagerly recorded, and whenever possible doctors were enlisted as advisers. Women were expected to use charm and tact to persuade doctors to allow them to labour without drugs and other interventions. But this strategy did not work. The late sixties and early seventies saw the introduction of more technology and obstetric intervention than ever before.

Some women welcomed with relief the introduction via France to Britain and the USA of Russian-style psychoprophylaxis. They strove above all to gain control over their own bodies, and trained for birth as they might for the Olympic high jump. If a woman screamed out in labour, asked for pain-relieving drugs or 'lost control' in some other way, she felt that she had 'failed'. She was drilled, with her husband as 'coach', as one American textbook put it, to 'react in a precise and orderly manner to uterine stimuli'.[23] The members of a childbirth class marched on labour like a disciplined army. In Britain birth was 'B-day'. Women trained as if for battle, and the victory was to be over their bodies and their own 'negative conditioning'. This method of birth education was often co-opted in a modified form by the medical system because it could then be taught as a series of exercises to large classes.

Yet as women shared experiences with each other there was more open and sharper criticism of hospitals and of the routine interventions that by the early seventies had become an established part of childbirth. Almost one in two British women could expect to have labour induced. This led to the need for drugs to reduce the pain caused by the artificial stimulation of the uterus and disturbance of the whole physiology of childbirth, which itself resulted in many other interventions.

Knowledge of alternatives and the right to choose between them was a concept that was slow to become accepted. In the early sixties the National Childbirth Trust (NCT) had resisted the establishment of the Association for Improvement in Maternity Services (AIMS) on the grounds that AIMS promoted the idea that 'women should be free to choose whatever way they want to have their baby'.[24] It took fifteen years or more for the NCT to shift its emphasis to the rights of every woman to make her own decisions.

During the eighties there was a radical shift of emphasis. The independent birth organizations stressed that a woman could have no internal control, could not surrender to the birth experience, if she was unable to control what other people did to her. The new focus was on the environment for birth, negotiation with care-givers, and on working out 'birth plans'.

In the early years, failures in communication, 'misunderstandings', had always been presented as an excuse for distressing birth experiences, the implication being that if the givers and recipients of care communicated more effectively everyone would be happy. Such an assumption ignored the power of the medical system and the relative powerlessness of patients, especially of childbearing women in relation to male obstetricians. By the eighties and nineties there was much more open criticism of obstetrics, and also a new alliance with midwives, who were becoming increasingly disenchanted with the obstetric way of birth. The result has been a new awareness that birth is a political issue.

Childbirth classes remain the one place where a pregnant woman and her partner can focus on the changes in emotions and relationships entailed in becoming parents, and on their own needs, where they can develop self-confidence, and have at least a chance of maintaining this when confronted with the power of the medical system. In Western culture these classes, with the opportunity they present to share hopes and fears with other pregnant women and to prepare for a major life experience, are the only ritual activity that focuses on the needs of women who are becoming mothers. It is a ritual that, significantly, has been created by women who are mothers themselves, rather than by doctors or other professionals within the medical system.

Childbirth education was started and has been developed by women striving for freedom in childbirth. As a result, it has a distinct character that clearly differentiates it from birth education in an autocratic system. It educates not only prospective parents but also birth professionals, and stimulates constructive change in women's health care.

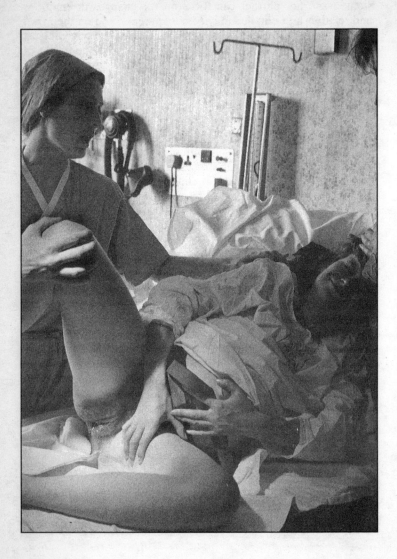

7

Birth – A Social Act

Birth is not just a matter of biology and primordial urges, but of cultural values. We have seen that in many societies the birth of a child is the consummation of marriage, rather than sexual intercourse, and that a girl does not achieve adult status until she has given birth. A baby has a profound effect on the relationship between a couple, and between them and other family members. The woman's identity changes too: she becomes a different kind of person – a mother. In highly segmented societies, such as India or South Africa, and in countries where there are extremes of poverty and wealth, such as Latin America, discovering what happens in childbirth at different socio-economic or caste levels can also tell us about the relative status of everyone concerned.

A woman knows how to get a baby born without ever reading a book about it or going to birth classes. There are elements in birth which she shares with other mammalian mothers, especially primates, powerful cues coming from inside her body which make her want to be upright and bend her knees, for example, and to hold her breath intermittently as she pushes the baby out, and then to reach down and touch her newborn child. But there are also strong cues coming from the environment, from those helping, and from her expectations about what she should be doing and about what her helpers should be doing as well. This is why childbirth is never simply 'natural'. Just as eating, drinking, excreting waste products from the body, sexual intercourse, puberty, old age and dying are culturally defined, birth reflects social values, and varies with each society.

A woman in labour may seem to be engaged in a purely biological and in many ways solitary activity. If things are going well she probably feels that what she is doing is entirely instinctive. But even though she may bear her child completely alone and unaided, society expresses through her its values about pregnancy and childbirth. Human birth is a cultural act.

Anthropologists do not write much about birth – possibly because they are often men and are not permitted to take part in the rituals surrounding labour, and because women anthropologists often delay having babies until after they have done their fieldwork. They have, however, written so extensively about the disposal of the placenta that we might be forgiven for believing that this must be one of the most important rites in childbirth. I suspect that the male anthropologist, not allowed to witness birth, waits outside the birth hut for the moment when someone emerges bearing the placenta, at which point he can at last make some useful addition to his notes.

From the evidence of female anthropologists who know something about childbirth, it is clear that it is rarely the casual 'dropping of a baby' which it is popularly believed to be in simpler societies. Instead it is surrounded and shaped by ritual and myth, injunctions, prohibitions and taboos, representing in symbolic forms 'the crucial values of the believing community'.[1] Just as table manners and emptying the bowels and bladder are closely regulated and follow unwritten rules, conventions and etiquette that control what is done, and where, and how, so too are attitudes to and behaviour in childbirth socially controlled.

In every physiological activity that involves the exits and entrances of our bodies, the way in which we behave is intimately bound up with ideas about the location, worth and workings of the different parts of the body. These include fantasies about our bodies' inner geography – the position, size, structure and function of various organs – which may be only vaguely related to fact. We have ideas, too, about our body boundaries, which are an essential part of our sense of wholeness and identity.

Each society has its own culturally approved ideas about how babies develop inside the uterus, how they are born, and how the mother and other people can help or hinder the process. When labour starts the woman and those helping her expect certain kinds of things to be done, often without even thinking consciously about what they are going to do, or why. This is as true for Western technological culture as it is for traditional cultures.

We must not imagine that childbirth is always easy in traditional cultures, or that women give birth without pain. There may be strict rules about a woman's behaviour in labour which make her family ashamed if she allows herself to cry out in pain. Her labour may be a testing time comparable to that of her initiation at puberty. Although many healthy women deliver in the fields or in between household tasks, and continue their work soon after, babies are often lost through miscarriage and stillbirth, too. And some girls who suffer from anaemia, protein malnutrition or endemic diseases such as malaria never reach childbearing age, or die before they safely deliver their first baby. So healthy women are picked out, by natural and cultural circumstances, to survive and become mothers. Even so, many of these die, too. Abortion is a major cause of death. The proportion of maternal deaths due to women trying to end unwanted pregnancies is approximately 20 per cent in Bangladesh, 29 per cent in Ethiopia, 64 per cent in Chile, and in Romania, a country where it has been next to impossible to obtain contraception, 86 per cent.[2]

Men and Childbirth

Childbirth, like menstruation, in many societies is thought to bring danger to men who encroach too near. In Judaeo-Christian thought that idea can be traced back to Leviticus. The seventh-century Archbishop Theodore of Canterbury proclaimed that a newly delivered woman must be isolated for forty days till clean, and that if any woman went into a church while menstruating she had to fast for three weeks. The Penitential of Archbishop Egber (AD 735–766) states that 'every religious woman should keep her chastity for three months before childbirth and for sixty nights and days after'.[3] This is not for the woman's sake, but because a newly delivered woman is dangerous to men. Not only is the menstruating or parturient woman ritually unclean, but her body products, nail parings, hair clippings and, most important of all, her secretions and blood, are taboo to men, and can result in illness or even death.

Even so, men are involved in birth, in a less direct way. It is usually considered important that a father is identified, even if he is not actually the biological father. Among Australian Aborigines, for example, the spirit of the baby appears in a dream to its father 'establishing the child's credentials by demonstrating a clearcut pre-natal connection between father and child', and so legitimizing the baby.[4]

There is a strict rule in many cultures that the father should stay away from the place of birth. Male and female elements must be kept separate. But even when he is not supposed to be there it is often believed that the baby's health and life depend to a great extent on his actions. He has a ritual responsibility to ensure a safe pregnancy and birth. If he goes off with another woman, or polishes his spear, or goes fishing on the day of labour, he is putting the baby's life at risk. He must watch his actions and in this way help the birth. So he participates actively even though he is not physically present. The Koran states that a father should offer prayers at birth, and he introduces the baby to the world by placing a piece of date in its mouth.

The Arapesh of New Guinea rely on the prospective father to contribute towards the health and welfare of the unborn baby by his own careful conduct, both in the way that he has intercourse – deliberately and thoughtfully in the early weeks of pregnancy – and in the emotionally supportive, stress-free environment he should create for the pregnant woman. In fact, the verb 'to bear a child' applies equally to women and men, and childbearing is believed to be as much a strain for the father as it may be for the mother. He is involved from the very beginning of pregnancy because the Arapesh believe that a man must really work at sexual intercourse in order for a child to be conceived, and continue doing this until his wife's periods stop. But once her breasts begin to enlarge the child is complete in miniature, and from then on intercourse is forbidden.[5]

In Thailand it is the father's responsibility to cut and stack the tamarind wood ready for the mother's 'fire-rest' after childbirth, when she lies on a board near a fire that protects her from evil spirits. In Northern Thailand he must also build a fence around the area under the house, which is built on stilts, directly under the birthing room, and place thorns all around this fence to keep out evil spirits. After the baby is born he cooks for his wife for the first two weeks or so. He prepares rice balls, sticks them on wooden skewers, and toasts them in the fire for her.[6]

In the few societies where the husband delivers the baby himself, as he does among the Bang Chan of South-east Asia, he must be specially protected from female forces.[7] He takes in his hands incense, flowers and a lighted candle, which allow him to cross over into the sacred world in which birth takes place. Then he prays for the help of the spirits to make the winds of birth strong in his body, for it is not he but the winds which deliver the baby, and he is there only to receive it.

In the custom of the *couvade*, which comes from the French 'to hatch', the husband either shares in the birth by acting it out at the same time as his wife is in labour, or he shares the lying-in period. Especially in societies in which it is uncertain who exactly is the father of the baby, this is a way in which a man claims fatherhood. An Arapesh father, for example, waits to hear the sex of the baby. Then he says 'wash it' or 'do not wash it', depending on whether he wishes it to live or not. In many societies abortion is the only effective means of birth control, and boys are usually preferred because they will grow up to inherit their father's land, while girls will pass outside the paternal family. If the Arapesh child is to be saved, it is the father who makes the decision, and he takes a bundle of soft leaves to his wife so that she can line the net bag in which the baby is suspended in a crouching position, a coconut shell of water for bathing the baby, and pungent leaves to keep evil out of her hut.[8] He also brings his wooden pillow and lies down beside his wife, and both have nothing to eat or drink for the first day after birth. They concentrate on performing magic rites for the welfare of the child and remain in seclusion for five days. The father must not touch his own body nor handle tobacco. He must eat all food with a spoon until a ceremony of ritual cleansing is performed at a pool in a leaf house built beside it. Even then his diet is still restricted, and he must not eat meat until the baby is a month old.

Although a father may be called upon to fill this supportive, sharing role, and male magicians may be summoned when things seem to be going wrong, in traditional societies the man as child-birth technician is unknown. There is no one who corresponds to the obstetrician of Western society. Birth takes place on female territory and is conducted entirely by women.

In all societies men who have engaged in midwifery have done so at their peril. In England the first male midwives were

95

not recognized until the seventeenth century. Up to that time a physician who was requested by the midwife to assist at a difficult labour had to creep up on his hands and knees and hide under the furniture, for it was considered disgusting for men to be involved with childbirth. The traditional English position for giving birth, on the left side, is said to derive from the woman's modesty at letting a man see her body, since in this position she has her back to the doctor and he need not see her face. Even when male midwives became accepted they had to grope under the bedclothes, sometimes with the sheet tied round their necks for decency's sake, when delivering a baby, and to rely entirely upon their sense of touch.

The God Sibs

Throughout the world it is the responsibility of women to help a friend, neighbour or relative in labour, except in a few cases where a woman goes off into the bush alone to deliver her baby. You learn how to help other women have babies just as you learn how to cook. In Elizabethan times in England a woman laboured surrounded by her 'gossips', a great deal of strong drink was consumed by all, including the mother, and 'there was often more merriment than at a feast'.[9] Much the same occurred in rural Japan, where the married women of the village gathered together at the house of a woman in childbirth and grunted and shouted in unison with her. This was called *goriki*: 'sharing'.[10]

The medieval term for these women was the 'god sibs', literally 'sisters in God', since throughout Europe they also had the religious function of being witnesses at the baptism. The term implies that they were not only practical helpers and comforters, but had a spiritual responsibility for shepherding the baby through the birth and into the community of faith. This gathering of women who came and took over the house was resented by men, who had no part in the birth nor in the lying-in afterwards, and in male usage the words 'god sib' gradually became changed to 'gossip'.

Woman-to-woman support in childbirth remained the dominant pattern all over Europe, as well as in the newly colonized lands of North America, right through into the twentieth century. A woman continued to select the people whom she wanted to be with her in childbirth. With the first signs that labour was starting she called on her friends, who often came from all around the neighbourhood, and who would then stay for at least a few days, and sometimes for weeks on end. It was the husband's responsibility to get messages to all the women who were invited to attend. An American father writing in his diary in 1740 records that:

> My wife had been somewhat ill all night but in the morning was so full of pain that I rode away to fetch Granny Forbush (the midwife) to her. The Snow which fell last night added to the former . . . made it extraordinarily difficult passing. I was overmatch'd with it at old Mr Maynards. Ebenezer Maynard and Neighbor Pratt took their horses and wife, and fetch'd Mrs How and Ensign Forbush's wife. Ensign Maynard brought his wife and fetch'd Mrs Whipple. Mr Williams also brought over his.[11]

Even after doctors came on the scene it was these women friends, neighbours and family members who orchestrated everything that took place in the birthing room. For a long time no doctor dared do anything that was met with disapproval by these women. Every intervention proposed by him had to be discussed by the women helpers, and he could go ahead only with their approval. When one nineteenth-century American doctor wanted to use the crochet, an instrument like a crochet hook, to dismember a baby and get it out in pieces, 'the women in attendance put their veto on the procedure and demanded that "the boy" as they sneeringly styled him . . . should be called in consultation.'[12] Young doctors with very little practical experience when they started out in obstetrics had to attend women in their own homes who were being cared for by other women with a great deal of birth experience, and who had strong opinions about what ought to be done. One doctor said that it was impossible to ensure sterile conditions and 'strip his patient and go at her with soap and scrub brush, lather and razor', as he wished, because 'there are five or six neighbor women and, perhaps, the mother of the patient – all mothers of large families of children.'[13]

Not only was childbirth a social occasion, but this network was maintained and strengthened every time a woman in the neighbourhood gave birth. This was important in colonial America, where migration led to the building of new communities in which these networks provided the basis of survival and, in the harsh conditions of birth in pioneer rural settlements and later in urban immigrant communities, meant that women had to rely on each other more than they had ever had to in the old country.

In traditional cultures today it is rare for a woman to give birth without support from other women. Anthropologists are sometimes at a loss to know who the midwife is because of the number of women attending a birth, and have to wait and see who actually catches the baby. A British midwife writing about the birth of a baby in a village in the Yemen, says:

> The room was crowded with other women who had come to give their encouragement and support. Some popped in and out between household duties and all took turns to physically support Miryam in whatever position she felt most comfortable. She was never at a loss of a shoulder to grip, a chest to lean against, or a strong hand to steady an ankle or knee. If one woman tired or had to return to her children another would quickly take her place.
>
> The atmosphere was cheerful and relaxed, with good-natured bantering between the women . . . As she tensed up for another contraction, the desultory chatter stopped and the women would again focus their attention on the labouring woman, getting themselves ready to support her in any way she wished. Sometimes she knelt or lay on her side and at other times stood with her arms around a friend's neck.
>
> During a contraction she would utter a long, loud but controlled call to God – 'Y'Allah!' – followed by pleas to God for help and protection. Her attendants would join in and echo her prayers, sometimes so earnestly that it was almost as if they themselves were enduring the contraction.[14]

Anthropologists are often shocked at what they see as a mêlée of women crowding the room. One who was observing a birth among the Gbaya of Zaïre was horrified by the crowd, who were 'literally cramming the hut . . . chatting noisily, laughing loudly, feasting, swilling down drink and smoking'.[15] Another counted sixteen women and children at a Seri Indian birth in Mexico, and said that most of them were sitting around 'in an aura of fiesta'.[16] Such gatherings reinforce the relationships between women through a celebratory experience in which they all share.

Once the baby is born, traditionally a woman is in a state of ritual seclusion, islanded with her baby, comforted and succoured by other women, and physically nourished and cherished by them. This period of puerperal seclusion is a women's time, too, an occasion for friends, neighbours and relatives to draw together in female solidarity. In traditional societies rituals of birth and lying-in are significant in defining the boundaries of an exclusive and concentrated female social space, something which, with the male take-over of childbirth, and the professionalization of care, has been lost in technological cultures.

The Place of Birth

Traditionally the birth place has always been women's space, either in the woman's own home, the menstrual hut or women's bath hut, or in a temporary construction built for birth only. In Sierra Leone birth often takes place in the club house of the Sande secret society, the organization that educates women for adult roles and responsibilities, and the midwife is the *majo* or headwoman of the society. In some villages the Sande Society runs a dormitory-style house in which mothers stay with their babies until they have weaned them, often at about eighteen months.[17] The Sri Lankan woman gives birth in a secluded northern- or eastern-facing room, and the house is completely shuttered, with the doors barred right through labour and for a good part of the lying-in time following.[18]

Among some native North Americans it was the practice to erect a palisade of branches with stakes pushed into the ground at measured intervals, forming a kind of pathway leading towards an inner sanctum. The woman walked through the palisade from stake to stake as her labour progressed. It provided visible evidence of the advance of her labour. When the pushing stage started, at last she achieved the protected inner space where she was to give birth.

An Ojibway baby was born in the temporary birth hut constructed by the father a week or so before the due date. Choosing a place near running water, he dug a depression in the ground and built a curved hut of white cedar, called the 'tree of life', over it. He fixed a clutching pole above the dip in the ground, and when labour started the depression was filled with soft, fluffy fern fronds over which the mother could kneel or squat.[19]

The space for receiving the baby has usually been constructed to be soft and warm. The Kwakiutl of British Columbia used to line their shallow birth pits with soft cedar bark, and the Pima lined theirs with rabbit skins. In making their own birth places, women in traditional societies continue in cultured form the biological process that other mammals and birds demonstrate when they select a secluded place and line their nests with soft hay or moss. In New Zealand the Maori birth hut was actually called 'the nesting house'.

In rural areas in traditional Japan the woman herself built her birth hut. It had to be very dim inside, because the coming and going of the soul needed a dark place, and birth required the participation of spiritual powers. The *Kojiki*, the classic book of Japanese legend and history written in AD 712, tells how the sea-god's daughter, her Augustness Luxuriant-Jewel Princess, built her birth hut at the sea's edge and thatched it with cormorant feathers.[20]

In Eastern Mediterranean countries women often used the communal bath-house, where they were accustomed to gather together to relax, exchange news and reinforce the bonds between them as women. In pioneer New England communities a quiet room at the back of the stove at the centre of the house was kept as the 'borning room'.

Making one's own birth space is an important, and in the technological West, usually neglected, element in human culture. Indeed, it is usually taken for granted in a modern hospital that this space is designed primarily to meet the needs of the professionals who conduct the birth rather than those of the mother, and that any comfort aids and personal touches are introduced as decorative concessions to her.

Body Fantasies and Birth Symbols

One of the most common body fantasies that crystallizes around the idea of danger is that the baby can go up into the mother's chest and choke her. To avoid this the mother's body may be stroked or massaged to direct the baby down, and long scarves or other pieces of cloth are wound round her to apply pressure to the top of the uterus and make sure the baby descends. In colonial days in America, and still today among peasants in Latin America, a strip of cloth is wrapped around the upper abdomen and back, and women on either side take turns pulling it. This puts pressure above the uterus and massages the woman's abdomen and back. The main idea behind it seems to be to make the baby go down rather than up. In societies where no medical help is available a long, obstructed labour may be terminated by the rupture of the uterus and the deaths of both baby and mother, and to those helping it must indeed look as if the baby has burst up out of the womb.

The fantasy about the body which corresponds to such ideas is that there is one long tube from the mouth down through the throat and chest into the stomach and uterus, which then separates out into the passageways leading to the orifices below. It is often believed, as among Jamaican peasants, that anything introduced through the vagina can emerge, possibly with dire results, from the throat and mouth. This is one reason why mechanical contraceptives may be unacceptable. When I was in Jamaica there were myths about how a condom could come off and work its way up inside the woman's body until it finally choked her.

A main concern of the helping women who attend a woman in labour is to reassure her and everyone around her that the baby is moving down the birth canal as it should. They do this not only through giving her comfort and companionship, but often through ceremonies and prayers which invoke supernatural powers to ensure a safe outcome.

In traditional cultures magic practices give some hope of controlling the physiological processes by harnessing the powers of ancestral spirits, gods or other spiritual forces. These practices have a logic of their own. There is contained within each system of magic an internal logical pattern, and in all magic there are clues to the values which are important in that society. In parts of East Africa, for example, a woman who is having a long and arduous labour may have her vagina packed with cow dung. It is an act which has significance in pastoral societies, where the main economic value is cattle. The dung is meant to encourage the birth of the child by letting it smell how wealthy its father is.

In other pre-industrial societies dramatic myths may be re-counted and re-enacted in front of the labouring woman in which

101

basic ideas about the human body and the relation of its parts and functions are expressed, and in which the particular act of giving birth is related to universal forces. The labour hut may be full of men banging drums and chanting and singing. What to the observer is a cacophonous pandemonium seems very different to all those engaged in the drama, including the mother. The saga symbolizes the encounter of the forces of good and evil and life and death in the woman's body. The goal of such dramatic myths is to achieve harmony between the spirit and physical worlds, thus freeing the woman to deliver her baby normally.

One vivid example of this is found among the Cuna Indians of Panama, when a shaman (medicine man) intervenes at the request of the midwife in cases of difficult labour and sings the baby out of the labouring woman's body.[21] The woman lies in her hammock and he squats underneath it. The song starts with a description of the problem the midwife is encountering, her request to the shaman to help, and his arrival on the scene. Then it goes on to describe the things he has done in the woman's hut in preparation for the song-drama: fumigating it with burning cocoa beans, praying, and making sacred wooden figures. The whole song represents a search, with the help of the sacred figures, for Muu, the god who created the baby. Muu dwells in the vagina and uterus, 'the dark deep whirlpool' of the woman in labour, and the battle to wrest from Muu the woman's vital essence (which the god has stolen) so that the baby can be born, takes place inside the mother's body. Each organ possesses its own soul, and everyone's vital essence consists of the harmonious co-operation of all the different souls within the body.

The shaman summons the spirits of alcoholic drinks, of the winds, the waters and the woods, and even the spirit of 'the silver steamer of the white man', and the woman's body is described in terms that relate it to the whole earth and all the forces of nature. Then he tells how the medicine men are penetrating her body to do battle with Muu, and lighting up the way. He traces the journey along the inner path in a sort of emotional geography of the internal organs, inhabited by monsters and fierce animals, and tangled by fibres intertwining and netting the uterus. The shaman calls the lords of the wood-boring insects to come and cut the threads. This is followed by a tournament, which he and his helpers ultimately win. Then he must make his difficult descent, with the aid of the lords of the burrowing animals. Although when they went into her body he and his assistants had to go 'in single file', on coming out they can travel 'four abreast'. The cervix is dilating as it should.

Through the psychodrama of myth the shaman gives to the labouring woman a metaphoric language in which her ordeal can be expressed and given meaning. This is a highly sophisticated form of psychotherapy, and no other treatment is involved.

In Malaysia, on the coast of the South China Sea, a midwife who is dealing with a difficult labour may call on the medicine man to sing a birth incantation that links the creation of the world with the birth of the baby. Where in the Cuna song a contest takes place in the woman's uterus, this song links the birth with the genesis of the universe.

The medicine man describes the time before creation, the vastness of unimaginable space:

> *The Light had not yet emerged from the Darkness . . .*
> *The Light was manifest within the Lord. The earth*
> *and sky had not yet separated . . . Then came three*
> *Utterances. The first Utterance became iron, the second*
> *Utterance became the breath of Life, the third Utterance*
> *became semen. The semen swelled and glistened like a*
> *white sail and became foam.*[22]

The imagery in this song operates at two symbolic levels: the sea of creation is the mother's blood; the winds and waves that sweep through her are the winds of desire. The golden country is her body; the tree is her vagina, clitoris and pubic hair. The universe itself is pregnant with life.

> *The foam was carried by the wind, tossed by the waves,*
> *by the seven rolling waves, by the groundswell. Where will*
> *the foam land? The foam lands on the banks of Desire*
> *where the young casuarina tree grows in the golden land*
> *in the kingdom of Rajah Bali Stream of Desire.*

The first human couple are created out of the foam. The woman is the 'Lady White Dressed in Flowers.' Then the Angel Gabriel carries the first seed of life and thrusts it into the father's brain for forty days, for throughout Malaysia it is believed that the father conceives and is pregnant in his brain for forty days before the baby descends into his penis and is ejaculated into the mother. 'Its name was Light of Allah. It fell to his eyes, Light of Light.

It fell to his chest, True Sultan, happy centre of the world. It fell to his big toe, King Phallus is his name.' The baby's development is described, and finally its birth:

> *You fall into your mother's womb, in your mother's womb nine months, ten days. The first month you are called Dot. The second month Light of Beginning. The third month Light of the Soul. The fourth month Light of the Countenance. The fifth month Light of the Womb. The sixth month Abdullah the Slow. The seventh month bow to the right, bow to the left. Bow to the right, you are a son. Bow to the left, you are a daughter. The eighth month Light of Birth. The ninth month your outline and measure can be seen. The tenth out you come . . . you know your mother's body, you open your eyes and utter three prayers. The first utterance lifts the soul to the breast, the second utterance, the Breath of Life to the breasts. The third utterance lifts the vital force. May all your feelings be good. You let yourself breathe in the five vital forces as you wave your arms.*

In this song the woman's pain and striving is given meaning and purpose. Her individual experience is transformed into the universal. In the timelessness of strong labour she is given mythical time. 'The harmony thus set up between the labouring mother and the outside world encourages the baby to emerge.'[23] The medicine man 'identifies the woman's reproductive powers with universal creativity, using the deliberate ambiguity of symbols, and gradually focuses upon the drama of birth taking place within a particular time and space and involving a particular mother and child. The woman retains the principal role; the Bomoh (medicine man) merely aids her in her completion of her part.'

The Sia of New Mexico also give ritual expression to the processes of dilatation and birth, but this is acted out together by family members and the midwife. The woman's father dips eagle feathers in ashes and throws the ashes to the four points of the compass. He then draws the ashy plumes down either side of the woman, and down the centre of her body, as he prays for the safe delivery of the baby. The midwife does the same, with a prayer that the child may pass down the road of life safely and quickly. The woman's sister-in-law then places an ear of sweetcorn near her head and blows on it during the next contraction. The prayer blown on the corn blows through the passageway of life.

In India it is the custom for a grain jar to be burst to let all the grain pour out, to show that the child will be quickly and easily born. The imagery can have a vivid effect on the mind of the labouring woman. In India, and in some Mediterranean cultures, a tight bud – the rose of Jericho is the flower used in Southern Italy and in Malta – is put near the mother. She watches it, and as the petals open so her cervix will dilate. In Southern Italy this flower is called 'the hand of the Mother of God', so it has deep religious significance. Images of grain being poured and of blossoms opening provide a focus for the mother's awareness. But they do more than that. There is a sense of unity between the body of the mother and the changing form of the flower, between her body and the rest of the natural world. When culturally significant symbols, such as the eagle's feather and corn, grain jar and flower, are used like this, the experience of the moment is linked to permanent values, and the labour is given pattern and meaning.

In many non-Western societies the psychological element in some childbirth difficulties is understood and techniques exist for encouraging better psychosomatic co-ordination. In African societies, for example, a woman having a difficult labour may be urged to confess her sins. These techniques are based not only on ideas about the body, about health and sickness and dirt and cleanliness, but also on concepts of good and evil. If the most disgusting thing that a woman can do is to break an incest taboo or to commit adultery, sins like these committed during pregnancy may endanger the life of the coming child, and so have to be confessed and expiated. Among the Manus of New Guinea, the husband and wife are exhorted to confess any hidden anger they may feel against each other. In Hawaii the midwife may perform magic so that the woman's pain leaves her and is transferred instead to an animal or someone else who lacks moral fibre (a lazy brother-in-law is said to be the favourite choice).

In the civilizations of the past prayers were often said to the goddesses of reproduction to protect the mother and baby, and religion provided a framework for emotional support. In the Mesopotamian invocation to Ishtar, the Goddess of Morning and Evening, birth attendants placed the labouring woman under divine protection:

> *May this woman give birth happily!*
> *May she give birth,*
> *May she stay alive,*
> *May she walk in health before thy divinity!*
> *May she give birth happily and worship thee!*[24]

When a Zuni Indian woman's labour was prolonged, a member of the Great Fire Fraternity helped by singing special songs to the Beast Gods to hasten delivery. Among Moslem peoples today the midwife may recite blessings from the Koran.

We have seen that it is generally accepted that every child ought to have a father, although the man who is a baby's social father may be different from the biological father. In Jamaica birth can be speeded up by getting the mother to sniff the sweaty shirt of the father of the child. The point about this is that a large proportion of babies in Jamaica are born to women who are not in a stable union, and the most usual time for a man to decide he has had enough and leave is just before or just after the birth of the baby. Having his sweaty shirt around is a fairly good sign that he is available to 'response for' the baby. Reminding the woman of her good fortune at a critical point in the labour probably has a positive psychological effect, giving her fresh strength.

All the same, it is important to realize that in peasant societies, as in our own, many customs associated with birth are based on empirical reasoning. In any peasant society where older women deliver babies they must rely to a great extent upon the practical experience they gain as they go along and the proven techniques they learn from other practitioners of the art. Most women in labour need only basic nursing, comfort and encouragement. Traditional midwives have developed many skills for giving this sort of help.

A wide variety of comfort techniques is used: hot towels wrapped around the body, massage of the abdomen, back and perineum, breathing patterns which the mother is encouraged to use during contractions and adjustments to the woman's posture or movements she is urged to perform (sometimes including marked physical exertion or even being shaken upside down to speed up labour). Tranquillizing herbal teas are employed or, as among the Manus, a sustaining hot coconut soup.[25] There are medicines to prevent bleeding, and in South America and the

Caribbean, techniques for assisting the expulsive reflex of the uterus by getting the mother to blow into a bottle, used when there is a delayed third stage of labour.

Movement

Women in labour are not normally expected to lie down. They move about, changing position frequently and carrying on with normal tasks in the house or outdoors for as long as they feel able. It is physiologically much better for both mother and baby if the mother keeps moving: her uterus contracts more effectively, pain is reduced, the blood-flow through the placenta to the baby is better, and labour is shorter. When I was doing research in a big Jamaican maternity hospital there was a constant battle between labouring women and midwives, the women wanting to get up and crouch down or rock their pelvises back and forward, with knees bent, and the midwives trying to get them on the bed, where they were expected to lie still and be good patients.

For hundreds of years midwives in Europe travelled to births with their own birth stools on which a woman could crouch to give birth in a position similar to that in which she milked her goat or cow or sat to spin. It was above all a work posture, and because the early stools had no back to them, and were like a horseshoe-shaped milking stool, she could move her pelvis freely. By the sixteenth century these stools had become more elaborate, and birth chairs were introduced which, because of their rigid framework, restricted movement, although they still enabled the woman to be upright.

Japanese women traditionally adopted many different positions for the second stage. The mother held on to a rope hanging from the ceiling, and moved between half-sitting and standing. She might kneel leaning against a pile of straw bundles and a quilt, or sit leaning back with the midwife or her husband holding her pelvis from behind, or she might crouch forward over a bed of rice, or kneel with her back supported by futons. There are myths that one empress gave birth to twins while leaning against a mortar, and that another delivered her son while holding on to a branch of the pagoda tree at a shrine.[26]

The Zuni Indians gave birth on a bed of hot sand, clean and comfortable, and symbolic of the lap of mother earth. The woman's mother put sand on the floor, patted it into a mound about twenty inches across and five inches high, and laid a sheepskin over it. It gave the woman firm support, and after delivery the sand was swept up and thrown away.

The Sia woman sat on a low stool, wrapped in a blanket with her back to the fire, and walked around when she felt like it. As she started to push she, too, knelt on a bed of sand, her hands clasped round the father's neck and her back supported by the midwife's body, who sat with her arms around her and massaged her abdomen. Dakota women used to give birth on a pile of sand in a similar position, with their feet supported against pegs and their hands holding other pegs at the sides.

Positions in which a woman is upright, kneeling, squatting, or with one knee and one foot on the ground, while supported in the arms of a helper, are the most common. In Uganda the Baganda woman gives birth in the garden of her husband's mother's home, where she kneels grasping a tree, supported by a female member of her husband's family, while the midwife, who is also one of her husband's relatives, kneels behind her ready to catch the baby.

On Easter Island, which is exceptional in that the midwives are male, the woman chooses either to stand with her legs apart or to sit, and the midwife stands behind her, supporting her with his body, while massaging her abdomen slowly and rhythmically.

The Manus of New Guinea give birth in special houses where the old women of the tribe live, built on stilts over the sea.[27] The labouring woman lies on her side on a mat on the floor, with her feet against a board. Three midwives support her, one on each side and one holding her back. The woman hooks one leg over a midwife's leg, changing sides frequently. Among another New Guinea people, the Usiai, the woman sits between the legs of her sister.[28] Her husband's father's sister sits in front of her with her arms around her, massaging her back, and the labouring woman rocks between the bodies of her two helpers.

In West Africa a labouring woman may kneel, with women holding her on either side. Or she may prefer to hang from the rafters, swinging backwards and forwards for part of her labour.[29] An alternative position is to crouch between two house posts, pulling herself up and down with her arms during contractions. For delivery she squats with a helping woman on each side with their arms crossed with hers, another midwife exerting pressure against her back, a fourth massaging her abdomen and two other women supporting her legs. This rounded back, crouching position with firm support from a helper's body is used – with various modifications – in most traditional societies. It is only in the West that women have been forced to lie flat on their backs with their legs in the air, like beetles on their backs, in a position convenient for the obstetrician, but often uncomfortable and difficult for the woman, because it means that she has to push the baby 'up-hill'.

The squatting position is spontaneously adopted by human beings for defecation, and childbirth entails release of the same pelvic floor muscles used in emptying the bowels. A woman's pelvic outlet increases up to 28 per cent when she squats.[30] So squatting or semi-squatting helps her to deliver more easily than if she were stretched flat. With modern methods of preparation for childbirth in the West mothers are again being allowed to adopt squatting and kneeling positions for delivery, to get on all fours, sit right up, stand, and explore any other position which is comfortable.

Touch and Massage

I have been in hospitals in the West where women in childbirth are touched only when necessary in order to palpate the uterus, to introduce a catheter or a foetal electrode or to set up a drip. I have watched women lying neatly in bed under a white sheet which has been carefully arranged by a midwife as if she had laid the table for dinner and did not wish it to be disturbed. Any physical contact has been instrumental, essential for the performance of the task. The touching has no emotional component, beyond perhaps a mild distaste, and no energy has passed through from the helper to the woman in labour.

In traditional cultures, in contrast, a woman is usually touched often. She may be held, massaged, pressed, stroked, caressed, rocked, swung, given hot and cold compresses, sometimes even pummelled, kneaded or bounced up and down. The traditional Japanese midwife, the *samba*, was also known sometimes as 'the massaging old lady'. A British midwife describing a birth in a small town in the Yemen says: 'Naomi supported herself against a bolster with the mother crouched between her knees and leaning back against her broad chest; with her hands Naomi supported Miryam's bottom and by doing this could feel the progress of the baby's head as it journeyed through the birth canal.'[31]

Indian midwives of Rajasthan massage the woman's lower back with melted ghee and glycerine, using circular and up and down movements. An anthropologist tells how a midwife straddles her and presses down at the sides of her pelvis with a kneading motion.[32]

This touching is qualitatively different from the kind of touch used to acquire information or to perform an intervention. Traditionally the contact between a woman in childbirth and her female helpers is sustained and intimate. They are joined as if in a dance in which they act in unison with the rhythm of her contractions. In Yucatan the labouring woman may lie crossways in her hammock, legs slightly drawn up and her feet propped in its folds. A woman helper or the husband, called the 'head helper', sits at her head end with arms around her shoulders and supporting her hammock-encased body in his or her lap.

> *Its flexible compactness permits the head helper to raise the woman slightly at the height of a contraction, lifting her almost to a sitting position. As the contraction fades away, she gently lets her down again to rest. Meanwhile, the midwife and another helper are occupied with rubbing her abdomen, her back, her legs, and pressing down on the thighs whenever a contraction comes on.[33]*

The traditional Malaysian midwife massages the mother's abdomen for hours on end, and if labour is difficult may use coconut oil over which she has recited charms. If there is delay when the baby's head is on the perineum she oils the woman's head and, lifting some strands of hair, says: 'If this hair is slippery, you will slip right out; if this hair is not slippery, you will not slip out', in this way combining imagery that is psychologically effective with the massage.[34] Malaysian midwives take their daughters with them when they visit pregnant women and to births, and when a girl is old enough she is taught how to massage, her mother placing her hands over hers and guiding her movements. She also teaches her how to palpate the woman's abdomen to discover how the baby is lying.

Throughout the Caribbean midwives massage the woman during labour, too. In Kenya the Akamba woman gives birth standing while other women holding her close grasp her shoulders and legs. In the Ivory Coast the woman squats between the midwife's legs and leans against her body while the midwife holds her shoulders.

Feet as well as hands may be used to massage. In Sierra Leone the midwife sits facing the mother and supports and massages her perineum with her big toe. In India she presses her heels against the mother's sacro-lumbar area, producing strong counter-pressure with her foot, leaving her hands free for massage and holding.

Birth is often a lonely experience for a woman delivering in a modern hospital in which she is more or less isolated from human physical contact. In contrast, birth in a traditional culture is almost invariably strongly interactive, and involves close and sustained physical contact to give comfort and encouragement and to relieve pain. In fact, in some cultures the midwife is known as 'the woman who holds'. This close physical contact, nurturing through touch, is basic to the help traditionally given by midwives. In Europe too, massage was an important element in the care offered by midwives. In one of the earliest manuals of midwifery, *The Byrth of Mankind*, published in 1545, the midwife is told to anoint her hands with the oil of white lilies and encourage the mother to 'patience and tolerance' while 'stroking gently with her hands her belly about the navel'.

Lubrication of the perineum to help the tissues fan out is practised in many cultures, and is described in the Talmud. Vegetable oils, the glutinous pulp of vegetables or fruit, whale blubber or any other kind of grease may be used. In eighteenth-century England Grace Acton and Letitia Owen referred in their household books written for female domestic managers to pork fat being used to massage the perineum.

Hot compresses and other forms of heat are often employed along with massage. In Jamaica pressure may be applied with a heated stone. In India a bag of warm sand or of dried, powdery cow dung is rested against the mother's abdomen. The Kwakiutl of British Columbia use hot seaweed placed over the abdomen and in the small of the back.[35] In Australia the Kiwi press heated leaves against the woman's sacro-lumbar region, in her groin and on her legs.[36]

Touch is employed not only for comfort but to correct mal-presentation, a skill which many doctors in the West do not possess because they have never had the opportunity to learn it. If a baby is breech, or if cephalo-pelvic disproportion is diagnosed, the easiest thing for them is to resort to Caesarean section. In many cultures where women are far from hospitals, and so Caesarean section is not a practical solution, traditional midwives know how to turn babies from breech to vertex, from transverse to a longitudinal lie, and from posterior to anterior. They do this externally through a combination of massage and repositioning of the mother. Brigitte Jordan is an anthropologist with specialist knowledge of Mayan midwifery. Her video-tapes of midwives in the Yucatan include a sequence of a midwife rotating a baby from posterior to anterior. These midwives also turn the baby when there is a shoulder presentation, as the mother lies in her hammock with her head tipped over the edge and her pelvis raised.

Dirt, Cleanliness and Purification

Ceremonies of cleansing are central to childbirth rituals. In much of Africa and India, for example, the mother gives birth in a special birth hut which no one other than those attending her may enter. This has the useful effect of isolating the mother and baby from possible infection. Both mother and baby need to be purified, and this is done with libations of oil, sacred signs or chants, purging, or bathing in water to which special herbs or colouring substances may be added.

A major threat to the life of babies born under unhygienic conditions is neonatal tetany, because the umbilical cord is often cut with a dirty or rusty knife, frequently one that has been used in the fields or for killing a chicken. Ritual cleanliness and freedom from pollution may overlap with but are often very different from practical cleanliness, just as immersion in the polluted River Ganges is spiritually purifying but may result in disease.

Purification rituals mark the crisis through which both mother and child have passed, and also guard them against the threat of the unknown, the powers of outer darkness. Some of these ceremonies involve actual physical cleansing, such as the customary squatting over a bucket of steaming water 'hot like nine nights' love' adopted among Jamaican women, which is a good method of cleaning the perineum without needing actually to touch the area. The newborn child may be bathed immediately, as in our own society. There is really no need for this, as babies are born clean. They are often covered with vernix, a substance with the consistency of curd cheese, which protects the skin inside the uterus, but the removal of this at birth does more harm than good. Cleansing of the newborn has ritual significance rather than hygienic validity.

Purging is a drastic method of cleansing popular in various forms throughout the world and especially so in the West, where regular bowel motions are considered essential for health and cleanliness and where the sale of laxatives has reached astronomical proportions. These attitudes to bowel functions are carried over to childbirth. In some technologically advanced societies the labouring woman is still given an enema or suppository to empty her bowels. In others she is given a dose of castor oil, a traditional way of trying to start off labour when it is delayed.

The placenta, or afterbirth, is the object most intimately associated with the baby, which it brings with it from its other – intra-uterine or spirit – world. So it is often held in reverence, and may, for example, be buried under a tree which is thenceforward that child's tree throughout life. In West Africa wise men are called in for placental divination. They examine it closely, rather as we might look at tea leaves in a cup, in order to foretell the child's future. The West Indian practice of counting the knots in the cord is closely connected with this: the number of knots is supposed to indicate the number of children the mother has still to bear. It is often thought that anyone obtaining the placenta can get power over the child, so it must be disposed of carefully and secretly, either by burying or burning it.

Midwives

The history of midwifery goes back to and merges with that of witches. Midwives are often attributed with magic powers in relation to fertility, the development of the baby, the labour, and the baby's survival. So the midwife was frequently also a witch, had power over the spirits of the newborn, and in many peasant societies is still consulted for charms and love philtres.

Universally the maintenance of health has been the responsibility of women. Health care in peasant societies, involving the use of bush teas and herbal medicaments, massage and psychotherapeutic procedures, has always been in the hands of women healers. Only when these measures fail is recourse made to the more dramatic methods of male experts, the shamans, witchdoctors, priests and doctors. The healing skills of these women is from one point of view an aspect of mothering. It grows out of the capacity to nurture and is an extension of the ability to support inherent processes of growth, while at the same time mediating between the natural and the supernatural. These are really not two separate functions, but one, for the right balance which is the foundation of health depends on an equilibrium between the natural and supernatural worlds. Because this is so, healers have usually also possessed magico-religious power. They have corrected not only the imbalance of physical but also of spiritual elements. This is why they are witches as well as being experts in the art of folk medicine.

In medieval Europe witches were believed to kill and eat unbaptized children. A Swiss witch is reported to have confessed that she killed babies in their cradles, or when lying beside their mothers, so that it looked as if the baby had been laid on or had died naturally. It was the custom of medieval midwives to leave the nail of one finger to grow extra long, and to trim it till it was pointed, in order to rupture the bag of waters when necessary in labour. There was a popular belief that there was a special opportunity for midwives to kill babies at the moment of delivery by thrusting this through the soft spot of the baby's head, or fontanelle, and into the brain. And the midwife who delivered a number of stillborn babies or ones who died shortly after birth was especially vulnerable to accusations of witchcraft.

The Catholic Church always viewed midwife-healers with as much alarm as those who were thought to do evil, for the power of the woman healer was a threat to the male authority of the Church. They functioned alongside and in opposition to ecclesiastical power and male medicine, which was itself regulated by the Church. Szasz writes:

> *Because the Medieval Church, with the support of kings, princes and secular authorities, controlled medical education and practice, the Inquisition (witch-hunts) constitutes, among other things, an early instance of the 'professional' repudiating the skills and interfering with the rights of the 'nonprofessional' to minister to the poor.*[37]

A leading English witch-hunter warned against 'all good Witches, which do not hurt but good, which do not spoil and destroy, but save and deliver.' He went on to state that 'it were a thousand times better for the land if all Witches, but especially the blessing Witch, might Suffer death.'[38] So both male-controlled medicine and the Church were implacably opposed to female-controlled healing and regulation of fertility. It is a conflict which persists to this day.

One fourteenth-century professor of theology, instructed by Pope Innocent VIII to assist the Inquisition in its persecution of witches, declared that it was all the fault of the midwives, who were enemies of the Church: 'No one does more harm to the Catholic Faith than midwives.' These women caused the death of, or allowed to die, unbaptized infants, who were souls lost to the Faith. The Pope announced that they had 'abandoned themselves to devils, incubi, and succubi, and by their incantations, spells, conjurations, and other accursed charms and crafts, enormities and horrid offences, have slain infants yet in the mother's womb.'[39]

This pattern of black and white magic, indissolubly intertwined, consisting partly of spells, prayers and incantations, partly of medicines and bush teas, and partly of faith healing, psychotherapy and the laying on of hands, exists all over the world. In peasant societies midwives are some of the most important people in the social group formed by women. For not only do they practise herbal medicine and healing, but they preside over the forces of fertility and the coming into being of each new member of society. So they are important to the society as a whole, and usually (but not always, midwives in India being a marked exception) have high status and considerable power.

In pre-industrial societies the real or apparent control of fertility has always been vital, and bound up with the welfare of the entire society. Those with power over fertility control the society. Mary Douglas says of the Lele people of Zaïre that she was struck by the way childbearing and hunting were always coupled together, and that if there had been a series of bad hunts villagers soon started remarking how few pregnancies there had been recently, and diviners were called in to right matters. Failure in hunting is always linked with barrenness in women, and when all is well again the Lele say: 'Our village is soft and good now. Since the diviner went home we have killed three wild pigs and many antelopes, four women have conceived, we are all healthy and strong.'[40]

This is why traditionally the power of midwives has extended far beyond their functions as helpers with childbirth. The whole of social life has depended on them because they controlled the balance between the male and female worlds. From the vantage point of Western society traditional midwives are often seen as dirty and ignorant crones. From within a peasant society, however, it is clear that these 'wise women' of the community are exceptional and often highly gifted. In countries where educational opportunities for women are few, it is often the most intelligent who find means of canalizing their skills so that they can be socially effective in this way.

In England the first men to take over as experts in childbirth were members of the barber surgeons guilds, which developed in the thirteenth century. By their rules only surgeons could use surgical instruments, and they were called in to dismember the baby when delivery was obstructed. These first surgical tools were hooks, drills, callipers and knives. In 1616 Doctor Peter Chamberlen introduced the forceps, although he and his family kept them a secret until 1733. Peter Chamberlen wanted to teach midwives himself, and planned to set up and control a Guild of Midwives. His proposal came in for much criticism from midwives on the grounds that he only did deliveries using instruments 'by extraordinary violence in desperate occasions', and that he knew nothing at all about natural labour. Both charges were perfectly true.[41] The forceps became the tool of trade for the emerging male midwives.

One of the earliest midwifery schools was the Hôtel Dieu in Paris, which was founded in the sixteenth century. Louise Bourgeois was its most famous pupil, and midwife to the Queen, Marie de Medici. She was one of the first practitioners to warn against cross-infection, over-reliance on medicines and the use of drugs that had not been thoroughly tested.

Another famous midwife was the Englishwoman Elizabeth Nihell, who in 1758 published her *Treatise on the Art of Midwifery*. She was strongly opposed to male midwives, and wrote:

> *A few, and a very few indeed of the midwives, dazzled with that vogue into which the instruments brought the men . . . attempted to employ them, and though certainly they could handle them at least as dexterously as men, they soon discovered that they were at once insignificant*

and dangerous substitutes to their own hands, with which
they were sure of conducting their operations both more
safely, more effectually and with less pain to the patient. [42]

Midwifery became popular for aspiring doctors because it was a way into general practice. Once a baby had been delivered the whole family might come to a doctor to treat their ailments. It was in the interest of all doctors to limit the power of midwives and to restrict their knowledge. The textbooks they wrote for midwives omitted a great deal of important information on the grounds that only doctors should know certain things. In one book, *The Midwife Rightly Instructed*, published in 1736, midwives were told that they need not know how to treat haemorrhage, and were warned not to aspire 'beyond the capacities of a woman'.[43] Presumably if the midwife was in an isolated home and could not get the doctor, her patient was to be allowed to bleed to death.

Male midwives charged two or three times as much as midwives, and it became fashionable for those who could afford it to call on them because it implied that a husband was doing the best he could for the mother and baby. By the second half of the eighteenth century even small tradesmen tried to show that they could afford to pay a doctor to do the delivery.

At the same time maternity hospitals were built as places where very poor women could go to have their babies while simultaneously providing clinical material for the doctors and their students. The most dangerous place to give birth was in these hospitals, where death rates for babies and mothers were high, and where even if a mother did not die during the birth she was exposed to the risk of puerperal fever afterwards. Between the years 1860 and 1864, 9,886 women were admitted to the Paris Maternité. Of these, 1,226 mothers died, a mortality rate of 12.4 per cent.[44] It was a good deal safer to give birth at home, even if home was a slum, and to be attended by a midwife.[45]

But male doctors had won the battle. Midwifery had become subordinate to obstetrics, and a midwife acted on the instructions of the doctor, prepared the patient for him and cleared up after him. The Ladies' Medical College, and Florence Nightingale's attempts to establish a training for midwives of the same standard as that for doctors, failed. There was to be no separate speciality. A woman either had to try to get training as a doctor or be a

117

midwife working under the authority of the male medical profession.

In the industrialized West birth continued to be full of dangers for women and babies well into the twentieth century, both from unnecessary intervention and from puerperal infection. Maternal mortality remained on a plateau from the 1850s until the mid-1930s. In 1898 a study conducted in one district of London revealed that the highest maternal death rates were middle class, and the lowest working class. A specialist in the history of medicine suggests that 'high maternal mortality was associated with doctors' deliveries and a low rate was found where midwives' deliveries were the rule', as in the slums.[46]

Analysis of maternal deaths in Leeds in 1920–29 showed that 3 per 1,000 women died in the poorest areas of the city, but 6 per 1,000 in middle-class areas. The *Lancet* reported: 'The midwife employing class expect to deliver themselves . . . The woman who engages a doctor . . . often does so in expectation that if things do not move quickly the artificial aid that is at hand will be immediately available.'[47] Analyses of statistics in Glasgow and Aberdeen and of national statistics produced similar results. General practitioners, who at that time were mainly responsible for conducting childbirth, were quick to use the drug pituitrin to accelerate labour, with the result that a woman's uterus often ruptured. They gave chloroform routinely, thus running the risk of anaesthetic deaths. They also frequently resorted to forceps delivery, but failed to deliver the baby and then transferred their patient to hospital. One in ten mothers and two-thirds of the babies died from the effects of FFO (Failed Forceps Outside).[48] This style of obstetrics continued into the thirties. In 1929 Henry Jellet, analysing the causes of the high maternal mortality rate, said that doctors had turned 'a physiological process in a healthy woman into a death trap'.[49] Birth did not become much safer until the Second World War. One explanation for this is that doctors were away serving in the armed services, so that responsibility for overseeing childbirth was returned to the midwives.

Women's concern about unnecessary and dangerous intervention in childbirth is no new phenomenon. Historically it has always been associated with the conduct of childbirth by doctors, rather than by skilled midwives.

8

Birth in Three Cultures

Birth under Communism

Within Communist social systems education for child-birth took the form of pregnancy gymnastics based on the Russian method of psychoprophylaxis, instruction about the Pavlovian psychology of conditioned reflexes, and some basic anatomy and physiology. 'Breathe *in*, one, two, three, four – stop – breathe *out*, one, two, three, four, five, six, breathe *in*! Breathe *out*! Relax!' Commands were rapped out as if by a drill sergeant. None of it bore much relationship to what a woman actually feels during childbirth. The idea behind it was to control her behaviour so that she was quiet and disciplined.

When Germany was still divided into two separate countries, I sat through formal lectures in psychoprophylaxis in two university hospitals in East Germany. They took place with the women sitting in orderly rows that fanned out from around an enormous boardroom-style table, presided over by the portrait of a bearded Marx gazing sternly on the scene of twenty or thirty hugely pregnant women silently drinking in complex Pavlovian theory. Expectant mothers were shown charts of conditioned reflexes and diagrams of salivating dogs, their maws gaping while saliva dripped into test tubes screwed into their cheeks. The instructress was not concerned with how it felt to give birth or a woman's own knowledge about her body – only with her *correct behaviour*.

In countries such as this the discipline of psychoprophylaxis has been used to teach Communist values and to regulate women's behaviour in childbirth. This last bastion of individuality, the

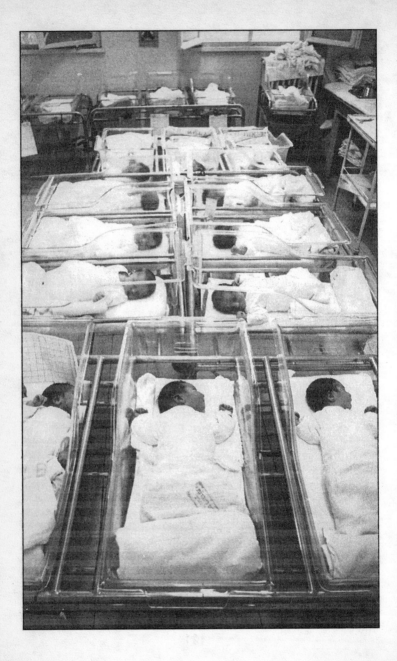

intimacies of psychosexual life, the inter-relationship between a mother and her baby, and between the couple and their child, was made to conform to norms which each woman fulfils successfully or fails to fulfil.

For many years throughout Eastern Europe the inculcation of socially approved attitudes to birth and training in techniques for coping with childbirth has had little to do with any personal wishes of the expectant mother herself. It is something done *to* her, rather than something she has decided to do herself. In the labour wards the women lie like sandbags, quiet and still, breathing correctly, softly moaning. They are tense but acquiescent. In one university hospital when I asked what women were taught about awareness and conscious control of their pelvic floor muscles (those that need to open up for the baby to be born and that need to be well-toned afterwards), I was led downstairs to the basement. There I saw women sitting in rows, their white hospital gowns drawn up to their waists, knees spread, while opposite them men in rubber suits aimed hoses of ice-cold water between their legs! As they gasped they involuntarily contracted their pelvic muscles.

In these Communist countries, together with those like Czechoslovakia and Poland, which until recently had Communist governments, the presence of fathers in childbirth is considered a shocking practice. Doctors rationalize their refusal to try it by making reference to germs, explaining bacterial attack on the human body as similar to the way in which undesirable influences can endanger the body politic. As with the body of society, so it is with the human body: childbearing women are perceived as at constant risk of infection. The West has for the most part discarded the elaborate ceremonial designed to kill an invisible force of germs poised to invade the woman's body in childbirth. Doctors and midwives can shield themselves from the HIV virus simply by wearing gloves and spectacles.

It is now accepted that careful, scrupulous cleanliness and avoidance of unnecessary pelvic examinations and other invasive obstetric procedures is the best way to prevent infection. The rate of infection goes up with the number of pelvic examinations following rupture of the membranes. In Eastern European countries, however, there is great faith in sterile garments, including hats or turbans, as barriers against infection, and strict segregation of women in childbirth and of new babies while still

121

in hospital from partners, family members and friends is enforced, since they are seen as sources of infection.

I was in Moscow in 1989 when an official order was issued by the Ministry of Health allowing visitors in hospitals, following open criticism of maternity hospitals in a lively correspondence in the press. Yet this still has not, for the most part, affected practice. Obstetricians and paediatricians were shocked by the threat to accept good practice, and anxious about how they were going to cope with that edict. It was reminiscent of how thirty years ago it was believed in Britain and North America that fathers in the delivery room would faint and cause chaos, and that newborn babies would die from germs brought in by visitors.

To be with a Russian woman in childbirth is to be stuck in a time warp. No fathers are allowed inside the hospital, let alone in labour wards. On admission, a ritual enema and complete shave transforms the woman into a patient, after which she is left alone, lying on a narrow, hard, high bed, to 'get on with it'. She is expected to be quiet and disciplined, and if she has had any classes in psychoprophylaxis, to use these techniques in order to control herself and not to make a fuss. So she lies biting her lips, moaning quietly, or writhing in silent agony. When it is judged that it is time for the baby to be born, she must climb on a table, and there is a hurried, violent delivery. She cannot hold and may not even see her baby, which is given vigorous resuscitation that is likely to do more harm than good. It is whisked away to the nursery as if the word 'bonding' had never been invented, and mothers are left on trolleys with ice-packs over their abdomens in the corridor for two to three hours or more before they even set eyes on their babies. In one Moscow hospital I noticed nurses nipping off for a quiet smoke in the rooms where the babies were lying 'under observation'.

It is strongly believed that mothers may harm and contaminate their babies if they are allowed to have them with them. Strict rules are enforced, and the experts must exert their authority. Anyone from outside the institution is considered dirty, so before a mother is allowed to touch her baby her fingers have to be painted with iodine in order to avoid conveying germs to her cocooned infant.

Midwives, nurses and doctors do not have to undergo this iodine ritual, although in any maternity hospital it is the staff themselves who are mainly responsible for cross-infection, as Semelweiss, the Viennese doctor who taught doctors to wash their hands, pointed out long ago. Yet in Russia the threat to the institution and its staff is seen as coming entirely from outside. The germs that mothers transfer to their babies are perceived as the primary source of the epidemics of infection in hospital nurseries. These in turn threaten the staff of the institutions. One professor of neonatology told me: 'I can remember when other staff of maternity hospitals would not shake hands with neonatologists because they considered them a source of infection.' In this way the medical system reflects the same dread of external contamination that was expressed in the Communist political system.

In Moscow, as in the rest of Eastern Europe, babies are fed according to the clock, a regime which was the rule in the West only thirty years ago, and which caused great misery for both mothers and babies. In the former East Germany I shocked doctors and nurses when I talked about feeding a baby when it cries. Apart from being disgusted at the slackness and indulgence in this approach to infant feeding, they were neither interested nor curious. They smiled kindly and said that *their* way was better: 'The child will become undisciplined. He will grow up a little tyrant,' they said, as we looked at tiny newborn babies in their cribs. (Later, in a different context, I happened to remark to my hosts that my children ran in from school ravenously hungry for their tea and was told, 'Ah, that is because they were not disciplined as babies.')

A State-issued booklet for parents instructed the father to 'use severe words to stop the soft-hearted mother from rushing to the basket at the first shriek of its occupant.' This belief about discipline was such an essential tenet of their faith that when I asked in one hospital what the nurses did when babies cried between scheduled four-hourly feeds I was confidently told, 'There *is* no crying here', information which I found difficult to accept at face value.

In Moscow for every birth a woman has between two and six legal abortions, usually consisting of dilatation and curettage without anaesthesia. (In Britain there is one abortion to every five births, and anaesthesia is used routinely.) For every three legal abortions, it is estimated that there is one illegal abortion, too. Thirty per cent of these illegal abortions end in the women's deaths. Abortion is available on demand until the twelfth week of pregnancy. Contraceptives are often unobtainable, and there is a great deal of suspicion about them. A young doctor said she would never take the pill because it was dangerous, and condoms were 'horrible'. Abortion she considered safer, cleaner and simpler. Close on half of all Russian gynaecologists do nothing but abortions.

Every maternity hospital performs abortions as well as births. It is as if abortion has become the model for childbirth. Birth is simply evacuation of the uterus. Women endure it as they must put up with all the other hardships of being a woman, living in flats shared between three or four families with only one kitchen, having to queue for nearly all food – not even knowing what is being sold till they reach the end of the queue – being forced to work outside the home because pay is so low, and sometimes doing three jobs piled one on the other just to make ends meet. They travel long journeys to and from work because public transport is slow and inadequate, and are landed with all the housework, usually without any help from the men. This is why a pregnancy can be a disaster, and certainly having a second child is a luxury that few women feel they can afford.

Even with the enormous political changes that have taken place in the former Soviet Union, any change in the condition of women and their health care has yet to come. Yet there are some obstetricians who are making efforts to give birth more personal significance for women. In one hospital the admission room is like the entrance to an abattoir, with a huge enema apparatus, an open lavatory, and two women being 'prepped' at the same time without any privacy. But there is also a ceremonial room (it looks like the parlour of an American funeral home) where the new mother meets her husband and family and introduces the baby to them before she is discharged. One whole wall is made up of a stained-glass picture, lit from behind, of a mother and child. First the woman goes to the adjoining swaddling room, where she is taught how to bind her baby, and the resulting package is tied with pink or blue ribbon according to the baby's gender. Then she emerges to a background of music, the father sees his child for the first time, flowers are presented to her, and family photographs with the new baby are taken. The music softens and a lyric female voice announces: 'Now the new life is in your hands. The baby is your dream and when you get home will grow up and take care of you. Good luck little baby! We want your parents to take care of you so well that you will grow up to take care of them in the future. Good luck, little citizen!' – and the national anthem blares out.

The meeting of a father and other members of the family with a newborn child, treated as a private and intimate event in Western countries, became in Communist society a formal and ritual entry into the culture, one in which the baby was symbolically exhorted, long before there was any possibility of understanding, to be a good citizen, and in which the parents were reminded of their duties to train the child well. Ceremonies of this kind serve a similar function to those of baptism and christening for members of the Christian faith.

A Peasant Birth in Jamaica

In traditional cultures birth has remained largely in the hands of women. 'Nanas' are the folk midwives who in the past delivered most Jamaican babies – they had to, because there were too few trained midwives. Their activities are illegal, however, and when a *nana* helps at a birth it is recorded on the birth certificate as 'unattended' or 'her mother delivered'.

There are three highly respected positions in any Jamaican village, all of which are held by women: the schoolteacher, the postmistress, and the midwife. They are the pivots of the social system and form the links between all the women in the community. And since traditionally it is women who maintain households and keep each family going, with the men often leaving, they are very important.

Midwifery practice in Jamaica is part of a system of folk medicine and healing derived in part from West African concepts of sickness and health and in part from European methods. From Africa (but also from Europe) came some of the ideas about 'unblocking' the body from sickness and removing lumps or clots of foreign objects which are stopping up the free flow of body liquids. From Europe, in the books of plantation owners of the eighteenth century, came ideas which had grown out of the medieval theory of 'humours'. A balance must be kept between hot and cold. All foods and drinks can be divided into 'hot' and 'cold', not literally hot and cold ones, but those that are spicy, pungent, which are supposed to heat the blood, and others that are mild and which cool it down. The nanas combine both of these traditions with great expertise.

As part of the research into childbirth that I did in the sixties in Jamaica I was able to interview some nanas, and found them impressive women with strong personalities. Many of them had daughters who were studying midwifery, some of them in Britain, who sent them back textbooks which, they said, kept them up to date.

When the *nanas* talked about their work they emphasized that it was the art of 'freeing' the body so that the baby could be born. For them a basic method of helping childbirth is through touch. It is really a laying-on of hands. When oil is used, as it often is, it is called 'anointing'. This does not start only in labour, for the nana visits the woman in her home from about the fourth month of pregnancy. There is a good deal of talking about local matters and about how the pregnant woman is feeling, and the *nana* does an abdominal examination, following this with massage with oil from the wild castor oil plant, so as to 'shape' the baby. She is helping the mother to 'grow it right'. She usually gives advice about diet in pregnancy, and urges the woman to eat iron-rich foods, plenty of fruit, vegetables and fish, and to drink bush teas. These herbal teas are prescribed according to the woman's condition: cerasee 'to clean the blood' or for high blood-pressure, 'fever grass' for headaches or, when mixed with rum, for vomiting, cape gooseberry, sometimes called 'wild tomato', to prevent miscarriage, 'granny humpback' or ruth upstick for indigestion, 'king of the forest' or soursop for high blood-pressure, convolvulus, called 'the love bush', as a laxative, 'strongback' for bladder infections, and 'shame root' as a sedative. She may advise against certain foods, particularly eggs, which are considered 'binding'.

By the time she goes into labour the woman and the *nana* attending her are friends, even if they have not known each other and each other's families for years before, which is usually the case. When labour starts both women prepare the labour room together by putting thick layers of old newspaper on the bed and covering them with a clean cloth, which may be an old cotton dress. They then tear up clean rags to make nappies for the baby. Water is collected in a pitcher from the nearest standpipe or spring. Paraffin lamps are filled, or special wood which burns like a bright torch may be used if there is no money for paraffin. The *nana* puts the pot on to make more bush tea. If contractions are not good this may be 'spice tea', made up of a mixture of different spices, which, according to one Jamaican medical practitioner, stimulates the uterus to contract.[1]

Any other children are sent out to neighbours, or if it is night they are bundled over to the side of the bed to give the labouring woman room to deliver, and a clothesline with a blanket over it may be suspended down the middle of the bed to serve as a curtain. The children lie listening to the progress of the labour and catch the first glimpse of the newborn baby as it is lifted up over the washline for them to see immediately it is born.

The usual drinks for the first stage of labour are mint or thyme tea. Both are thought to speed up labour. Thyme contains a cardiac glycocide, which may have the effect of increasing the efficiency of contractions and of uterine muscle tone.[2] Doses of castor oil may also be given if labour is slow. The *nana* uses wild castor oil, which is a good deal weaker than the commercial variety.

The *nana* massages the woman's abdomen with oil or the slimy scraping from 'toona' leaves. She helps to get the baby into the right position by doing this. As contractions get stronger she tells the woman to breathe lightly and rather quickly or there will be 'too much hackling' (she is probably suggesting that if her breathing becomes too strenuous the mother will hyperventilate). 'Do not take deep breaths in, or the baby will go up out of the belly,' she tells her.

If the mother is getting tired or if contractions are weak and ineffective the *nana* may wrap her round in hot towels, 'giving the whole body a souse down', and then follow this by massaging her lightly with olive oil all over. If she has backach the *nana* will use a strip of cotton cloth about one foot wide and pull it from one side to another, producing friction in the small of the woman's back. As the mother approaches full dilatation the *nana* also uses hot compresses – sometimes a heated stone – over her lower abdomen, or may make quick, light patting movements with a rag soaked in hot water over the place where there is pain, all the time speaking to and soothing the mother. 'You have to coax them,' one *nana* told me, 'give them good words and cheer them up.' She encourages the woman to 'blow out' until she can see the top of the baby's head in the vagina, meanwhile 'bussing' the perineum with oily hands to help it relax. If the baby's father

127

is present the *nana* asks him to get up on the bed behind the mother to support her back. 'You push gentle,' said one *nana*, 'and you give a little rest and you push again. Pushing hard brings in weakness. Let it open gradually.' The mother usually delivers the baby sitting up in bed, her feet on the bed and her hands on her thighs. If it does not cry immediately the *nana* lights a cigarette and blows the smoke on to the fontanelle, 'for the spirits'; this is one expression of her ritual function in interceding between the human world and that of the ghosts of duppies. Once born the baby is handed immediately to the mother.

Nanas are very wary of taking any active part in the third stage, because they know that if the woman has a post-partum haemorrhage they will be thought to have caused it. So they usually give her thyme tea and let her deliver the placenta herself, cutting the cord only after the third stage is completed. If the third stage is delayed, they ask her to squat over a bucket and blow into a bottle. This causes the diaphragm to press down on the top of the uterus and the abdominal wall to press in on it, and is an effective way of encouraging separation.

Once the placenta is delivered the perineum is cleaned, the woman crouching over a bucket of steaming water 'hot like nine nights' love' – a very effective way of cleansing the perineum without touching it and introducing infection. The *nana* washes the baby in cold water, which is thought to make it hardy, rubs asafoetida into the baby's fontanelle to protect it from duppies, treats the cord stump with finely ground nutmeg (which is slightly antiseptic) mixed with talcum powder, and gives it a prelacteal feed of 'Jack-in-the-Bush' or mint tea which helps to clear out mucus. The baby lies on the bed beside its mother, close against her body, and suckles at will. The *nana* makes cornmeal porridge for the mother and perhaps for the other children, and clears up the room. Before she leaves she tells the mother to stay indoors with the baby for a week, lest the duppies come for the child, and bind her hair in a turban and not wash it so that she does not get 'baby chill'. Neighbours come bringing food for the family, and boys and girls are sent off on errands. If the family can afford it there will be some rum drinking to celebrate.

The *nana* cares for mother and baby in the first few days after delivery and may also look after the other children and do cooking and washing if the woman's own mother or an aunt is not available. In other words, she simply takes over and mothers the new mother.

The Jamaican *nana* gives a good deal of emotional support to women in pregnancy, labour and the puerperium. She provides for the mother a continuing personal relationship, and herself fills the role of a mother who accepts responsibility from early pregnancy on, who is known in the community, and who meets the expectant mother at the grocery store and the market, in church, washing clothes down by the river, and gossiping with other women under the shade of a tree outside her homestead. She may give advice casually during pregnancy as they pass the time of day. She knows exactly what sort of life the pregnant woman is leading, what her worries are, and about family difficulties and money problems, housing and ill-health. The result is a prototype for family and home-centred maternity care.

Birth in South Africa

In segmented societies where there is a culture clash between forces representing the powerful and the relatively powerless different styles of childbirth reflect the conflicts in the social system. This is strikingly the case in South Africa.

The African ideal of childbirth is represented by the traditional Zulu way of giving birth, which is rarely possible today in the townships but remains the ideal. According to Zulu custom a witchdoctor should be present to bless the ground on which the firstborn is to be delivered, and to help in case of need, but is not necessary with second and subsequent births.[3] Unmarried girls smear cow dung on the floor of the grandmother's dwelling, where labour usually takes place. 'When the child is born it must look on something beautiful, for this will affect its life',[4] so coloured beads and special childbirth carvings decorate the room. 'The first minute of life is the most important.' If the woman bleeds too much, the witchdoctor orders a red calf to be sacrificed and she is made to drink some of its blood. After delivery she is always given a special dish of spinach to make the blood strong. A retained placenta is delivered by getting the woman to blow into a bottle (an almost universal practice in peasant societies for dealing with a delayed third stage). It used to be the custom for a male witchdoctor to deliver his own child, so that it might inherit his spirit, but a witchdoctor informant told me that the hospitals make this impossible, for doctors and nurses 'do not realize that the forces that activate the birth are much older than humanity itself. They turn birth into a spiritual nightmare.' But still wherever possible Zulu children are taken to see a birth 'to instil in them respect for human life' and so that they learn 'to regard birth and death as part of life'. This is considered an important part of their education.

In the third month of pregnancy the Zulu woman is taught how to breathe 'to give life and strength to the child'. Each morning she goes outside the hut, and, facing the east, takes three deep breaths, followed by a long breath out, to breathe out all evil. In labour the woman concentrates all her energy on breathing alternately through her mouth and her nose 'to lessen her consciousness of pain'. Traditionally there is an opening through to the sky in the central point of the roof of all Zulu dwellings, and it is on this that the labouring woman focuses: 'She must kneel, concentrating on this space, through the hole where she can see the stars. We say of a woman who is in labour: "She is counting the stars with pain."'

The Shangaans and the Tswanas, like the Zulus, kneel in labour. But among the Bushmen the mother makes a space in the bush, like a nest of grass, and tying a rope to the branch of a tree, bears down while holding the rope.

Many home deliveries in the African townships are reported as 'unattended'. These babies are usually delivered by traditional midwives. In the customs they adopt can be seen an area of 'culture contact' between traditional African practices common to all the tribes and Western-style methods. One of the traditional midwives who talked to me had been a nurse in a large American-style hospital for seven years before she had gone into midwifery among her own people, and had also started training as a witchdoctor. She combined Western techniques acquired as a professional nurse, but with which she had been dissatisfied because of their isolation from traditional social values, with Zulu tribal healing and the cult of spirit possession. She described to me the importance of asepsis but was also convinced that it was important for the mother to drink herbal teas in pregnancy 'to make the baby play free inside'. She was familiar with methods of obstetric intervention, but explained that if labour is prolonged one should deliver a child by smearing one's hand with bone marrow and helping the baby 'get through the road that is closed'. Both mother and midwife 'must follow the pain, keep quiet, and listen'. The woman should handle the baby and kiss it at delivery, for 'the child must know who is the mother'.

Within several miles of the homestead where I talked with these traditional midwives, there exists the enormous modern hospital for African patients. Maybe it has changed now, but in the seventies when I was there the delivery ward was full of groaning, writhing women – the majority of them labouring alone. Oxytocin drips and pumps were in widespread use. This was the meeting place of the old Africa and the new technology of the West. Pools of blood lay on the floor like sacrificial out-pourings, and African nurses were happy to leave them there as witness of the blessings of the earth, while they busied them-selves with technologically sophisticated modern equipment and ignored the labouring women as far as possible, which it was not so difficult to do, as they did not speak the same languages anyway.

All normal births took place at home or in the Soweto clinics: these hospital mothers fighting to give birth were selected from the township as potentially complicated cases. Birth was very far from normal here, and it was conducted in a way I had seen before in American hospitals that catered for black 'clinic patients' from large urban ghettos: impersonal, conveyor-belt obstetrics accom-panied by a plethora of technical innovations and machinery.

In South Africa childbirth for white women is very different from that for African women. An obstetrician who delivered his upper-class patients in the most luxurious private maternity home of the city said, 'There's the woman, varnishing her nails, a box of chocolates at her side, the radio blaring and the baby hanging at one breast, and she is supposed to be trying to feed it . . . they're spoiled little rich girls in here!' One nursing sister told me: 'Lots of mummies are silly. They handle their babes as if they were little china dolls. They go home with a sister, and often two sisters, one for the day and one for the night; and when they leave, an African nanny takes over.'

I asked what education was provided for women (and fathers, too, perhaps) in caring for and relating to their own babies, and she said, 'Mummies like to cuddle too much. They spoil the babies.' Indicating the glass doors leading from each mother's bed through to the nursery with its three or four cribs, she remarked, 'Of course we lock the hatches when the daddies come. They are not allowed to touch the babies.' I wondered who was colluding with whom, since it was not surprising that parents who were not encouraged to explore and handle their babies failed to develop confidence. 'But,' protested the obstetrician, 'we can't have women molly-coddling their babies!' At night, according to the paediatrician, the mothers were fed several sleeping pills and the babies removed to the central nursery. The women woke up 'with breasts like footballs'.

At another maternity home, the supervising nuns sat in a circle with beaming faces and fresh white habits, offering tea and cakes. This was the private clinic where Grantly Dick-Read introduced what were then his revolutionary ideas of birth without fear. But here babies were not with their mothers at all, but in a solid mass of plastic cribs in rows like those in cemeteries for the war dead. 'Oh, it's rarely that a mother asks for her baby,' Matron explained; 'we believe mothers need a rest.' The nuns glowed as they tended 'their' babies. Fathers were taboo, and although some were present at delivery, most were sent to the fathers' waiting room downstairs where they smoked and worried together and viewed – what was then the latest development of modern technology – deliveries on a television screen.

When I undertook my research in South Africa in the seventies it was clear that African women had little or no choice about maternity care. All mothers, white as well as black, were effectively denied the opportunity to decide how they wanted to have their babies and what kind of post-partum care they preferred. It was a maternity system where the consultant obstetrician was king, and where midwives were undervalued and had few links with any midwifery associations outside South Africa. The mother was subservient to the direction of her obstetrician, and later to her paediatrician, and both of them followed the autocratic, interventionist style of their American counterparts. As women reach out across continents to help each other, as they find a voice in their own health care, all that is bound to change.

9

Ritual In The Western Way Of Birth

The modern hospital, no less than a traditional society, evolves its own culture. Some practices are empirically based. Others are enshrined in the mystique of hospital protocols. They are linked with social expectations and medical assumptions about what a patient is and how she should behave. In this chapter I want to look at some of the customs of the modern Western hospital, and see what social functions they fill.

'Good' Patients

Most obstetricians in the West are men, which is odd to start with. When a woman goes to an obstetrician she comes up against his ideas about how a female patient should behave and what mothers should be like. The relationship between doctor and patient is asymmetrical, and he is dominant. Her preconceptions about what doctors are like and how they behave figure in this transaction, too, but are unlikely to be expressed openly in his presence.

Because birth is a medical event, the woman is supposed to be a 'good patient', and her responsibility is limited to this. She is meant to be quiet, placid, polite, appreciative of what is being done to help her, quick to respond to instructions, and able to comprehend and remember what she is told without requiring the information a second time. She should be clean, neat and self-contained, and should not disturb other patients or the staff

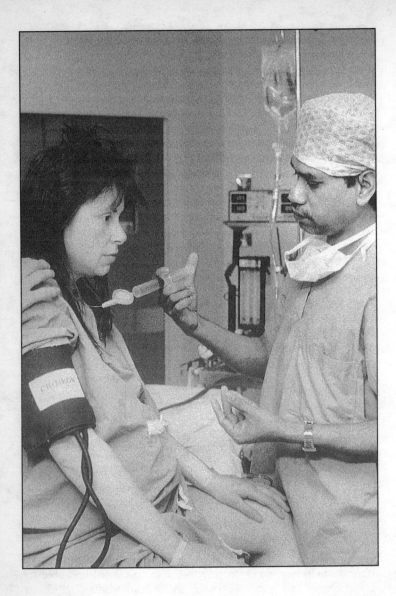

by expressing strong emotions of any kind. The word 'patient' itself derives from 'passivity'; a patient is someone to whom something is done.

In almost every circumstance where I have sat with women who are in labour in Western hospitals I have noticed that nurses are most satisfied with the management of a case when they can write on the record sheet 'patient resting peacefully', whether the labouring woman is in fact relaxing well or whether, under the influence of narcotic drugs, she is quietly moaning and groaning but still not disturbing anyone else. The ideal patient of the case sheet is a woman tucked up in bed, more or less inert. In writing 'patient resting' on the card nurses offer the obstetrician an assessment of which he approves, for this is his aim, too.

Any male obstetrician tends to make assumptions about female psychology which derive from his view of his own mother, sister, wife or girlfriend. He may assume, or be taught as part of his medical training, that the act of coming to him puts the patient in 'a parent-child' relationship. As one textbook puts it: ' . . . by the patient's dress, walk, make-up and attitudes in answering questions, a judgment of her personality begins . . . The physician notices whether the patient is reacting to the interview in a feminine way or whether she is domineering, demanding, masculine, aggressive.'[1]

Obstetricians are sometimes perplexed and threatened when patients do not behave according to the stereotype of the good patient. If a woman questions obstetric procedures or hospital routines a doctor may reply: 'Just leave it to us'; 'Don't worry, we know what we are doing'; 'It's a very good hospital'; 'The midwives will make you as comfortable as possible'; or 'I'm sure you will like it here.' On the other hand, a doctor's anxiety may be expressed in verbal attack on a patient who questions his judgement, and in threats that unless she relies on him she is endangering her baby's life: 'You don't want to harm your baby, do you?' or even 'Do you want to kill your baby?'

Psychological factors which profoundly affect patient-doctor interaction in the antenatal clinic and maternity ward include prior assumptions about each other's roles, the doctor's and the woman's anxiety, and poor communication between them. Obstetricians are well aware that there are frequent breakdowns in communication. But they often do not acknowledge their own anxiety, and the way in which it can permeate the patient-doctor relationship.

A doctor's whole training can be seen as providing a protective barrier against the patient. This process starts when a medical student begins to dissect a body and has to forget that it was once a person. It is reinforced by medical humour, much of which focuses on the subjects of death and the female body. The ward round, with the big chief progressing from bed to bed trailed by a small crowd of doctors and students to whom he turns to ask questions about 'interesting cases', further refines the skill of talking about people as if they were not really there, and of evading personal contact. Moreover, the career structure of medicine is such that the doctor depends on superiors' and colleagues' approval and trust, and far less, in a hospital structure, about what patients think.

In hospital a doctor enters a total institution, one which dictates his own behaviour rigidly – how long he can reasonably spend with each patient, for example, or whether Sister will disapprove of him sitting on a patient's bed; and sometimes, more subtly and pervasively, whether it is acceptable to touch a patient other than when examining her and, if it is, but only sometimes, what conditions must first be met (for example, is it all right to put an arm round a patient who has had a stillbirth?).

Problems in the relationship between women patients and doctors are not only a matter of psychological stresses or because women find it difficult to be assertive and to negotiate skilfully. The management of pregnancy and childbirth is a *political* issue, and one that cannot be solved by individuals. I mean by this that the interaction between a doctor and a patient, however sympathetic and woman-centred that doctor is, cannot but be affected by the power wielded by the medical establishment and women's relative powerlessness.

One consequence of this powerlessness is that women are denied their own definition of pregnancy and birth. The 'meaning' of birth is to be found in medical records. When a woman is dissatisfied with or distressed about what is done to her, and wants to find out what happened, she must turn to experts and learn their construction of events. Her experience is treated as personal, eccentric, aberrant, uninformed, unbalanced – and even, perhaps, hysterical. Once the obstetric 'facts' are known, the touchstone of truth has been provided. The only accepted reality is the medical construction of pregnancy and childbirth.

Doctors are often genuinely astonished, and hurt, that their patients should perceive the events of pregnancy and birth in a way that conflicts with their own perception. They have done the best they can. They have made their skills available. They are baffled that women should react critically. Even those who are women themselves, and who have given birth, are often unwilling to accept a patient's definition of her experience. It is sometimes claimed by doctors that women are vulnerable, fearful and easily upset by minor occurrences, attaching too great a significance to casual remarks or ordinary routine procedures. They therefore see their main role in psychological terms as being to 'reassure'. It is implied that everything will be all right, there is a 100 per cent guarantee that the baby will be fine, so long as the patient 'trusts' the doctor. An important element in medical demeanour is the 'show of normalcy', by which the professionals suggest that, whatever happens, they are in control and there is nothing for the patient to worry about.[2]

Birth ritual is not just something that people act out in the Third World. We have our own complex ritual that serves to reinforce the power of the institution in which birth takes place and the control that doctors and other professional attendants have over women in childbirth.

Hospital Birth

One of the most dramatic changes that has occurred in childbirth in the last fifty years is that women rarely have the option of giving birth at home. They must become hospital patients. By the very act of entry to a large institution the nature of childbirth is changed, and women become subordinate members of an institution designed to process them through a system that is organized according to a mechanical ritual of production, just like a factory. Babies are the goods to be produced, women the containers, the packaging.

Hospital rites of passage into motherhood entail separating the pregnant woman from 'normal' people going about their everyday lives, taking control of her body and her behaviour, exposing the most intimate parts of her body to men and strangers, and subjecting her to alarming and sometimes painful procedures at

137

which she must not flinch because they are 'for the sake of the baby'.

Rites of Admission

Entry to hospital involves a complex ritual that inculcates the dominant values of a technological society. An expectant mother goes into hospital as a woman with a baby inside her who is about to be born. She is transformed into a uterus that holds a foetus, which is contained within a pelvis that is located inconveniently inside a patient, who is classified as 'at risk'. With this rite of passage the physiological act of birth-giving is redefined as a technological process. Not only are her uterine contractions and baby's heart rate monitored electronically, but her body is treated as if it were a piece of faulty electronic equipment, with the obstetric team as the trouble-shooters and data analysts.

Some of the constituent ceremonies by which this transformation is achieved are well-established initiation rites. Removing a woman from her home environment, separating her from her family, shaving her perineum, giving an enema to empty her bowels, taking away her own clothing and putting her in a hospital gown, thus turning her into the property of the institution; allowing her partner or other companions only to be present on condition that they are submissive and do not 'interfere', sticking an intravenous catheter in her arm through which drugs are fed straight into her bloodstream, thereby denying her the right of freedom of movement, all were standard procedures before the electronic age in obstetrics.

While some of these ceremonies have all but disappeared in many hospitals in the West, others persist tenaciously, and new ceremonies have been introduced to take the place of those discarded. In the seventies the setting up of an intravenous drip was restricted to women believed to be at special risk. Now, in some hospitals, every woman must labour with an IV in her arm, 'her umbilical cord to the hospital, signifying her now total dependency on the institution for her life, telling her not that she gives life, but rather that the *institution* does.'[3]

The first ceremonial on entering hospital is that of the admission procedure. A couple are often separated while the labouring woman undergoes 'prepping', consisting of the recording of data about her condition and that of her foetus, together with other predominantly ceremonial rites: still, in many European hospitals, shaving of the pubic hair, an enema, a shower, being dressed in impersonal hospital nightwear, and being confined to bed.

While this is being done by uniformed strangers, verbal exchanges may take place which serve to further define her role as patient. These at first sight may seem the stuff of normal conversation between equals, but in fact entail forms of what social anthropologist Erving Goffman, the first person to analyse relationships within the 'total institution' of a hospital, calls 'presentational deference'.[4] The midwife makes a complimentary remark about a patient's hair or the pattern of her sponge bag, or asks, 'What do you want, a boy or a girl?' These appear to be expressions of sympathetic concern and friendly interest, but in effect, because of their context, they invade the individual's personal reserve:

> which becomes clear if it is the patient who pays the member of the staff these compliments or asks the midwife or doctor about their families. Taken together, these rituals provide a continuous symbolic tracing of the extent to which the recipient's ego has not been bounded and barricaded in regard to others.[5]

It is all part of the making of a compliant patient.

Let us look more closely at exactly what is done when the patient is 'prepared', starting with the shave – either just a trim or a complete shave, turning the woman's perineum into an object resembling a hardboiled egg. There is no evidence that shaving reduces the amount of bacteria on the skin. Research back in the sixties established, in fact, that chances of infection are increased because the razor is bound to scrape surface skin cells and allow the introduction of bacteria.[6] Perineal shaving is a way in which the labouring woman is de-sexed and the area around her anus and vagina ritually returned to its pre-pubertal state. The implicit message is that she is no longer an adult woman, no longer a sexual being, but a docile little girl.

In a technological culture female energy in childbirth, women's powerful sexuality must be sanitized and disguised so that birth can be under medical control. Women's sexuality is perceived as dangerous, and so threatening that its very existence in relation to childbirth may be vigorously denied. Birth, it is implied, is simply *pain*, and doctors can manage pain.

The purging of the expectant mother with an enema is rarely insisted on now in North America and Britain because it is acknowledged as useless. But until only a few years ago it was done routinely. Where it persists it is an act of ritual cleansing and purification. It involves the taking over of personal bodily processes by an external institution, and thus taking control of that which is most intimate. The regulation of bowel functions is maintained throughout the hospital stay, and nurses make regular rounds with laxatives, asking who has 'been', and continuing institutional control over elimination.

If the woman's cervix is already three centimetres dilated, or in some hospitals if the midwife or doctor can manage to introduce even one finger, the membranes are likely to be artificially ruptured. That is, the protective bubble of liquid in which the baby is lying is punctured. The rationale for this is that it accelerates labour, though there is no evidence that this is the case, unless the woman is already nine centimetres dilated.

There is rarely any medical reason why the father should not be present throughout childbirth, nor why women friends and family members cannot help give loving support, as in peasant communities. Yet still in some hospitals the father is told to wait outside during the admission procedures, whenever the mother is examined, and sometimes throughout the whole of the second stage of labour and the birth. The message behind this is clear. The woman's body has been appropriated by medical personnel. To permit the presence of those she loves is to confuse two categories of social identity, that in which the woman is wife, sexual being, daughter and mother, and that in which she is a patient whose actions are under the control of the doctor. In order to avoid confusion between these two social categories modern obstetrics takes labouring women out of their own homes, separates them from other members of their family, and sometimes, too, from the father of the child, and puts them through what amounts to an initiation process on entry to hospital which has the effect of ritual subjugation.

Induction

Induction is the artificial initiation of labour by surgical or medical means, or by a combination of these. Rates of induction of labour rose to close to 50 per cent in British hospitals in the late sixties and early seventies, in spite of the fact that there was no evidence that it was saving babies' lives.

It is not a new idea for doctors to trigger labour artificially. Looking at the history of induction and speeding up of labour can give us some idea of what women have suffered at the hands of those obstetricians who treat the uterus as a fascinating thing to play with rather than part of a woman. *Accouchement forcé* was practised in the nineteenth century; and in the early twentieth century one obstetrician tried used children's balloons to open the cervix. He pushed them inside, then poured water into them, and pulled. Another method was to use castor oil, large soapsud enemas, repeated doses of quinine (the drug employed to treat malaria), and injections of pituitary extract (a hormone excreted by the pituitary gland). One advocate of this method said that if the woman did not start labour after doing this repeatedly for three days, it was safe for the obstetrician to go away for the weekend. It was estimated that quinine, which is a poison, killed 5 per cent of the babies.[7]

Acceleration of labour with ergot, a drug obtained from the fungus that grows on rye, was introduced in 1808, and the doctor who did so commented, 'Rarely have I been detained more than three hours.'[8] But within a few years it was found that the stillbirth rate had increased alarmingly as a result of this practice. Then sparteine, another drug that causes muscle spasms, was tried, but that led to the uterus contracting strongly in an uncoordinated and acutely painful way hours after the last dose was given, and it was found that it could also slow and sometimes even stop the baby's heart.

Modern methods of induction have become possible both because very few women have a seriously malformed pelvis nowadays, and because of the discovery of penicillin to treat pelvic infection. The oxytocin drip was first introduced in 1947 and since the seventies it has been common practice in Britain to convey a synthetic uterine stimulant straight into a woman's blood system in order to induce labour or to speed it up. To this has been added another method, prostaglandin induction, which – though widely used in Britain – is considered potentially dangerous in the USA. One problem with induction by intra-venous infusion of oxytocin is that unless the dosage is carefully regulated the woman's uterus can go into a state of hypertonic spasm, that is, it clamps down onto itself. This results in a

141

reduction of blood flow to the placenta, and the baby may become distressed, or even die. The uterus of a woman who has had a previous Caesarean section, and which is therefore scarred, and that of a woman who has already had a number of babies, may rupture with induction unless contractions are monitored meticulously and the drip turned down or switched off if they get too powerful. This is why women having induced or augmented labour should always be carefully monitored.

Induction rates vary greatly between different hospitals, and even between different consultants in the same hospital. Whereas some obstetricians reckon to do no more than 10 per cent inductions, others select anything up to 75 per cent of women. It has not been shown that high rates of induction save babies. In Cardiff in the early seventies there was a high induction rate, but the conclusion drawn from lengthy research was that 'there is no evidence that a woman in Cardiff having a baby in 1973 was any more likely to end up with a live child than in 1965'.[9]

As women told others about their experiences of induced labour, and further information was published in medical journals in the seventies, there was a strong and angry reaction on the part of many women. Some obstetricians explained this as engineered by the press and television, and even by research. It was not, they thought, 'real': 'I do not believe that . . . we are seeing other than the response of a relatively vocal minority of the patient population. If the vast majority of patients were not encouraged by the media, and by questionnaires, to express disappointment and frustration, and discontent, they could be effectively dealt with.'[10] Nevertheless, once public disquiet was expressed, the high induction rates of 1971-4 were dramatically reduced over a short period, and in at least one large teaching hospital a rate of over 40 per cent was in a few months reduced to 25 per cent, without any rise in perinatal mortality. It looked as if women's voices were at last being heard.

The Tethered Body

The room in which a woman has her baby in a modern hospital looks very different from the dwelling or forest clearing in which a woman gives birth in a pre-industrial society. Whereas the traditional mode of childbirth places the woman in the centre of the unfolding drama, modern childbirth involves advanced and sophisticated technology and cumbersome equipment, compared to which the labouring woman seems dwarfed and insignificant. The delivery room is an obstetric shrine, the high altar on which the obstetrician and his acolytes enact their ceremonial. The signals which the obstetricians amd midwives receive and interpret come not directly from the woman's body but from monitors and other machines which fill the delivery room. It is on the screens and the unwinding paper chart that all eyes are fixed. 'An eventual aim,' said one professor of obstetrics, 'must be for every woman to have her baby in an intensive care situation.'[11] Another obstetrician remarked to colleagues: 'Labour wards now look like some scientific hell-holes with instruments everywhere, wires everywhere . . . If we used telemetry and got rid of the wires (we can monitor a man's heart on the moon) surely we could monitor a baby without having a wire attached.'[12]

Not only have machines taken over the centre of attention, but they have also immobilized the woman in labour, who cannot get up and walk about, or even change position freely in bed. In no traditional societies are women completely immobilized in this way. In contrast, helping-women encourage the mother to adopt different postures and to move around so as to help the descent of the baby's head. In the West restriction of a woman's movements has been accepted as necessary because of the new technology, with little research into the effects of this change. Iatrogenic interventions are giving rise to conditions which in their turn have to be treated by still further new obstetric techniques. Inserting an electrode through a woman's vagina and cervix and clipping it on to the baby's scalp allows monitoring of the foetal heart, for example, but introduces the risk of infection, prevents the woman moving and produces data in the form of a print-out which may be interpreted incorrectly and result in an unnecessary Caesarean section, may cause an abscess on the baby's scalp, and sometimes leads to the spread of HIV infection.

Perhaps the most powerful ritual act that is now accepted as routine practice in many hospitals is that of wiring up a woman to a continuous electronic foetal monitor. It may be done for a set period of time and then discontinued, or the electrode may remain in place for the whole of labour. The ceremony of wiring up a woman in labour gives her the message that her body is not to be trusted and that it is in constant danger of malfunction.

Electronic foetal monitoring (EFM) also serves to convey the message that obstetricians have achieved cultural control over birth, just as traditional midwives and witchdoctors in pre-industrial societies communicate cultural control through prayer, chanting, magic, divination and the laying-on of hands. All eyes turn to the flickering print-out rather than to the woman. It is as if the machine were giving birth, not her.

There is no evidence that electronic foetal monitoring saves babies' lives, nor that it produces better-quality babies. It has been acknowledged for some years that its value cannot be demonstrated in low-risk labours, but it has continued to be used routinely 'just in case', and everyone has agreed that even if it was not needed for normal births it obviously could be life-saving for babies at special risk, particularly for those born pre-term.

In fact, the opposite seems to be the case. A study of pre-term babies demonstrated that the risk of a baby suffering cerebral palsy was a good deal higher following electronic foetal monitoring than after intermittent monitoring with a stethoscope. Cerebral palsy was diagnosed at eighteen months in 20 per cent of the children who had EFM, but only in 8 per cent of those who had received intermittent monitoring. In the editorial section of the *New England Journal of Medicine*, in which this study was reported, the comment was made that 'clearly, the hoped-for benefit from intrapartum electronic foetal monitoring has not been realized. It is unfortunate that randomized, controlled trials were not carried out before this form of technology became universally applied.'[13] Now that trials have at last taken place it is too late to limit its adoption in hospitals worldwide, as obstetricians feel nervous when they do not use it. Thus electronic foetal monitoring is a failed technology that continues to be used primarily for ritual purposes.

The posture which a woman may be required to adopt in the delivery room is symptomatic of the relation between obstetrician and patient. It is easier for the obstetrician to examine and to intervene when the patient is supine. She lies flat with her legs raised in lithotomy stirrups, and, in the USA, sometimes with her wrists and ankles tied or clamped, or with a shoulder restrainer holding her firmly in position. It is only in our Western technological culture that a woman having a baby has to lie almost flat on her back with her legs in the air, and try to push her baby up-hill and out through a perineum stretched tight by legs in that unnatural position.

Drugs for Pain Relief

The most commonly used analgesic agent in Britain is Pethidine (Demerol in the USA), which is a narcotic. It was first introduced to take the place of morphine, since it was claimed by the manufacturers that only small doses were needed (25 or 50 mgs) and that it was non-addictive. In fact, it is an addictive drug, and the doses now given start at 100 mgs and go up to 200 mgs. Since it is injected several times, in many labours women are getting as much as 500 mgs of Pethidine, a knock-out dose. Although in some hospitals mothers control their own pain relief, asking for it as and if necessary, in many others Pethidine, and Pethidine in combination with other drugs, are given as routine, and the patient does not really share in the decision-making.[14] Pethidine sends women into a drowsy stupor in which labour can take on a nightmare quality, reducing the ability to cope with pain and making it impossible for them to control their breathing and relaxation.

Regional anaesthetics, of which the best known is the lumbar epidural, have been hailed as the answer to pain in childbirth. An epidural can give painless and even sensation-free labour, and is safer than a general anaesthetic. But some women experience a swift and dramatic drop in blood-pressure which is bad for them and the baby. Some have an allergic reaction to the local anaesthetic used. The possibilities of the mother having difficulty in breathing, becoming unconscious or remaining paralysed are exceedingly remote, but they exist nevertheless. A much more common problem is that the baby will have to be delivered by forceps, and in most maternity units where elective epidurals are available the forceps rate has shot up.

An epidural also usually means that urine must be drawn off from the bladder by a catheter, since the woman has no sensation of wanting to empty her bladder. This lack of sensation may persist for the first day or two after the delivery, so during this time too she may need to be catheterized. Infection is far more likely when a catheter is used: 29 per cent of women who have catheters passed suffer an infection, as compared with 3 per cent of those who have not. A forceps delivery also makes urinary tract infection five times more likely.[15] Some obstetricians believe that an additional disadvantage of epidural anaesthesia is, in the words of one, 'the need for constant observation of the patient',[16] an objection which should be discounted if we think that all women should be watched over and cared for in labour.

An article describing the advantages of epidural anaesthesia published in a midwifery journal[17] was illustrated with a photograph of a laughing mother sitting up in bed watching television, oblivious of her labour, and explained that this patient delivered shortly after the photograph was taken. (Although it was strange that the test-card seemed to be giving her such pleasure, the claim that the woman need feel nothing of the labour holds true.) Obstetricians often pride themselves on having a patient who is 'talking, laughing and joking' while delivering a baby, and engaged in what, for the woman who has not had regional anaesthesia, can be a psychosexual experience in which talking and joking would only be distractions, just as they would be at the height of lovemaking. For these doctors, having a patient in pain is to go back to the Dark Ages. Complete absence of sensation is offered to women as the modern way of giving birth.

Ceremonial Garments

The donning of special clothing – gown, head cover, mask, overshoes – is a device familiar in religious ceremonies, and by this practice the ritual act of birth is dramatized. It also has the effect of segregating the woman who is giving birth from her everyday existence, isolating her from her normal social relationships and of depersonalizing both her and her birth attendants. She is surrounded by anonymous masked figures officiating as at an altar.

Studies of ritual aspects of the use of masks and other uniforms in hospital show that the higher up in the hospital hierarchy an individual is, the more often sterile clothing is dispensed with.[18] The senior obstetrician may approach his patient wearing his ordinary suit, only donning sterile clothing for an obstetric manoeuvre. Conversely, the lower an individual is in the hierarchy the more special clothing he or she is required to put on, and the more consistent its use. A woman's partner comes at the bottom of this hierarchy, and is often required to be muffled up

146

in cap, gown, overshoes, perhaps a beard cover, and at all times a sterile mask, although one kept on for longer than fifteen minutes no longer prevents the passage of bacteria. The function of these sterile garments is purely ritualistic.

In many countries the labouring woman is still covered with sheeting. She looks like a sofa draped with dust-covers, no longer a human being. The only visible object is a plate-sized area of shiny swabbed flesh and a vulva exposed under bright lights, ready for delivery. When an obstetrician isolates with drapes the lower half of a woman's body, it becomes his sterile field. But it is clearly neither his, nor, because of the juxtaposition of vagina and anus, sterile. It is a convenient fiction however, by which he asserts his rights, insists that the woman keeps her hands off her own body, which becomes out of bounds, and serves to render the genital area depersonalized and to de-sex birth.

This depersonalization provides protection for the gynaecologist. The woman is no longer a sexual object. This is not a man looking at a woman's naked body, but a doctor confronting 'a case', detached, objective, professional. It provides armour against his own feelings, not only disruptive sexual emotions, but often also those of tenderness, compassion, sympathy and friendship. It may be only in the presence of another man who is allowed to have these feelings, the woman's partner, that an obstetrician can allow himself to relax and let some of the barriers down. Now that fathers are more and more frequently present the armour no longer serves its purpose of creating a protective barrier between doctor and patient. Obstetricians often say that they enjoy having the woman's male partner there because his presence permits a more 'normal', easy atmosphere.

A Production Timetable

Each stage of labour may be pharmacologically regulated in order to ensure that it fits a timetable. Uterine activity is made to comply with a superimposed itinerary, and if there is deviation from this schedule oxytocin is introduced into the woman's bloodstream through an intravenous drip (IV). In many large hospitals an IV is set up 'just in case', so that drugs of different kinds can be dripped straight into the woman's circulation. Dilatation of the cervix is assessed at regular intervals with probing fingers, and the results recorded on a partogram or labour chart. Lines on

147

the graph paper register the statistical norm for dilatation and for descent of the presenting part, and the strength of uterine contractions is adjusted if necessary so that labour conforms to this standard. If dilatation is slow or the baby is not delivered within the time limit a Caesarean section is performed. Retrospective audit by senior obstetricians in one English teaching hospital revealed that 30 per cent of Caesarean sections were unnecessary.[19]

Delivery as a Race to the Finishing Post

Once full dilatation of the cervix is reached it is 'action stations'! The expulsive stage is treated as an assault course on delivery. The aggressively managed second stage is marked by bullying, violence and the dehumanization of both the woman and her attendants, and all attention and effort is directed towards evacuation of the uterus at top speed. In many countries it is the rule that delivery must be managed by the obstetrician, so obstetric nurses summon him and lay out the instruments and other equipment he may wish to use, tethering the woman's legs and raising them in lithotomy stirrups to make his work easier. Her legs are draped, her perineum swabbed down with antiseptic, a bright light is directed on her vulva, students and other observers flood in and stand around the lower end of the delivery table, and all eyes turn to the bulging perineum and offending orifice. The woman is instructed to push strenuously 'like going to the toilet, dear', to hold her breath for as long as she can, and push again as soon as she has the breath to do so, in order to get the baby delivered as soon as possible. Her cheer-leaders stand round, urging her, often imploring her, to push longer and harder.

Many women become exhausted with the prolonged breath-holding and straining. They suffer the effects of dehydration, hyperventilation and ketosis (the accumulation of acids resulting from the burning up of fat). They burst blood vessels in their eyes and faces, are drenched in sweat, and all their muscles ache as if they have a bad dose of flu.[20]

This kind of pushing leads to fluctuations in the mother's blood-pressure which can be serious and can reduce the oxygen available to the baby.[21] The stress to the baby may be picked up on the monitor print-out as a 'type-II' dip, and this has the

148

effect of triggering further commands to push so as to get the baby delivered quickly. It is a vicious circle.

The management of the second stage represents in microcosm the authoritarian control claimed by modern obstetrics over women in childbirth. A woman doctor, shocked by her experience of residency in an American teaching hospital, believes that 'the medical birth is pornographic. The woman is degraded. The physician intimidates her and forcefully takes from her both the act of birth and that which she herself has nurtured.'[22]

Episiotomy

The final flourish in obstetric delivery is an incision of the mother's perineum to enlarge the birth opening – an episiotomy – and then, in many countries (the USA, Germany and Italy, for example), the obstetrician may use fundal pressure to force the baby out, pushing with a powerful hand grip or with an arm pressing down on the woman's abdomen where the top of her uterus is. Birth is thus transformed into a combination of surgical operation and brutal assault, and a wound is produced which must be sutured. An episiotomy involves cutting through layers of skin and muscle with a pair of scissors – which are often blunt, so that tissues and muscles are crushed and mangled. The repair involves pushing cotton swabs inside and then probing and stitching the most sensitive part of a woman's body, often with completely inadequate anaesthesia. Suturing can take anything from fifteen minutes or so, as is usual in North America, to an hour or longer, as is often the case in Britain, where episiotomies are usually made *across* layers of muscle rather than straight down through the natural division that extends vertically from vagina to anus. This has been described by an obstetrician as 'one of the least considered and most painful of all operations performed on the human female. Far too many women leave hospital with the memory of perineal pain, which they aver was far worse than the pain of parturition.'[23] It is a ritual mutilation through which the majority of women in our society pass in order to be mothers. It is the Western way of female genital mutilation.

Doctors often say that they perform episiotomies to avoid the baby being brain-damaged, and because it is the only way to get a baby out without tearing the mother's pelvic floor. They believe it prevents her having a prolapsed uterus or bladder, or stress incontinence. Yet there is no evidence that episiotomy is effective in preventing injuries of these kinds, and good reason to suspect that it is the ritual of forceful pushing and straining in the second stage that puts stress on the ligaments supporting the woman's cervix, the tissues lining her vagina, her bladder and pelvic floor muscles, and her perineum. The ritual of episiotomy can be justified only as a way of limiting the damage done by the misconduct of the second stage of labour.

Though sometimes a woman's perineum is especially rigid, and some babies need to be born quickly, routine episiotomy for close on 100 per cent of women, as in the United States and Eastern European countries today, is only necessary because the obstetrician wants to get the task over and done with as quickly and efficiently as possible, without wasting professional time or relying on the vagaries of nature, or on biological rhythms which do not readily accommodate themselves to hospital schedules.

Nor is it only the 'memory' of pain with which many women leave hospital. Pain following the wounding and suturing of a perineum often persists until the third post-partum month, and sometimes for much longer.[24] Both the pain of suturing and the pain of the months following is often not acknowledged by doctors, and little or nothing is done to help a woman cope with it. In women's words: 'The stitching was painful. The doctor said it wasn't painful.' 'It hurt, but the doctor said it couldn't possibly hurt as there were no nerve-endings in the vagina.' If infection, granulation and breakdown of the scar occurs the woman is left with a gaping wound that must be re-sutured: 'The midwife examined me to cut the stitches and found that they had fallen out and some were in the wrong place . . . She said that I was gaping like the Mersey Tunnel.' When nothing anatomically wrong is visible, a woman may simply be told, 'What do you expect? You've just had a baby!'

Episiotomy serves as a demonstration of medical power over women. The medical hierarchy is in most countries male-dominated. Thus episiotomy is the ultimate assertion of the right to mutilate and torture so that a woman may be fully female, and of men's right to use women's bodies in any way they like.

Clearing Out and Cleaning Up

The delivery of the baby is often followed by rapid 'housekeeping' to empty the uterus of all further products of conception and to get the delivery table free for the next patient. Given the violent conduct of the second stage of labour, there may be a case for the active management of the third stage and evacuating the placenta quickly with an injection to stimulate contractions in order to avoid haemorrhage. Other interventions have far less justification. It is the standard practice in some American hospitals, for example, especially those located in cities in which there is a large proportion of immigrant women, to complete the labour at top speed by extracting the placenta with a combination of pulling on the cord and fundal pressure, the obstetrician then putting his arm, up to the elbow, into the uterus, 'to make sure there is nothing left'. He pulls the uterus down with forceps to 'visualize' and check for tears in the cervix. This is done regardless of the woman's pain because it is assumed that all patients have had an epidural or other anaesthesia. The woman's body is treated as a machine that must be emptied of its contents, cleared out and inspected before allowing it to pass along the assembly line.

The Defusing of Female Power

Almost universally a woman is seen as having a threatening power which can weaken and emasculate men, and, as we have seen in Chapter 4, her sexuality and the products of her body are considered dangerous. She is like a bomb which can be defused only by denial of her sensuality, by carefully circumscribed behaviour on her part, and by meticulously avoiding her during those critical periods when her body opens up and its fluids and other substances emerge, or at those times when a man is engaged on some task which involves special skills and concentration. The shame which women feel in Eastern Mediterranean countries, the ritual offered by husband and wife during her unclean time in Judaism and Hinduism, and the taboo on sexual intercourse typical of tribal societies before going into battle or on an important hunt, engaging in a community activity of great significance or making sacrifices to the ancestors, indicate that woman is at once the creator and the destroyer, the terrible Hindu goddess Kali, who bears life in her hands. Perhaps this is how all children feel at some time about their apparently omnipotent mothers. Girls grow up and start to menstruate themselves and develop the power to bear babies in their own bodies. But boys can never do this.

The obstetrician, as distinct from the midwife who was traditionally, and usually still is, less interventionist, seeks to take control of childbirth. It is then almost as if he, and not the woman, gives birth to the baby. Technology has defused the bomb, and childbirth has been de-sexed. The previously mysterious power has been annexed, harnessed to a masculine purpose and according to a masculine design. It may be that the actions of those obstetricians who manage childbirth aggressively can only really be explained in terms of their fear and hatred of women and their uterine envy.[25]

Controlling Women

Why do women put up with all this heavily ritualized treatment? Why do they tolerate an invasive technology that takes birth from them? Why do they often seek it out? For in hospitals where these rites are less frequently enacted there are women who feel that they are not getting the best treatment. 'They don't care in that place. They didn't even bother to shave me.' 'They kept asking *me* if I wanted things. Don't they know what to do? I don't think they know what they are doing in there. They've got their minds on other things.'[26] These are really the same questions we might ask of boys being initiated into manhood in the African bush, who endure circumcision, scarification, having their teeth knocked out and other ordeals conducted by tribal elders to turn them into adults and prove their manhood. We could ask why mothers in Somalia put their seven-year-old daughters through the suffering and mutilation of clitoridectomy and infibulation.

In childbirth obstetricians act as our own tribal elders controlling a perilous life passage. The mechanisms by which women are conducted through this transition to motherhood result in their feeling safer when undergoing these processes than when they are not performed. This is one of the important functions of ritual. In a dangerous transitional state ceremonies enable the individual who is in limbo, to feel secure, in good hands, guided each step of the way.

A woman who is becoming a mother, especially for the first time or after a previous miscarriage or a difficult birth, is anxious not only for herself but for her baby. She may have deep fears as to whether the baby will live, and whether it will be normal. These are exploited to keep her in line, and emotional blackmail is employed that has the effect of injecting further fear as well as a keen sense of guilt and helplessness. She must put her trust in the experts.

One highly effective mechanism of control is confusion and ignorance. The patient is by definition less informed than the doctor, but she may receive advice that further disables her. She is warned not to listen to other women's birth stories, and told to approach birth without any 'preconceived ideas'. A doctor who perceives a patient as anxious because she is asking many questions or presenting a detailed birth plan may stress his skill and length of training and urge her to trust him, may mock her for her ridiculous notions, refer her to a psychotherapist as in need of counselling, or label her a 'difficult patient'. A National Childbirth Trust teacher who glimpsed her case notes was amused to see the caution underlined in red ink 'NCT teacher. Handle with kid gloves.'

Along with this conscious and deliberate ploy to control women, there is the power and mystique of medicine in general, which has something of the solemnity and sonorous purpose of church ritual. It seems at least bad taste, and at worst possibly dangerous, to object to a procedure or to question the portentous ceremonial, rather like interrupting a communion service. The medical system has provided the modern world with a new priesthood, which with impressive ritual guards the gates of life and death.

Joking Behaviour

There is a lighter side to all this. When doctors feel threatened by women's changing expectations of birth they ridicule new practices and assert professional solidarity. The medical student gang show or annual hospital cabaret lampoons patients who present the doctor with birth plans, or who want to give birth in the dark or in a pool. Doctors are shown groping around in the dark with goggles, flippers, and other underwater gear. A *Sunday Times* report on the 1989 British Congress of Gynaecologists reviewed a sketch which left the medical audience 'fighting for breath'. It was *The Good Patient Guide*, a parody of my own *Good Birth Guide*,[27] in which 'doctors were offered marginal symbols as a

153

key to the patients they were handling . . . black square (patient has to be delivered in total darkness), stethoscope (doctor's wife), half a stethoscope (psychiatrist's wife), capital O (overweight), 007 (she wants to bond), thumbs up (member of BUPA), thumbs down (member of the National Childbirth Trust), oil well gushing up (sheik's wife) . . . little notebook (woman journalist), little notebook with black hat (woman journalist from the *Guardian* woman's page). Difficult patients explained why so many intelligent, middle-class obstetricians were forming self-help groups and reverting to "natural obstetrics", a method of doing without patients altogether (loud applause).'[28]

In an asymmetrical relationship, one between individuals of unequal power, the dominant individual is free to engage in licensed familiarity and joking behaviour. A doctor may treat a woman patient as if she were a child, talking slowly and using words like 'waterworks' and 'down there', for example, and, depending on the specific culture, addressing her as 'sweetheart', 'young lady', 'dear', or by her first name only, although she is expected to address the doctor in more formal terms.

In traditional societies joking is one way of diffusing hostility in a difficult relationship, and the victim is expected to accept it submissively. There is often an element of this in the behaviour of professional care-givers towards childbearing women. An obstetrician replies to a woman who asks if she can be free to move about in labour, 'You can swing from the chandeliers as far as I am concerned,' displaying a privileged offensiveness characteristic of joking relationships. A woman has a second Caesarean section, with epidural anaesthesia. The surgeon cuts out the old scar: 'They took this thing and threw it towards a bucket; it fell on the floor and someone asked "does anyone want it to go fishing?" '[29] Humour may also be used in a punitive way. A midwife says to a woman who is writhing in pain, 'It's a bit different from what you were doing nine months ago, isn't it?'

Sex is a taboo topic in childbirth. This does not mean that no one mentions it, but that it can be referred to only through joking. The Italian sociologist Franca Pizzini has analysed the joking language used during painful interventions in childbirth.[30] It may be employed with privileged offensiveness, used to fix a woman in the patient role, and to persuade her to submit to practices that she might otherwise experience as intolerable. Shared between

154

the professionals, it also helps to assert their solidarity *vis-à-vis* the patient.

The doctor who has just finished suturing a woman's perineum pats her on the leg and says, 'There you are. Better than new!' or 'Your husband will be pleased. He'll think you're a virgin again.' One who examines an episiotomy made by a subordinate which has extended, tearing into the patient's rectum, comments, 'What a dog's dinner!' A woman is rigid with pain as her cut vagina is swabbed, and the nurse smiles and asks, 'Do you act this way when your husband touches you too?' When the woman shakes her head to this the nurse replies, 'Naughty girl! When her husband touches her she's all relaxed, but when we touch her she gets tense!' A doctor is performing a painful obstetric manoeuvre and the woman screams. He asks, 'What will your husband think, that I am torturing you? Afterwards he will want to settle accounts with me.'[31]

Midwives and staff lower in the hospital hierarchy are less likely to engage in this kind of banter, and patients least of all. But women sometimes make jokes directed against themselves such as, 'I hope you didn't stitch me up entirely.' The function of remarks like these is to placate, rather as a dog grovels as a way of pleading not to be punished. In general, however, joking behaviour is the prerogative of those who wield power, and is a means of reinforcing authority over the powerless.

The Depersonalization of Birth

In pre-industrial societies the unfolding script of an individual's life cycle, with its transformations, becomings and peak experiences, provides the scenario for the ritual representation of changes in social status. Physiological and biological processes present images in which the individual's relationship to society is conceptualized. Central to these rituals is a complicated metaphor which uses the great experiences of being born and dying as archetypes which occur again and again in dramatized form, to symbolize acts of creation and renewal on the one hand and destruction and departure on the other. In the majority of these rituals both are involved, since each person must die before he or she can be reborn into a new social state. Rites of rebirth from the mother form major themes in many religions from East to West. Having a baby is not just a biologically nor even simply a socially significant process. It has many layers of meaning, and provides one of the most important and richest themes of all ritual.

In the West we have 'emptied the notions of death and birth of everything not corresponding to mere physiological processes and rendered them unsuitable to convey other meanings.'[32] In achieving the depersonalization of childbirth our society may have lost more than it has gained. We are left with the physical husk; the transcending significance has been drained away. It may be the price we pay for reaching a goal implicit in all highly developed technological cultures, scientific control over human life and the obliteration of all disturbing sensation.

10

The First Encounter

Babies, unlike tadpoles or tortoises, survive only because there are mothers (or others able to take their place) who can respond to them in a nurturing way. Much of this maternal response is learned, and is acquired from the culture. The apparent dichotomy between 'nature' and 'nurture', and the old argument as to which is most important, is highly artificial. All behaviour depends on both organic and environmental factors.

A human baby has to be born at the end of about nine months, or its head, containing a brain which has a volume of between 375 and 400 cubic centimetres – as compared with that of a chimpanzee or gorilla, which measures only about 200 cubic centimetres – would be too large to pass without difficulty through the mother's pelvic cavity.[1] This is one of the penalties we pay for our greater intelligence, which necessitates a larger brain, and for our upright stance, which has tilted the pelvis. As a result a baby is born in a much more immature state than are many other baby animals. It can take eight months or more for babies even to be able to crawl, and another six months or so before they can walk. It is not just a question, then, of the human baby being born immature, but of its development being very slow compared with that of other animals.

In this chapter I want to focus on the transition to motherhood, and to draw on evidence from the study of animal behaviour as well as from social anthropology. Learning about motherhood takes place in two phases. The first occurs during the female's infancy and youth, and develops out of her own experience of

157

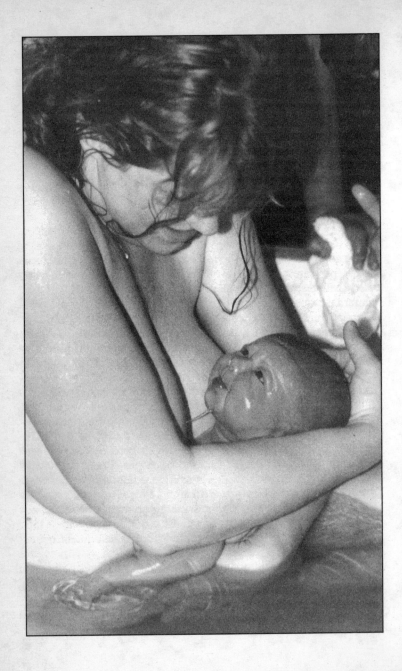

being mothered and her relationships with others; the second, intensive learning phase is triggered by pregnancy, birth, the presence of the newborn young, and the mother's interaction with them.

At the beginning of life the human baby's appearance and behaviour provide very effective signals for the mother which stimulate her caring reaction to the child. The rounded shape of a newborn baby's head, the short face and large forehead, plump cheeks, the smell of the skin, the fixed attention which comes from the eyes of a vigorous (and undrugged) baby, rooting for the nipple, the hunger cry, exploring hands and mouth and the uncoordinated movements of the limbs are all evocative signals for maternal attention. In the baby, too, there is a special kind of attachment between mother and neonate.[2] It bears some resemblance to, but is a good deal more complicated than, the imprinting described by the ethologist Lorenz, who watched geese and found that when the chicks were hatched they would follow the first large moving object, whether it was their mother, another animal, or even the investigator himself.[3] A similar imprinting phenomenon has been observed not only in other mammals (sheep, dogs, deer, zebra, cows and buffalo, for instance), but in insects and fish as well. If these attachment mechanisms are interrupted the young develop abnormally.[4] Even so, it is of course very different with a human baby – otherwise newborn babies would be emotionally attached to the midwives and doctors who delivered them, and mothers of adopted babies, or women parted from their babies because of illness, would never be able to fall in love with them.

It used to be thought that if a baby was born healthy and was physically well cared for there was no reason why it should not grow into a normal adult. The primary function of parents was to protect the newborn from harm, provide food, keep it warm and clean up its waste products. When the Emperor Frederick the Great unwisely decided to discover what kind of language babies would grow to speak if no one spoke to them as children, he did not realize that the orphanage children he used for his experiment would die, 'for they could not live without the petting and joyful faces and loving words of their foster mothers.'[5]

So little understood was a baby's need for loving, tender care that as late as the 1920s, and in spite of all the attention given to providing a hygienic environment for babies in foundling homes, many died, and in some institutions there was a death rate of almost 100 per cent.[6] Such attitudes changed slowly, and even in the 1950s Gesell, in his work on the development of children, implied that the unfolding of a child's abilities took place in an environmental vacuum.[7] Nothing could be further from the truth. For although for each species there are pre-existing, genetically determined patterns of development, they unfold only if environmental conditions are right.

One important element in the environment is stimulation. Special kinds of stimulation are necessary for optimal social and emotional development. Babies need the stimulus of things to see, moving objects and people to follow with their eyes, patterns to explore, voices and other sounds to hear, and hands to hold them. Ethology (the study of animal behaviour) has increased our understanding of human development. Although we cannot infer that because a particular stimulus is right for a rat, human infants need similar treatment, ethological research does raise questions about human mothering. When chimpanzees are reared in the dark they are slow at learning later, and are unable to discriminate between friends and strangers. If puppies are reared in small cages, unable to see either human beings or other dogs, and are let out when they are eight to ten months old, and then treated normally, they are overactive and nervous, of low intelligence, are easily dominated by other dogs, and suffer mental and social retardation for years after.[8] Deprivation in infancy for any species seems to have definite long-term negative consequences.

Baby rats develop and actually grow faster when they are handled frequently. This seems to be because they utilize their food better and have a higher output of growth hormone when they are handled.[9] The work of Harlow with baby rhesus monkeys is well known.[10] When reared without a mother, these monkeys much prefer a surrogate mechanical mother which is soft and which rocks to one which is hard or stationary, even if the latter supplies milk. Soft body contact and rocking generate feelings of security, resulting in 'well-balanced' adult monkeys.

From the earliest moments of life the human baby's development is similarly affected by and unfolds from his relationship with his mother. The stimuli which the baby receives from his mother, and those which she gets from her baby, play a significant part in the baby's development, and the episodic nature of a newborn baby's sucking, in intermittent bursts, provides plenty of opportunity for 'conversations', and the beginning of human socialization.

In many hospitals in the USA and elsewhere silver nitrate drops are inserted into the newborn baby's eyes to prevent gonorrheal blindness. The liquid stings, so the baby closes her eyes, and this intense interaction between mother and newborn cannot take place. (Erythromycin is just as effective and does not irritate the baby's eyes.)

Newborn babies are most alert when they are well propped up or upright. When you put babies less than two weeks old down on their backs they tend to get drowsy.[11] The way a baby is handled from birth affects her alertness and therefore the amount of learning that takes place. In most cultures a baby is carried around close to her mother in a semi-upright position against her body. Babies can smell their mothers, too, and can soon distinguish their own mother from anyone else. Aiden MacFarlane did an experiment with pads soaked in breast milk, and found that a five-day-old baby preferred a pad soaked with her mother's milk to a clean one, and usually by six days turned her head more towards one soaked with her own mother's milk than with milk from another woman.[12]

But more than biology is involved, even from the very earliest moments of life. The relationship between a mother and her baby reflects the family and society. The baby's behaviour is part of an interactive system.[13] This is so with animals, too. When a mother monkey has never herself been adequately mothered as a baby, and especially when as a motherless baby she has not been able to play with other monkeys, she does not respond correctly to her baby's cues, and either neglects it or becomes hostile. Her ability to mother well depends on her having been mothered herself, and having learned the give and take of living with her peers. Normal relations in adulthood, including mothering, grow out of social contacts experienced in infancy.

Immediately following birth the mother begins to learn, if she is given the opportunity of uninterrupted contact with the baby, the signs by which she is soon able to recognize her baby as distinct from any other. For this to happen the baby must be with her, to be watched, heard and touched. During this period the animal mother maintains physical contact with her young. When a mother cat has given birth she immediately starts to lick her young all over, and then nudges them in the direction of her nipples so that they can suckle. A goat first licks the amniotic fluid from her newborn, hears its bleating, and then responds to this by further nuzzling, tasting, smelling and exploring of the kid's body. Stimulation of the face and anus seems to be particularly important in mammals, and what looks like cleaning of the newborn is an important factor in the bonding of mother and baby. If an animal mother is anaesthetized at delivery, or immediately following it, before she has started to lick her young, or if they are removed at this time, she never recognizes them as her own. If a kid is taken away from a mother goat, for instance, for two hours after birth, she does not accept the kid as her own when it is brought back.

A human mother, too, responds to her baby's cry, and this response is not only 'mental' ('I ought to attend to the baby') but also physical. Her baby's cry, heard on tape on the third post-partum day, immediately increases the temperature of her breasts as shown on thermograms of the chest wall, and this is followed by a sudden heavy dripping of milk. So communication between mother and baby during the time when lactation is getting established is very important, and feed times should relate to the baby's crying rather than to the clock.

But this kind of interaction does not occur in a vacuum. The mother is partially prepared for it by endocrinological changes which occur in her body at the end of pregnancy, and also by her emotional readiness for labour and the baby. Even being in labour may help this readiness. Perhaps this is one reason why women who have had Caesarean sections with general anaesthesia, and without experiencing labour, sometimes face more difficulty in breastfeeding. It is not just that they are uncomfortable when they hold the baby in their arms because of the pain of the abdominal incision, or that they are still recovering from the effects of anaesthesia, but often the baby is presented to them like a package, a gift provided by the hospital, and it seems as if the child cannot have been born from their own bodies: the continuity is broken. The phrases they often use in describing their experience are: 'It was a shock . . .' and 'I couldn't believe he was mine.' The result is that they may not yet be emotionally ready for interaction with the baby. It is important that they have time alone to discover and get to know their babies and to begin to feel themselves mothers. The same thing can happen when labour is induced before term, or

162

at any rate before the expectant mother has reached the stage, common in the last two weeks of pregnancy, of feeling that she has had enough of waiting, wants to get on with the birth, and longs to push her baby out into the world and have it in her arms.

When labour starts spontaneously the woman is not only physiologically ready, with a soft and partially dilated cervix, but is also emotionally 'ripe' to become a mother and to respond to her baby in an appropriate manner. If she cannot start labour spontaneously, or when she has an elective Caesarean section (one planned ahead of time), the environment in which she gives birth and meets her baby can often make up for a physiological and emotional lack of readiness. Sometimes she does not have the baby in her arms until the third or fourth day, but then experiences the extraordinary sensation of the 'let down' reflex, which precedes the rush of milk to the nipples, a spontaneous and uncontrollable response to the stimulus of her baby crying or actually sucking.

A woman who had a long series of obstetric interventions starting in early pregnancy, each of which necessitated the next, and then an emergency Caesarean section, found herself unable to relate to her baby. She felt 'an incongruous emotional numbness. I had no real awareness of motherhood . . . I sat holding the baby awkwardly, trying to feel something.' But there was one midwife who gave her emotional support and helped her start breastfeeding. She led both the parents 'into a room with a low chair, made me comfortable with pillows', removed their masks 'and showed me how to hold the baby and – the miracle occurred. He was my baby – he sucked! . . . and then, tact upon tact, she left us! John touched his son for the first time . . . He was ours.'

Human mothers share in a pattern of interaction with their new-born young typical of many other species. It is an intensely powerful bond which impels the mother to action to protect and cherish and feed her baby. Often it is a further development of mating behaviour and of relations between the mother and father, and is part of the bond between them, too.

Mother mice and rats are very sensitive to any disturbance in their environment. If the nest is disarranged the mother mouse rushes to rebuild it, or if the pups are removed, seeks to retrieve them.[14] But the mothers only do this because they are already in a 'maternal state', which is partly the result of endocrine changes,

163

but also of stimulation from the pups (pregnant female rats do not attempt to retrieve another rat's wandering pups). In the three or four days after birth the mother initiates all interaction with her pups – she has to, because the pups do not yet have their eyes open and have little hearing, so that they depend on physical contact for stimulation. If the pups are removed during this period, the maternal state quickly fades. During this time stimulation from the pups is an important factor in keeping the mother in a maternal state. At the end of the second week the pups begin to walk and start to leave the nest, and at this stage they initiate suckling and interact with each other. If the pups are removed during this time the mother's maternal state does not wane so quickly; it is less dependent on stimulation from the pups. Finally there is a stage starting at four weeks when the pups become independent, and the mother is less likely to retrieve and suckle them. The maternal state gets weaker, even if the mother's own pups are replaced by other, younger pups.

When I analysed eighty-six labour reports I had received from mothers who had attended my own childbirth classes and who had described in detail their first encounter with their babies, I found that many used words descriptive of touch. They commented on the delightful feeling of the infant kicking against their inner thighs as it was being born, or lying across their legs or bodies immediately following delivery. Many talked about the baby's appearance, and a few felt rather negative about it at first, but the predominant theme in the majority of accounts was the excitement resulting from touch, including the pleasure of holding the baby in their arms. Even if they had thought before that the baby looked odd or ugly, there then occurred a sudden flood of feeling, with laughter, tears or kisses, in which their partners, who were present at the birth, were also involved. After complicated and difficult births this meeting-through-touch of mother and baby initiated a rush of feeling in a woman who until then had felt numb, and often exhausted. A woman who had a Caesarean section under general anaesthesia woke up to find the baby waiting to be put in her arms, and, holding him, 'washed him in tears of joy'. Another said, 'I didn't feel any emotion when I first saw Catherine lifted out and heard her cry, but as soon as they gave her to me to hold a few seconds later I thought she was fantastic.' The mothers themselves often wanted most of all to touch their babies: 'I did so want to cuddle and touch her before she was wrapped.'

When a newborn baby is handed to the mother and she is allowed to get to know him in her own way, there is a definite sequence of events, a kind of emotional 'unfolding', sometimes slow and gentle, sometimes in a passionate rush.[15] The mother may start by touching the baby hesitantly with her fingertips, and then, four to eight minutes later, she starts stroking the baby, with her whole palm caressing the infant's body (or at least she does this if the baby's body is left uncovered). She tends to run a fingertip over the baby's hair and feels its silkiness. She traces the contours of the baby's face and profile with a finger. She may at first hold the baby rather stiffly, as if he were a bouquet of flowers, but soon her whole hand is in maximal contact with the baby's trunk, and later her entire arm is involved in holding him.

Much of the psychological material written about a mother's first meeting with her baby treats it as if the woman were an electronic machine programmed to respond correctly. When that response is inappropriate the researchers look for a fault in the hardware, the mother. But she is not acting in an environmental vacuum, and the management of labour (including the drugs she was given) together with the setting within which she meets her baby – whether she feels at ease and is surrounded by friends, for example – must affect the way in which she begins to get to know her child. The way birth is conducted and the people present have a powerful influence on how a mother greets her baby.

Among all primates, if the birth environment is stressful a mother may never learn how to nurture. It was discovered at the Yerkes Primate Research Center in the USA that only one-third of gorilla first-time mothers cared for their young. The others ignored them or beat them up. At first the researchers thought that this must be because the gorilla mothers had been captured as infants, but it turned out that it was because they were socially isolated at the time of birth. When a gorilla mother has a cage-mate, either male or female, she does not harm her baby, and when another gorilla is put in the cage of a mother who has been abusing her infant, the aggression stops. If other adult gorillas are around when a baby is born they all help care for the baby. It is misleading to talk about the interaction between a mother and her newborn baby without taking the environment into account.

Human mothers, too, need support from other caring adults. In focusing exclusively on bonding between mother and newborn it is easy to ignore all that has preceded these initial moments of contact. Aiden MacFarlane has recorded these first encounters on videotape, and there is wide variation in the degree to which mothers relate to their babies and feel free to touch and explore them. When certain midwives assisted at the birth there was more expression of emotion and more flesh-to-flesh contact between mother and baby, not because the midwife told the mother that she should touch her baby, but because she provided an environment in which the woman was able to express spontaneously whatever she felt, and to do whatever she wanted to do.[16]

Harlow's work with monkeys has demonstrated that the fact that the baby clings to the front of the mother's body, and is face-to-face with her, plays an important part in the attachment which grows between them.[17] In this position there can be eye contact, another significant element in the development of attachment between human mothers and babies and a major 'social releaser'.[18] Human mothers who do not play with their babies very much suddenly begin to do so when, usually during the fourth week of life, their babies' eyes focus more easily and they start looking straight at them.[19] Many mothers have no idea why they find them more interesting at this stage, but some say that their babies seemed strangers to them until they began to feel that they were recognized.

A baby's initial response is often described as 'undiscriminating', but such a description takes no account of the searching gaze of a healthy newborn infant (who has had a gentle birth) when placed in its mother's arms immediately after delivery. Although the baby cannot yet 'know' the mother, he is clearly intent on finding her out.

In Touch

The general pattern of care in pre-industrial societies is for a baby to be with and close to the mother and to remain with her, day and night, for some months after birth. In forty-five out of sixty-four cultures studied in cross-cultural perspective, children sleep with their mothers all through the time they are breastfeeding, and that may be for three or four years.[20] The baby is often fixed to the mother's body in one way or another, bound by shawls, slung in a net or special carrier or wound into a strip of cloth, apart from the time when he is lying beside her, and frequently they are in flesh-to-flesh contact. Life outside the uterus is treated as a continuation of life inside it. The Ndembu of Zambia call the cloth which attaches the baby to his mother's back 'the placenta'; because the baby is exposed to the malevolence of other jealous women, he is shielded from danger under the mother's clothing. In Mexico the baby is completely covered (face too, lest his spirit escapes from his mouth).

When interviewing mothers in traditional societies I have often found it difficult to explain why this is not done everywhere in the world, for they say that of course babies must be with their mothers, for how else can they survive, and who else can the baby possibly belong to? I have met with reactions of disbelief from mothers deeply shocked to hear that in our own society babies are often separated from their mothers and put in communal nurseries where they are looked after by women who are not even related to them. When a mother is confronted with rows of babies lined up in identical plastic containers, sees lines of newborns packed like sugared almonds in a box behind the glass wall of a nursery, and listens to the wails of half a dozen other women's babies who are left to cry it out since it is not yet feeding time, she is prevented from being able to form an intense relationship with one unique individual.[21] If she cannot have her baby with her, for as long as and whenever she wishes, and cannot care for her herself, it is more difficult for her to relate actively to the baby, and thus to experience the important psychological change that enables her to pass over the emotional bridge into motherhood.

The modern hospital environment represents a departure from a universally accepted norm. Everywhere else there are the loving hands of women in the family to greet the newborn, and a grandmother, aunt or older sisters and brothers to cherish and help tend it. In many cultures acts performed by the mother and those assisting her involve close observation of and contact with the baby, including a great deal of touching. In some the baby is immediately massaged – in India, for example, the head or limbs are 'shaped' by patting, kneading or pressing, lest the child grow up 'crooked'. In other societies the baby is anointed with oil, bathed, or rubbed with ashes as in the Philippines, or has patterns painted on her face and body.

Prelacteal Feeding

In some traditional cultures babies are not put to the breast immediately after birth, but they are either fed alternative foods or breastfed by other women for the first two or three days. The mother's colostrum is milked and thrown away, and may be considered poisonous. Commonly, the midwife or other helper has the baby suckle gauze dipped in a syrup, or spoons herb tea into the baby. Western advocates of breastfeeding may be non-plussed by and highly critical of this practice. It is often assumed that it must result in breastfeeding problems, since in the West women who, because of hospital practices, have to delay putting the baby to the breast, are likely to find breastfeeding much more difficult than do those women whose babies are allowed to suckle straight away.

Next to nothing is known about the advantages and disadvantages of this widespread practice of prelacteal feeding. It obviously does not reduce women's ability to breastfeed in traditional cultures. It looks as if the firm expectation that she will breastfeed successfully is much more important for a mother than any specific breastfeeding practices, and that women can breastfeed under apparently impossible conditions if they are convinced that they will be able to do so.

Seclusion

The mother and baby are usually segregated from the rest of society because they are in a marginal state of existence, and so are 'unclean' and believed to be dangerous and contaminating. The period of seclusion is terminated by a rite of purification which often takes the form of a bath.

Until the eighteenth century the Christian Church treated women as polluted by childbearing. If a woman died in pregnancy or childbirth she might be denied burial in sacred ground, and was interred in that part of the graveyard which was kept for murderers and suicides. A new mother was re-incorporated into the fellowship of believers only through the ceremony of 'churching', in which her uncleanliness was removed from her. She was not allowed to enter a church until thirty-three days after

168

the birth of a boy and sixty-six days after the birth of a girl. Babies were baptized without the mother being there, since she had not yet been purified. She was not supposed to fetch water from the well in case she accidentally poisoned it, and in some rural areas a woman who appeared in public before the purification ceremony was warded off with a broom.

There was a good deal of theological argument about whether this was the right way to treat women. Pope Gregory told St Augustine 'This is to be understood as an allegory, for were a woman to enter church and return thanks in the very hour of her delivery, she would do no wrong.'[22] But the effect of the 'allegory' was that the new mother was free from her usual services as a wife, and instead stayed in bed attended by her 'god sibs', or neighbour women (see Chapter 7). They prepared special delicacies and nourishing food for her. Alcoholic drinks were an essential element of the lying-in both in Europe and later in the American colonies. When eighteenth-century doctors in New England were insisting on thin water gruel, women were still demanding their sugar, tea and rum.[23]

Even then, at a time when the lying-in had been reduced to one week in the American colonies, women's body products in childbirth were still treated as tainted. In her biography of a Maine midwife, the historian Laurel Thatcher Ulrich describes how midwives 'touched the untouchable, handled excrement and vomit as well as milk, swaddled the dead as well as the newborn . . . and presided over neighbourhood gatherings of women.' 'The female world of love and ritual' around childbirth grew from an ugly root, the belief that birth was polluting.[24]

In many traditional societies today the new mother's impurity means that she and her baby are left alone together, or with only one or two women companions. Food may be passed under the door or through an opening in the wall. She is often fed special delicacies, as well as foods to make her strong and to increase her supply of milk, while other foods are scrupulously avoided because they are thought to expose her or her baby to risk. In southern India the Adivi mother stays with her baby in a hut made of leaves and mats for ninety days. If anyone touches her they themselves become outcast and are expelled from the village for three months. But she is not completely isolated; her husband makes a hut fifty yards away and stays to watch over her. This ritual seclusion of mother and baby is today giving way to modern practices learned from the maternity hospital. One result is that both mother and baby are exposed to infection as they never were before.

The Acholi woman in Uganda keeps to her house for three days if she has delivered a boy, and four if it is a girl, and is looked after by either her mother or her husband's mother. Nobody is allowed to enter, for it is thought that should anyone else cross the threshold the baby may get ill or be blind, or the mother become infertile. The Dusun of North Borneo segregate mother and baby for eight to ten days and nobody except the mother may touch the infant.[25] In North America, a Hopi mother and baby remained for eighteen days in a darkened room. Every day a mark was made on the wall and an ear of corn placed beneath it. On the nineteenth day the mother ground the corn for the ceremony of purification and celebration on the following day.[26] For most North-west Coast Native Americans there was a twelve-day seclusion which the husband shared, together with the helping women. In Europe, gypsy culture treats a new mother as polluted for some weeks, and she has her own special tent and crockery. At the end of the period of seclusion both tent and bedding are ritually burned. She is still not allowed to prepare food for men until some weeks after that.[27]

Traditionally in Japan the mother's food was cooked by women family members exclusively for her in a separate pot over a separate fire. In the Edo era in the seventeenth century the woman was secluded for thirty-five days, and the father, too, was considered polluted. When a boy was thirty-one days old and a girl thirty-two days old, the grandmother presented the baby at the shrine. At the end of the period of pollution the mother passed through a rite of purification. If she lived near the shore she immersed herself in the sea. Otherwise this ceremony took place in a bath, or she and the baby were sprinkled with salt. Even today a Japanese mother must not visit the shrine for thirty-five days, and babies are rarely taken out of the home until they are about a month old.[28]

Seclusion means different things in different cultures. Often it means that the mother rests in bed and that other women visit her from all over the community, bringing gifts and admiring the baby. In these cultures there is seclusion from men but it is a great social occasion for women. Bedouin Arab women are

170

supposed to stay in the home for forty days, are not allowed to cook or do housework, and are meant to rest and eat well and be visited by other women. No woman who is menstruating may visit, however, in case she 'closes the womb'. In urban areas early in the morning women can be seen leaving their homes swathed in black cloaks to visit women who have had babies; they spend the rest of the morning drinking tea and coffee and discussing their childbirth experiences, and then they all eat lunch together. They take for the mother a gift of money which they tuck into the newborn's swaddling clothes. When this visitor has her next baby she will be visited in turn, and will be repaid what amounts to a loan. Most of these women are illiterate, yet are capable of very complicated sums, remembering exactly who gave what and the interest that is involved. When women visit like this they represent their men, so it is an important way of linking families together. 'Women trace out the choreography of the connection between families through their visiting patterns.'[29]

The Fire Rest

Fire is often used to keep out evil spirits and to protect the mother and her new baby in their marginal state, and, together with steam and herbal baths, as part of a healing process after childbirth. In Malaysia a woman's body is considered to be in a chilled state following birth, so the *bidan kampung* (the traditional midwife) first bathes the mother in warm water to which 'hot' scented leaves have been added. Meanwhile the men of the family erect a slatted frame called the 'roasting bed', the women heat a smooth flat stone and wrap it in cloth for the mother to rest over her uterus, and they light a wood fire in a pot that will go either beneath or beside the slatted frame on which the mother lies. In the hot season the fire rest is a ritual observance that takes only a short time, but in the monsoon season, when it is cold, the mother finds great comfort in lying over the fire.[30]

In Guatemala the native women of Santa Lucia take either a herbal bath or sweat bath. The sweat bath is built of adobe and constructed adjacent to the house. The woman sits on a wooden board while other women throw water onto heated stones and fan steam towards her with branches. The midwife also massages her while she is in the sweat bath. Latino women in the same area sit over a pail of hot water containing herbs, cover themselves with a cloth, and steam the perineum in much the same way as do Jamaican women (see Chapters 7 and 8).[31]

Although the use of heat comes under much criticism from professional care-givers in the modern health system, it persists in rural areas in many different parts of the world, and women seem to appreciate the comfort it brings and to believe that it makes them safe from the forces of evil.

Nurturing the Mother

During this period of seclusion the midwife usually visits to massage the mother and her baby, or female members of the family may do this. In some cultures this is a regular feature of the puerperium. In others, such as the Mayan culture of Yucatan, massage and binding is a rite that terminates the period of lying-in. Puerperal massage involves lifting the uterus and ascertaining that any internal organs which may have been displaced by the birth are in their correct position.[32] The firm stroking movements help the involution of the uterus (that is, its return to almost its pre-pregnancy size), and can thus reduce bleeding. They stimulate the circulation, assist restoration of muscle tone, and are comforting to the mother and help her feel good about herself. In Thailand, for example, the midwife 'restores the belly', lifts the womb back into its 'cradle' and 'soothes the womb'.[33] In Guatemala, too, the midwife's massage is designed to return the uterus to the right place, to encourage it to contract so that involution is rapid and bleeding is reduced, and to relieve post-partum pain. The midwife may also massage the woman's legs downwards from the thighs and upwards from the calves to encourage circulation. To 'close' the pelvic bones an abdominal binder is tied around the lower abdomen. Medical personnel oppose these practices and consider them harmful.[34]

The traditional Malaysian midwife, the *bidan kampung*, massages the mother's abdomen with a paste which may be made of simply salt and turmeric or be a mixture of ginger, garlic, tamarind and lime – 'hot' substances, which are thought to encourage rapid involution. She then binds the mother with a long sash. Even women who have delivered in hospital look forward to this massage and confident care given by the *bidan kampung*.[35] The use of abdominal binders is very common in traditional cultures, and until the 1970s was advocated by many midwives in Europe as well.

A Malaysian mother and newborn baby are both vulnerable to attack by the earth spirits, who are attracted by the sweet smell of blood, and by the spirit of the afterbirth, who may be jealous of the baby. This spirit is the baby's older sibling, and when a baby smiles and coos for no apparent reason it is because the spirit of the afterbirth is playing with him.

There are well-established, culturally-anticipated ways of dealing with post-natal mental illness, which is attributed to spirit-possession. If a Malaysian woman is emotionally distressed in the post-partum period it is thought that she has been attacked by evil spirits. They cause postnatal depression by entering the open gateway of the body. Treatment is by means of incantations, magic water and limes, but if the depression is severe a seance is held to raise the spirits. This may last between one and three nights and requires the services of a shaman, his assistant, a drummer and a cymbal player. 'The shaman, in trance, first takes on the personae of the inner forces or guardians of the body, his own and those of the patient. He strengthens and restores her *semangat* [vital forces].' The spirits are encouraged to speak through the mouth of the shaman and are persuaded to leave. The woman is encouraged to go into a trance, too, and in this state she may laugh, cry, sing, dance, and express all the emotions that are welling up inside her. 'She emerges from the trance refreshed, greeted by the approval of her friends and relatives who have been watching the ceremony. Their overt show of concern and the opportunity to express her feelings in an appropriate and unthreatening setting, usually serves to cure the post-partum patient.'[36]

Traditional cultures have often evolved complex and highly sophisticated ways of caring for women, both physically and psychologically, through the transition to motherhood. In diverse cultures seclusion of mother and baby together, and their special nurturing by women who are in a close relationship with them, affirms the woman's new identity as a mother and provides a sanctuary after giving birth. It also facilitates the 'tuning in' of mother and baby to each other and their emotional bonding, and may be an important factor in survival of the newborn in conditions of extreme poverty and deprivation.

It may be useful at this stage to look in more detail at what

173

happens between a mother and baby in the time immediately after birth in one particular peasant society, and to see how this has the effect of helping the woman get to know her baby and feel herself a mother.

A Traditional Lying-in

The Jamaican baby who is born at home is delivered either by the local trained midwife or by the *nana*. Even if the delivery is conducted by the trained midwife a *nana* may be called in to give guidance during pregnancy, and again afterwards to care for the mother and baby, as well as the mother's other children. We have already seen that there is continuity in care, which lasts throughout the pregnancy and for the first post-partum week or two. Since the *nana* is almost invariably a neighbour, the contact is in fact a good deal more prolonged even than this, and the *nana*, as the district nurse used to in rural areas of England up until about thirty years ago, lives surrounded by 'her' babies, who have grown up and had babies of their own whom she has delivered in their turn. So there is a secure and familiar environment for birth both in terms of the actual setting and the people involved.

After birth the *nana* puts the baby in bed beside its mother. Ideally, birth is followed by nine days of ritual seclusion for both mother and baby in which they are cared for by the mother's mother – the 'Grandy' – or by the *nana*. They remain together within the darkness of the dwelling, windows or jalousies tight shut, the child because it needs peace, darkness and rest, and so that the duppies or ancestor spirits may not know of its presence, and the mother so that she is protected against the dangers of 'baby chill' (puerperal fever), and in order to allow her back 'to mend' or 'knit up'.

Devout mothers often also use incense or 'holy water' (a symbol of the holy spirit in the local revivalist church). They concentrate on making the setting ritually right for the baby. Loleta, for example, had a baby a few hours old when I visited her. The room was heavy with perfume and she explained, 'I burn some sweet-smelling incense. With the sweet smell it keep good spirits.' The duppies represent the old pagan religion which has been swept away and replaced by Christianity, but like the agents of any other underground religion, their subterranean power remains and they are never quite vanquished by the Christian angels. Another newly delivered woman asked me for advice on keeping duppies away and attracting the good angels. I told her that a wise mother kept the house clean, and in that way she could make the angels welcome. Her eyes lit up, and she exclaimed, 'Yes! Keep the angels manifesting by cleanliness!'

Maternal behaviour in these nine days is ringed round with dietary and other taboos. Above all the mother must avoid catching a cold, and since her head is particularly vulnerable, her hair is covered by a turban made out of a kerchief. She must keep her hair from getting damp at all costs, and must not allow rain to get on to it – which keeps her indoors for an especially lengthy time if it is the rainy season – nor wash it for as long as three months. She must be careful to avoid backache from overexertion and must not 'hackle' – become exhausted from work or get emotionally overwrought. The result is that mother and baby are secluded together in a darkened, familiar environment removed from everyday worries. Often what actually occurs is far from this ideal, and women have to cope without anyone to care for them, and may immediately return to looking after a large family. But this is how Jamaican peasant women believe that it should be.

The baby only gradually emerges from ritual seclusion, and if the duppies make it ill, it is withdrawn into the dwelling hut again. It is normally kept in the shelter of the home for anything from six to twelve weeks, although towards the end of this period it may be brought out into the swept mud-patch in front of the hut whilst the sun is up. If a mother leaves her baby, even for only a short time, the separation is ritually safeguarded by placing a Bible open to the twenty-third Psalm by its head, and often, too, a tape measure is left nearby to 'catch the duppy' (perhaps to 'take its measure'), sometimes with a pair of open scissors (which may be to 'cut off its retreat').

The shared seclusion of mother and baby means that the very important first days and weeks of life are passed within the dark and shadowy world of the household dwelling. The two are islanded in an exclusive and intimate relationship. One of the most important rules is that the baby should never be left to cry. No Jamaican woman would think it right to make a baby wait for a feed. One of the main reasons given for this is that if the baby cries the duppies will hear and will come and fetch her; the baby will sicken and may die. So babies are immediately 'hushed' with the breast. At night the mother lies with the baby beside her in the bed, and this continues to be the case for as long as she is lactating, and often after she has officially weaned the child. Thus night feeds continue long after breastfeeds in the day have been dropped. This is a general pattern in traditional societies. In Papua New Guinea, a study of babies who were sleeping on the floor beside their mothers revealed that right through the night the longest interval between bursts of sucking was only twenty minutes in duration.[37]

For three months the baby must be protected not only from the other world but also from those women who are themselves in a marginal state. Therefore no menstruating woman may hold it or it will get constipated, nor may any pregnant woman handle another woman's child. Consequently the number of other people able to care for the child is severely restricted, and the result is that the mother-baby relationship is reinforced. Thus the initial learning time in which mother and baby become attached to each other is safeguarded and given special ritual significance by the culture.

Mother and Baby and the New Technology

There is an enormous difference between the first few hours of life in a peasant culture such as that of the West Indies and the beginning of life in any modern maternity hospital. The woman having the baby moves out of her home, the equivalent of the mother animal's nest, and gives birth among strangers. It is one reason why there is often a crisis at home-coming, when for the first time the woman has to accept responsibility for her baby, respond to its cues appropriately, and take on her new role of 'mother'. Moreover, in a modern hospital the woman's body may in a sense no longer 'belong' to her, but function only because of things done to it and not spontaneously of its own accord.

A baby born in a modern hospital may suffer emotional deprivation from the moment of birth. Far from being a learning time for the mother, the experience of the immediate post-partum days frequently involves segregation not only from society, but from her own baby. It is as if the baby is the hospital's property, not the mother's.

In the USA, for example, babies are still often automatically

176

removed to a nursery immediately following delivery and kept there for six to twelve hours, and following this are not allowed to be with their mothers except at scheduled feed times. Some hospitals do not permit the mother even to hold her baby after delivery, or if they do allow it, may insist that she holds it the other side of a sheet, so that no bacteria on her hands or body can be conveyed to the baby, and hence to the communal nursery.

Even in those hospitals that allow rooming-in after normal births, babies are usually taken to the nursery after Caesarean delivery, and one in eight mothers in the UK and one in four in the USA now have a Caesarean section. Private patients have more Casesarean sections than those in any national health scheme. In Brazil, for example, 75 per cent of the private patients are delivered by Caesarean section, compared with 25 per cent of the clinic patients. So the most privileged mothers are the least privileged when it comes to contact with their babies.

It may take a long time for a woman to love her child when the beginning of their relationship has been interfered with by outsiders. When the baby needs special care and is taken to a nursery to be looked after, the estrangement may be complete, so that it may be difficult for her to feel that this really is her child, and sometimes she even rejects the baby when at last she is supposed to care for her. Marshall Klaus and John Kennell, paediatricians who originally worked with mothers who were not allowed to handle their premature babies for a full three weeks, remarked that when at last they were permitted to touch them they 'looked as if they were picking fleas off their babies'.[38]

The Effects of Active Management of Labour

Medical intervention in labour, especially stimulation of the uterus with oxytocin, is associated with a high degree of separation of mother and newborn baby following birth. In some hospitals babies are induced as a matter of policy ten days after the expected date of delivery, or even before term, on the principle 'better out than in after thirty-eight weeks', or when the mother's blood-pressure is slightly raised, or for social and administrative reasons. Babies are more likely to have low Apgar scores after delivery and to be admitted to special-care baby units if oxytocin has been used to induce labour.[39] Even if all is well at delivery, induced babies have a greater tendency to develop

177

jaundice,[40] and this usually means that they are separated from their mothers for phototherapy when a few days old.

Only about 10 per cent of women really benefit from having labour induced. Where more women than this are induced (and in some British hospitals the rate is 70 per cent) we can take it that this is being done for very minor reasons, and that the babies of these mothers would not normally need to go to the special-care baby unit. If more than 10 per cent or so have to be parted from their mothers we can infer that something in the process of induction has harmed these babies.

I explored the experiences of 249 women who had received oxytocin either for induction or to augment labour, and compared these with the experiences of 206 women from the same childbirth classes who had had no uterine stimulation. When labour was induced or speeded up the mother and baby were more likely to be separated afterwards for at least a few hours, and the baby became what has been described as a 'one-day-old deprived child', isolated in an intensive care unit.[41] Twenty-four per cent of the women were separated from their babies in this way, compared with only 6 per cent of those women who did not receive the drug. These intensive care units were often on a different floor of the hospital from the postnatal wards, and sometimes in a different hospital. Forty-six of the women whose babies were in intensive care units described their first sight of the baby but did not mention holding it immediately after delivery, and the phrase which they used again and again was that the baby was 'whisked away' from them.[42]

It has been known since at least the early seventies that a baby who has received from his mother's bloodstream a high dose of pain-relieving drugs during labour may be virtually stoned for hours after birth.[43] Ninety-two per cent of the women I studied who received oxytocin had also received drugs for pain relief, compared with 59 per cent of those who did not have oxytocin. Many of those who were induced had Pethidine, and said that they became 'woozy' or were 'knocked out' or 'unconscious'. We have already seen the effect that this drug can have on the experience of labour, but it can also affect the way in which a mother reacts to her baby, for if the drug-induced somnolent state persists throughout the second stage of delivery she may be a passive partner in the meeting with her baby. The mother may have held her baby, but only knows she did because her partner has told her about it later. Her next meeting with the child, then, becomes in effect their first encounter. Thus, in 42 per cent of the births studied the normal mechanisms by which attachment is initiated between mother and baby were delayed.

These women often described vividly their reactions to their first sight of the baby. One woman said: 'I was absolutely shattered and exhausted. I wasn't at all interested in seeing the baby. All I wanted to do was to go to sleep.' Another remarked: 'If I had not woken as the baby was being born I would never have believed him mine.' This feeling persisted with one woman and merged with her later depression: 'I find myself going to pieces. Withdrawn into myself.' In a letter written when the baby was several months old she described how she found herself hitting him 'without reason', and said that she felt very frightened. Some of these mothers asked not to hold the baby after delivery because they felt 'too tired', 'exhausted', or 'drugged', because they were vomiting, or were afraid they might drop it.

There are many accounts in which the mother reported on her feelings after the birth and said things such as: 'They took her away. I did not really mind. I was completely exhausted'; 'I was utterly exhausted. I heard a baby cry. Unfortunately, I was still drowsy, so the memory is hazy.' Sometimes it was the father who woke the woman up or somehow got a response from her to acknowledge the baby's birth, as did the man who shook and slapped his wife, who was 'hopelessly muddled with Pethidine', so that she should be 'conscious enough to be aware of the birth itself'. Other women reported coming out of 'a haze' to see their baby hanging upside down in front of them, and described how they were 'stunned' by this sight, or sometimes 'coolly disinterested'.

The husband of a woman whose baby was cot-nursed for thirty-six hours reminded staff that the mother had not seen him at all, and the mother said: 'The baby appeared to react violently against me when he met me eventually [she was the only one of the 249 who'd never held a baby before] and against breastfeeding attempts. The staff were annoyed by my messing up hospital routine by taking so long to try and feed him . . . Only gradually could I "unfreeze" towards him inside.' She went on to tell how she had remained 'detached' from the baby for 'over a year'.

One woman said of this experience: 'I've had it taken from

me like a prize wisdom tooth by the dentist,' and another: 'I felt intensely estranged when the baby was brought to me eventually.' These women sometimes described how they tried to put the baby to the breast, but it was 'grabbed', or 'snatched away', someone told them they must not do it as it would 'make the baby sick', or took the baby away because it had to be weighed, bathed, Apgar-rated, clothed, put under a heater or given to the paediatrician. Other mothers said that they were not allowed to hold their babies immediately because 'they were too busy with the placenta'. These mothers surrendered their babies reluctantly, and some experienced helpless anger.

The most positive expressions of emotion about the baby occurred when the mother saw the head as it was being born, or even before it had fully emerged: 'I sat up and leaned forward to watch the head being born. Fantastic!' and when she felt the baby moving against her thigh or lying on her abdomen immediately following delivery. Here again, it seems to be a matter of physical contact reinforcing sight and sound.

Some of the mothers who had epidural anaesthesia, so that they had little or no sensation in the lower half of their bodies, said that it was like watching a scene on film or a TV documentary. 'I felt terribly detached watching in the mirror, and a little guilty because I felt that everyone expected me to be overwhelmed with joy,' said one woman who suffered from depression for several months after giving birth. Another, completely without sensation from an epidural which had been topped up, delivered in a labour ward bed and did not realize that she had had the baby, except that the sister called out for someone to come and help, at which point she heard a baby screaming and then saw one picked up from between her legs. She could not believe that it was her child, and asked whether it was really hers. In other reports where epidurals had worn off for the expulsive stage, these mothers too used words descriptive of touch, such as 'wet', 'slippery', and 'kicking'. In some accounts the baby was removed at birth, but the all-important contact had already been made, and the mother felt and knew that she and the baby belonged together.

The active management of labour can occasionally be a life-saving procedure. It is clear, too, that some babies need to be given special care after delivery, although in many cases this is possible at the mother's bedside, in the way that it is being done at present in some progressive hospitals. But even though a minority of mothers and babies benefit from the sequence of events which starts with artificial stimulation of the uterus and culminates with the baby in the nursery, it is questionable whether this justifies the practice of submitting the majority of women to what many of those I interviewed described as the misery of enforced separation from their babies, and equally questionable whether we should permit modern technological innovations to risk interfering with the basic human patterns of attachment between parents and their young.

It would be wrong to suggest that it is only drugs affecting the baby's behaviour at birth that interfere with the interaction between a mother and her new baby. Some babies are born in a drowsy or irritable state, making it hard to get to know them, because their mothers could not help reacting physiologically to the stressful environment during labour. When this happens a woman's tension and fear may lead to her uterus contracting less effectively, so slowing labour down, and produces a chemical imbalance in the baby's blood.[44]

Both the mother and her baby have suffered and are left dazed and shell-shocked by birth. A woman who feels like this may not be ready to hold her baby, and should never have the child thrust at her. She needs to be nurtured lovingly in whichever way she wants at the time and be allowed to get to know her baby in her own good time. The baby can be held close and quietly by the father or anyone else who can give the mother time to recover from the birth.

The time immediately after birth is treated by many hospitals not as a special period in which important psycho-biological needs of the mother are met by the staff, and in which she has the opportunity to get to know her baby, but as one during which both mother and child are medically screened before they can be pronounced 'not at risk' and discharged back into society. This is taken to be the main function of the hospital not only in industrialized but also increasingly in developing societies. The traditional ways of birth and the culturally accepted manner in which the mother first relates to the baby and the baby to her have been destroyed and replaced by Western methods. The focus of obstetric and neonatal care is almost exclusively on disease and potential disease. We do not yet know whether this wholesale replacement of traditional ways of caring may have a harmful effect on women, on babies, and on the quality of family life.

The West exports its technology with as much vigour as the Victorians did their religion and forms of administration. Doctors tend to believe that if a machine to regulate labour or an obstetric procedure is right for a baby who is at risk, it is also an appropriate technology for a birth in which a baby is not at risk. It is part of the same kind of confused logic that if it is advisable to separate some babies from their mothers for observation in a nursery, then it is right to separate all babies from their mothers.

Many people are persuaded that only if every new technique and every available machine is used are they giving their babies the best chance. One consequence is a failure of confidence in handling and relating to the baby, a basic lack of trust in the ability to mother one's own baby. This is so familiar in the West that we hardly comment on it any more, anticipating that a new mother will be awkward, unsure of herself, anxious and quickly distressed. But this particular psychological reaction to motherhood is almost unknown in traditional cultures, where birth takes place at home and where the new mother cares for her baby from the moment of delivery with the help of other women members of her own or her husband's family, and where everything that is done takes place in her presence.

The time immediately following birth may include some of the most important hours of the baby's, and also, perhaps, of the mother's life, because mother and baby are literally 'getting in touch' with one another. Even in the West, when births take place at home, as one-third still do in the Netherlands, for example, a quiet time for meeting with the baby occurs naturally after delivery. Although it may not come so easily in hospital, in many hospitals it is being discovered that it is possible for mothers and fathers to experience this quality of environment there, too.

Close holding and the spontaneous stroking and massage which occurs when parents explore their new baby, cuddling her, feeling the firmness of her limbs, stroking her silky hair and 'breathing in' her reality, involves emotional 'work' which may be no less important than the physical work of labour, and it is one which we should not allow to get crowded out by the busy activity of a hospital. Mothers do not need to be told how to do it. They do need, however, in their own good time, and whenever they are ready, to be handed the unclothed baby, to be left in peace, and to be free to do whatever comes spontaneously.

11

Learning To Be A Mother

Childbirth may be the grand finale of pregnancy. But it opens the door on a completely new experience and on a lengthy learning process that never finishes, however old the children are.

The Romance Trap

A woman who marries and is looking forward to having a baby may think that she has made a personal, careful and entirely private choice – and, perhaps, that she is just doing what is 'natural'. Yet she is conforming to a pattern imposed by a society that is intolerant of women who do not become wives and mothers. In Christian culture spinsters are approved only if they are nuns and therefore 'married' to Christ. In the Middle Ages, women who were not attached to men, because they were spinsters and widows, were those most likely to be accused of witchcraft and to be burned at the stake or drowned in the ducking pond.

From the vantage point of Western technological society it is easy to see that women in traditional societies, such as those of the Eastern Mediterranean, the Middle East and Asia, are under enormous social pressure to be mothers. A girl is reared to become a mother. It is perceived as the natural course of events, and the family's honour depends on her being a wife and mother beyond reproach, one who surrenders herself in service to her husband and children. Prior to marriage her virginity must be kept intact. Arab girls are taught to avoid strenuous exercise, never to jump from a height, and not to sit on a hard ledge, lest they inadvertently tear the hymen. The parents' primary duty is to ensure that a daughter remains a virgin until her wedding day. Her hymen is more important than her eyes, arms or legs.[1]

It is tempting to believe that women in the West are free to make their own decisions, and, with modern contraception, that we can choose to have a child when we want one, to delay motherhood or to avoid it entirely. In Western culture, where concepts of shame and honour are more muted, and where a woman's worth is less obviously connected with the virtue of daughters and sisters and the fertility of wives and the wives of sons, it is *romance* that propels girls into marriage and mother-hood, and is responsible for many unwanted pregnancies. It is more or less taken for granted that every little girl will grow up, fall in love, marry, have children and, as in fairy stories, live happily ever after. It is an effective way of moulding young women into a pattern and making them available to serve men and bear children. Romance makes women value themselves only as they are seen in men's eyes, and leads them to package and present themselves so as to be attractive to men, and to believe that having a baby will be an extension of that romance. It is a trap set with honey.

A few years back, an organization called The Responsible Society produced a film to be shown in some British schools and youth clubs. It was supposed to teach girls how to say 'no' to sex, and to wait for their prince to come. The story-line follows June, a good-time girl, who gets pregnant, fails her exams, has an abortion and goes into a dead-end job. Linda, on the other hand, says 'no', gets into college and has a white wedding with all the trimmings – while June watches, envious and miserable. The message is clear: 'Good girls wait, virginally intact, until a ring is on their finger. Bad girls enjoy themselves, have abortions and end up unloved and without a man.'

In novels written for the teenage market girls are offered a glittering fantasy, the tinsel and star-dust of romance, and it is implied that once they have their man everything will be happy ever after. A lotus land is offered in place of the boredom of life as an office junior or at the supermarket check-out and, for many youngsters, the emptiness and hopelessness of life when unemployed. 'His lips were moving against her skin and his breath caressing sensitive areas,' I read as I browse in my local newsagents. 'Glenna closed her eyes to try to shut out the wild sensations pulsing through her veins.' 'In my dreams my mind became filled with the perfume of your body,' the hero murmurs; 'I could feel the roundness of your breasts in my hands . . . I'd wake up hungry for the taste of your lips.'

Romance is to do with possession, not just the romance of novelettes like these, but the love stories and novels that sell well to an exclusively female readership. While women read these, men read pornography. Romance packages sex with love and ties it up with the bonds of fidelity and monogamy. Pornography is packaged with violence and has to do with exploitation and promiscuity. Neither romanticism nor pornography treat sex realistically, and neither acknowledges a woman as a person. In each she is *used* to serve a man's needs. It may not be so blatantly obvious with romance as with pornography – 'With a groan he bent his head and was kissing her hungrily . . . forgetting everything but his deep, intense need for her . . .' – but it is there all the same.

Romance is about a man claiming a woman and having her at his service. It is the path along which girls are led within Western society in order to settle down to being good housewives and mothers. It is precisely this kind of deception that makes a girl vulnerable to the fumbling youth who wants to show his mates that he can 'lay' a girl, or the exploitative older man who is just 'playing around', both of whom in her eyes are transformed into knights in shining armour. Many teenagers who get pregnant by accident have been confused and misled by such fantasies into believing that this was Mr Right. Any agony aunt has a pile of letters every week from young women who *meant* to say 'no' and who did not think they needed contraceptives.

Through romance, society programmes girls to fit a social system in which women tie themselves to men in order to nurture and tend them and bear and rear their children. This is not to deny that there are happy wives and mothers, or that children bring joy. Yet many women are slowly suffocated by family life and by a lop-sided partnership in which the wife services the man and his possessions while he wields power and achieves success in the big world outside the four walls of home.

It is not only that a steady diet of romance conditions young women to be exploited by the first man who comes along and convinces them that he is Prince Charming, but that it snuffs out a woman's own potential to be herself and do what *she* wants in life. Self-worth becomes something conferred on a woman by a man, and lasts only as long as she is loved and wanted by him. A woman who does not have a man is 'on the shelf' and becomes an embittered 'old maid'.

Another theme of romance is that a woman must find a man to 'awaken' her sexually. It is only through him that she becomes aware of sex and able to enjoy it. Female sexuality is meant to lie dormant until the prince arrives. That is the theme of the Sleeping Beauty story, reiterated time and time again in novels, films and our own fantasies. Yet human beings are sexual from the moment of birth. Though we cannot know exactly what babies feel, baby boys have erections, and the vaginas of baby girls become lubricated. You have only to watch a baby at the breast, sucking steadily, pausing for a moment, then eagerly grasping the nipple again, little hands and feet curling and uncurling in delight, enjoying the experience from top to toe, to realize that this is the kind of thing we know of as a sexual experience. Babies love being patted, stroked, kissed and cuddled. Later they love exploring their own bodies and getting good feelings when they rub or stroke their genitals. It used to be the fashion to reassure mothers that this was just intelligent curiosity, because adults shied away from the startling revelation that babies, too, have sexual feelings.

When the adolescent girl has a passionate friendship with another girl or an older woman, it is frequently treated as trivial and silly – a 'passing phase' – because women are not supposed to love other women or to get strength and support from them, but to look to men for the satisfaction of their needs, especially in order for sexual feelings to be aroused. Girls are under pressure to be heterosexually active from a society which treats sexual expression as necessary for happiness. Unsure of themselves, they use sex to obtain proof that they are of value, and that somebody wants them.

Through advertising and the media Western culture tells women over and over again that they are not good enough. Any teenager who is lacking in confidence is particularly vulnerable to this message. Her body seems wrong. It is too fat, too thin, too pear-shaped or top-heavy. Her breasts are too small or too large. Advertisements and beauty and fashion features

188

in women's magazines promise their readers that they can be remodelled so that they become more attractive to men. Love comes with a shampoo, a face cream or skin-tight jeans. If she uses a particular brand of soap or cosmetics the teenager will suddenly emerge from her chrysalis, a poised, beautiful woman.

Some teenagers risk pregnancy because they think that at least if they have a baby they will have someone to love who will in turn love them. They look to the baby to give them the sense of worth which is lacking in their lives. Others become pregnant accidentally because they never thought it would happen to them. Studies have shown that most adolescent pregnancies are unintentional. Teenagers often do not begin to use contraception until they have been having intercourse for anything from six months to two years. Many myths surround conception: it cannot happen if the couple do it standing up, or if the girl does not have an orgasm, or if the boy is drunk – and it certainly cannot happen the first time a couple have intercourse. Even when contraception is ready to hand in the form of condoms, girls often do not check whether a boy has them because they feel less guilty if sex takes place unpredictably. If she is 'carried away' it is forgivable. It is planning ahead – doing it with forethought – that is wrong. In this way, romance is directly responsible for unwanted pregnancies, and it is the 'good' girls, who do not 'intend' to have intercourse, who end up pregnant.

The Romance of a Baby

Where in traditional societies a baby is seen as a link with ancestors, a seal on a marriage, evidence of a woman's worth, and an investment for the future, in wealthy Western countries today a baby is increasingly treated as a personal accessory to the romance between a couple who, once they have established a home together and acquired a car and a stereo, acquire a baby, or even, when that romance is fading, look to a baby as a means of reviving and enhancing it.

With little previous direct knowledge of babies, a girl from a two-child family is at risk of growing up unaware that babies need constant attention, that they make messes and smells, that they can cry very noisily indeed, that they take over your life, and that they are, quite definitely, non-returnable. The babies she has glimpsed in magazines and in films were pink, plump and smiling adorably, gurgling with delight as they were bathed or powdered. A young woman may never have actually seen a dirty nappy changed, never had to listen to a baby crying all evening.

All pregnant women have fantasies about their babies hidden within them, but today there is a widespread delusion about what babies are and how they behave. This is reinforced by the media. Photographs of delightful babies sell products ranging from perfumes for men to sweaters, washing machines and cars. The 'new man', muscular, hirsute and gentle, is often depicted along with this adorable baby, for he is part of the same theme. Men are not really rough, tough and exploitative, the picture tells us. They have an untapped tenderness, and a baby will at last bring this out in them.

When a woman fantasizes about her baby, she also fantasizes about how she will be as a mother, and the two dreams mingle. The image of motherhood which we are offered is saccharine-sweet. I have often confronted this misty image when a book of mine is about to be published and we are at the design stage, discussing photographs for the jacket. The design department presents its chosen photographs, yet the woman I am offered is a stranger to me. She is the stereotype 'new mother' in soft focus, sitting in the lamplight with her baby at her breast (but without any of her breast actually exposed), placid in a rocking chair with light filtering through the leaves of the tree in bloom outside her window, walking on the seashore with her face upturned to the sun, or in a frilly négligé, her long blond hair falling over her face as she gazes at her sleeping baby. Both the men and the young childless women in publishers' offices are delighted with these gossamer images. In some strange way, even when the woman depicted is pregnant, she is incorporeal. You cannot imagine her ever having intercourse or giving birth. Her only emotion is that of gentle pleasure.

There are many variations on this theme in our images of motherhood, all of them romanticized. There is the myth of the powerful goddess who is creation and life, instinctively in touch with the fount of being and therefore profoundly wise, the myth of the mother as all-loving and nurturing, the myth that mothers know exactly what to do with their babies because it is all instinctive, and that mothers, as a consequence of the biological act of birth, adore their children all the time and have only tender feelings for them. The myth that mothers are selfless and giving and experience supreme satisfaction in sacrificing themselves is crystallized in the Christian image of the Virgin Mother sitting in placid serenity with her infant son on her lap. She is untouched by anxiety or passion, and represents the purity of woman given in service to her child.

We express our own infantile view of the mother as the property of the baby when we create this dichotomy between real feelings and the idealized vision of sanctified motherhood. At the back of every image of the mother as goddess is that other mother who personifies all the hatred which has been repressed. She is the witch, the wicked stepmother who gives her child a poisoned apple to eat or commands a shepherd to kill it and bring her its heart.

When sexuality is divorced from the emotions involved in mothering and an antithesis is created between them, a romanticized model of motherhood is erected with which women cannot possibly identify. They then experience the hopelessness and failure of trying to act a part which they know they cannot play and for which they feel temperamentally unsuited, and end up saying: 'I haven't any maternal instincts.' Alex Comfort contributed to this false antithesis between sexuality and motherhood when he stated that parenthood was incompatible with exultant sex: 'The best modern sex is unreproductive . . . The development of a recreational erotic life needs privacy. Sexual freedom just isn't compatible with a childbearing lifestyle.'[2]

In spite of having real mothers, children grow up clinging to a romantic version of how a mother 'should' be. With adolescence the image begins to be shattered once and for all, and boys and girls have to come to terms with their flawed mothers and establish a new relationship with them as human beings and not just as 'mothers'. At the same time parents have to learn that their children are not simply their children, but people. One of my daughters, when she was about eleven, said to me with evident surprise in her voice, 'I didn't realize that mothers had personalities! I thought they were just mothers, and the main thing about them was that they were motherly.'

Even those of us who are feminists, and who are determined to see ourselves realistically, may start out with unreasonable expectations of ourselves as mothers, and then experience disillusion as we face the challenges of motherhood, and discover that not only is the baby different from the one we expected, but – more disturbing in many ways – that we are not the mothers we hoped to be, however hard we try to act the part.

The feminist writer Sara Maitland has one child, but says that she planned to have eight:

> *Originally I would breastfeed them until they weaned themselves, teach them to read before they were toilet-trained, and be a very creative mother, baking bread, going for long walks with them, stimulating them through educational play – and be a great writer.*

She goes on to say that she discovered that:

> *I was selfish and mean, even towards this beloved person. When she screamed sometimes I could not comfort her even with my warm, milk-filled and loving breasts; I could not make her happy and I felt guilty . . . Sometimes I would go to pick her up feeling furious and resentful and at the touch or sight of her I would collapse, melted by physical love and tenderness. Sometimes I would be playing with her quite happily when a complete and profound anger would come over me and I would want to kill her.*

Her conclusion is a simple one: 'I am obliged to face the fact that I am not Superwoman.'[3]

The First Baby

Not only does a woman find that she is not the kind of mother she wanted to be, but the baby may turn out to be different from the baby of her fantasies. With the birth of a baby the romantic image is shattered. The new mother encounters a squashed-up little creature, vernix sticking in all his skin folds, with a high-pitched, demanding wail, a blotchy face, receding forehead, flattened nose, skinny, tortoise-like neck, and flailing arms. Psychological studies of mothers' reactions to their newborn babies suggest that it is common for women to feel alienated and anxious.[4] The baby is a stranger, and may seem like an invader from outer space.

192

Even so, in a heightened state of awareness, with the oxytocin surge that a triumphant birth stimulates and an emotionally supportive setting where she is able to get to know her baby in her own way and her own time, a new mother soon becomes intrigued and fascinated, enjoys her baby and develops self-confidence. Unfortunately, many women do not have that kind of environment for birth and the days after, and some find it really difficult to fall in love with their babies, because their own need for nurturing is overwhelming, and they feel disempowered, and often mutilated, by the birth.

Then after five days or so a woman is discharged from hospital, and suddenly has complete responsibility for caring for this new person. Her own wishes and needs cannot be met; the baby's needs must be paramount. Where in traditional societies older, experienced mothers and other women with babies in the same village or household community nurture and support her, a woman in the West is often totally alone, enduring what has been called 'the jet-lagged bewilderment of early motherhood'.[5] The fantasy, the romance of having a baby, the whole gossamer dream must fade, to be replaced with the real baby in its mother's arms.

In interviews that I have conducted with first-time mothers a few weeks after childbirth, they often talk about their shock at the disruption of established living patterns once there is a baby in the house: 'We were never really prepared for this' . . . 'We were ready for the birth but we didn't think how it would be after' . . .'My whole life revolves around the baby, attending to her needs, worrying about her, trying to find out why she's crying, trying to do things right' . . . 'I hadn't realized how much work a new baby was. How do women with more than one child ever manage? My time is completely taken up just with one. I sometimes don't know whether it's day or night. All I know is that he's either asleep or awake. If he's awake he's plugged in and sucking. If he's asleep I'm snatching the time for chores or trying to catch up on sleep myself' . . . 'I have never felt so tired in my life. I had no idea it was like this!' . . . and 'I have come to the end of the lollipop, and all I've got left is the stick.'

A baby brings an emotional challenge for both parents. One study of new parents disclosed that the birth of the first child frequently cuts conversation time between them in half.[6] They

193

may feel that they are drifting further and further away from each other.

During the three months following birth many women feel tied to the baby by an emotional umbilical cord. It is as if this period forms a fourth trimester of pregnancy, in which mother and baby are still united in a symbiotic bond (particularly if the mother is breastfeeding, as most mothers are the world over) and during which the well-being of each is inextricably linked with that of the other.

This symbiosis is well recognized in most agricultural and hunting societies, where a child is held close to its mother's body, day and night, almost like an extension of herself, and where suckling takes place in a casual and spasmodic manner, with the baby frequently dropping off to sleep while still at the breast. It is almost a marsupial phase of existence for the baby, who has emerged from the uterus into an extra-uterine stage, but who is still thought of as being part of the mother. Just as the baby kangaroo comes out of the pouch but still clings to its mother, so the human infant is slung or cradled on the mother's back or hip, in the folds of her shawl or other garment or, in New Guinea, in a basket or carrying net suspended from her forehead. In pastoral tribes of South Africa a baby is strapped to the mother's back or seated astride her hip in a sling made of goat or antelope skin. When a Sotho mother stoops to lift up her baby the child spontaneously raises his arms and legs at right angles in order to mould his body to his mother's back. The baby is rocked with each movement the mother makes as she washes clothes down by the river, tills the earth, or walks carrying water or firewood on her head.

Since nutritional survival depends on breastfeeding in these societies, and the baby fed on artificial milk is at risk of dehydration and death, this marsupial stage of existence has obvious survival value. When a mother and baby are close in this way the mother is also able to learn from and about her baby in a way that is much more difficult for a woman who puts her baby down in a cot, or even in another room, attending to it only when it sends out distress signals.

There are two basically contrasting mothering styles in the West. A woman may employ other people to care for her baby so that she can live relatively independently of it. Her breasts, arms and body remain her own, and the baby is not going to

194

disrupt her life in any way. Or she may change her whole life so that she is herself the baby carrier, the baby nourisher, the baby comforter, the child's life growing out of hers and physically contiguous with it. There are, of course, many points along the continuum between these two extreme positions. At times each mother probably feels guilty or anxious that she is not mothering in the other way. The woman who goes back to her job leaving the baby with other caretakers may feel anxious about not breastfeeding and being at home with her baby. But the one who gives herself to the baby without restriction may also feel anxious and guilty about her sudden rush of uncontrollable resentment at being so sucked into and taken over by motherhood.

The Nuclear Family

The urban family into which a baby is born in many industrialized societies today is likely to be small; the baby will have one or at most two siblings. Family members are dispersed, and even close relatives outside the immediate family form a collective unit only on ritual occasions when their relatedness is celebrated, such as at birthdays, anniversaries and funerals. A study done in the sixties revealed that for 62 per cent of the middle-class Londoners interviewed the effective 'kin set' – that is, those with whom there was regular contact – stopped at first cousins or closer relatives.[7] Even in the major life crisis of the birth of a baby a couple may have to cope alone. Forty per cent received no help from anyone in the family. The woman's mother was the person most likely to come to help, and did so in 50 per cent of cases, whereas the man's mother assisted only rarely. A woman's sister gave help in less than 10 per cent of cases because she was often employed or busy with her own home. But help was not really expected, and when it did come was often considered 'of dubious value'. Now that more women are working outside the home, and grandmothers are likely to be committed to their own jobs, help is even less available than it was in the sixties.

Perhaps we have an idealized view of how families once were – in a *Cider With Rosie*-style rural England that was always sunny. The comfortable solidity of the large interacting extended family was a luxury of the Victorian middle and upper classes, and less often a reality for the poor. Once the Industrial Revolution was under way there was little time for working-class families to bother with relatives, or any relatives not directly involved in the economic unit of the immediate family, and men, women and children worked throughout the daylight hours, and often at night too, in factories or in cottage industry.

Learning to be Parents in Pre-industrial Societies

In peasant cultures the care of small children traditionally takes place in women's groups engaged in domestic or other productive tasks. Women kneel by the river rubbing clothes on the stones and pounding and pummelling them while at the same time caring for children. They spin and weave with the children beside them, or prepare food for cooking, sew skins for garments, build dwelling huts, or work in the fields. The distinction between communality and privacy does not exist.

In many hunting-and-gathering societies dwellings are shared by several families. The Nootka of the American North-west Coast had large cedarwood houses common to four or more families. Each corner was inhabited by one family, with others ranged along the sides. Apache extended family groups shared one large tepee. The Ongre Negritoes of Little Andaman Island have enormous oval thatched houses, also shared by several families, each of which has its own fireplace, and Indians of the Amazon basin still live communally in dwellings of this type. Even where families do not live completely in common, they frequently have inter-connecting houses. The Ainu of Japan sometimes had pit houses which were linked with each other by tunnels. In these dwellings the family life of each member was open to everyone.

In agricultural as in hunting societies, children are the responsibility of all adults. The children of the band, tribe or village are 'our' children. Mothers share child-rearing tasks. Andamanese women pass babies round and cuddle them, and each lactating woman may suckle the child whilst it is on her lap. There are always other women willing to take over the mothering role. In some societies children are sent to the grandmother's house to be weaned. In Jamaica, where women work in domestic service and in shops and offices in the towns, it is customary to send first-born children back to 'me mada in de country', who by the time she reaches middle age expects to have a second family consisting of her grandchildren to rear, and who although she grumbles about the responsibility and hard work sees this as

196

providing social insurance for her old age. In societies such as these, children learn what mothering is not only from their own mothers and women of her generation, but also, and even primarily (as is frequently the case in the West Indies) from their mother's mother.

Every peasant child has the experience of caring for still younger children, siblings or cousins. As soon as a child can walk easily she may have a baby strapped to her back, and small 'mothers' play, run, jump, imitate household tasks and help their mothers with babies permanently clinging to them. A peasant girl learns very early what it is to have a baby almost as an extension of her own body, and boys, too, are expected to do their share of baby-minding. For the girls, however, the tasks persist long after the boy has left home and joined peer groups of other boys intent on adventure, whether these are neighbourhood gangs or, as in East African societies, formally constituted age sets. In many cultures the boy even sleeps away from home with the men, or in special huts in which he learns what it is to be a man in his society. Girls tend to be much more home-centred, whether from choice or necessity, and close to their mothers.

There is a wealth of folklore to teach a mother how to keep the child healthy, to use herbs and correctly enact ritual, as well as giving guidelines to the normal development of a child. But this is the common currency of women, and simply confirms what they all know already. In crises the peasant mother seeks help from the old rituals of witchcraft, magic and religion, or from the new, potent rituals of science and medicine. But in day-to-day family life she acts without reflection and without doubt.

Images of Parenthood in Western Society

An expectant mother in Western industrial society may never have touched, or even seen, a newborn baby before. The appearance and needs of a tiny baby may be as much a mystery to her as the breeding of giant pandas. She will probably have read the occasional article in a magazine, but she is aware that in having a baby she is starting to do something about which she knows nothing. She could go to her own mother for information, but this is often impossible in a highly mobile society in which a couple starting a family may be hundreds or thousands of miles away from the homes of the prospective grandparents. A woman

197

may feel, too, that this is not a subject about which her mother could be up-to-date, and given the speed of technological change associated with baby care she is probably right.

Our educational and child-rearing systems put great emphasis on the development of individuality and self-direction. The pregnant woman wants to do things her way, and even if her mother is available she may not wish to ask for help. When expecting the first child a couple may not yet know any others with babies, and although they see parents in the supermarket or the High Street they have no idea of what it feels like to have a baby in the house, or how it may affect their own relationship. A woman may worry about her lack of information. She often does not realize that even more important than technical know-how is some understanding of the emotional, relational, and self-image changes inevitably involved with becoming a mother.

Expert Opinion

Mothers are not short of advice. They are barraged with it. Sometimes it seems that everyone knows how to care for a child better than the mother herself.

The advice given by Dr Truby King in the twenties is typical of the prescriptions handed to new mothers by experts, most of whom have never themselves been mothers, and many of whom are male. Truby King, a New Zealander whose system of 'scientific' infant feeding was based on one he developed for dairy calves, denounced the unnecessary handling of babies because he reckoned it gave them indigestion, overstimulated them and led to 'nervous disorders' later in life. He taught that babies should be fed strictly by the clock on his special 'scientific' formula, and, to find out exactly the quantity of milk they were taking, that they ought to be weighed before and after every feed.

He was the man responsible for instituting the nipple rituals which have caused women to do extraordinary things to their breasts in the hope that thereby they would be better able to breastfeed. He taught that nipples must be 'prepared' for feeding by rubbing with a loofah or rough cloth, and that mothers must wash their breasts before and after every feed. He invented all the rules – with strong eugenic and moral overtones – about how babies should be fed on the dot every four hours, and their sucking time strictly rationed. He medicalized the whole subject of infant feeding, and in doing so destroyed women's confidence in breastfeeding and made loving mothers feel inadequate and guilty.

He said that a baby should be allowed to suck for only two minutes on the first day after birth, three minutes the second, four minutes the third, and up to ten minutes each side thereafter. He believed that in this way cracked nipples would be avoided – a notion still held by many nurses, who don't understand that it is not the length of sucking which matters, but whether the baby has a good mouthful of breast; if a baby can't latch on, the jaws champ on the nipple rather than the breast, so of course the nipples then get sore.

Truby King told women that what they had been doing for centuries all over the world – feeding their babies for as long as they wanted, soothing them when they cried and cuddling up in bed with them at night – was terribly damaging: 'The waking of a baby to take food, at any time between midnight and sunrise, is unnatural,' he warned. 'Any baby can easily be spoiled and made a cross, fretful, exacting little tyrant.'

One kind of maternal behaviour that he denounced in his book *The Natural Feeding of Infants* was 'the injurious or excessive handling or stimulation of babies', and in this he included cuddling, all the games that parents spontaneously play with their babies, and the simple act of patting a baby rhythmically to help her drop off to sleep. Babies should never be patted, for instance. 'Many women thoughtlessly and almost mechanically pat a baby to soothe him whenever he is uncomfortable or fretful, and in this way they may insidiously bring on serious indigestion accompanied by inability to keep down a sufficiency of food.' He implied that mothers could inadvertently starve and even kill their babies with uncontrolled love.

Truby King further asserted that swinging and rocking makes the baby giddy and that babies arrived at his hospital 'suffering from emaciation, vomiting and grave nervous debility due almost solely to this one factor'. His treatment was to take them away from their mothers and put them 'to the charge of a quiet, sensible, trained nurse'. The implicit message to mothers was: 'You are incompetent. Professionals know how to care for your baby better than you do.'

The great doctor's ideas were popularized in books for mothers by Mary King (his adopted daughter), Mabel Liddiard and Mrs Frankenburg. An important part of this creed was the belief that to give a baby everything that he or she wants is to lay the foundations of a criminal character. Mrs Frankenburg, who sat on the juvenile bench, wrote that 'the baby who "won't" lie in his cot becomes . . . the toddler who won't play alone, the schoolboy who won't get up when he's called, the adolescent who won't come in at night.' The only way to escape this was to have science take over child-rearing. Unless women were doing it by the book, they were doing it wrong.

Truby King was adamant that mothers should not allow their babies to be in bed with them. Mrs King, her husband's devoted disciple, records in her diary his meeting with a mother: 'Fred was expatiating on the enormity of mothers keeping their babies in bed with them when Mrs H.'s curly-headed little girl, who was sitting on her knee, burst into tears and hid her face in her mother's bosom. Her mother clasped her close and said, "Never mind, he won't take you out of mother's bed and arms." Later she said to us, "None of my children were brought up on a system." ' Mrs King added: 'We are afraid she will not be teachable.'

All those warnings that people shower on new mothers: 'You're making a rod for your back', 'Show the baby that you are master', 'Let him cry it out. It's for his own good', 'She's only crying because she wants attention' – ideas which still intrude on and destroy mothers' sensitive awareness of their babies' needs – rise from this New Zealand doctor's conviction that human babies should be treated as if they were dairy calves. The evidence from history and from cultures all over the world is that, by and large, women – ordinary, spontaneous, loving mothers who are alert to learn from and respond to their babies – do better than all the experts put together.

Mothers Who Cannot Mother

No one knows how much violence is expressed against children in pre-industrial societies. In the Caribbean physical punishment is often a normal part of family life, and in developing countries such as India, Turkey and throughout Latin America children are often cruelly exploited for their labour. The phenomenon of repeated violent assault on a baby or small child because a father or mother has lost control of themselves is, however, something which, although well known in our own society, has not been com-

200

mented on by anthropologists working in pre-industrial societies. Writing about the Ik of Uganda – probably the most unpleasant people an anthropologist has ever had to study – Colin Turnbull described how mothers shrugged their shoulders when a baby was devoured by a wild animal and urged the men to kill the animal, as it would now be fat from eating the baby and so make a good meal.[8] But even he did not suggest that there was any of the violence against children of the kind we know so well in the West.

When I interviewed mothers in Jamaica one subject I was interested in was how you 'grow a child right'. Although these women all thought discipline was important if the child was not to grow 'rude' (the neighbour's children were usually provided as an example of this), everyone stressed that a child should never be slapped till it 'knew sense', and that meant when he or she was talking well.

Whenever children are considered the personal property of their parents, objects which they possess and which demonstrate how successful or powerful they are, the way is open to child abuse. The institution of the family in its modern, Western form enables adults to abuse children in private, behind drawn curtains and locked doors, in a way that is almost impossible in traditional cultures.

In the Caribbean I met mothers who were suffering from mental illness, and whose children were neglected, but never one whose inner turmoil found expression in violence against a baby. I am sure that such women exist, but in a peasant society, as distinct from life in a city, it is impossible to seal the doors and windows and conduct family life in isolation behind the walls. Neighbours and relatives would soon become involved and take over care of a baby if a mother proved incapable of mothering her child. Perhaps this is the important thing about family life within a traditional society: it is lived out in public, and sanctions created and exercised by the larger community control and to a certain extent safeguard actions within it.

Babies have personalities and some babies are hard to love. A 'good' baby helps; a crying baby may make it just too difficult. There are babies who are unpredictable, and others who are mentally retarded, hyperactive, or who are suffering from a handicap which makes it difficult to 'warm' to them. This is why child abuse is often directed only at one child in a family, the

201

one who is picked out as 'bad'. Sometimes this is the child who is different because he or she is especially intelligent or bright and lively.

A woman may find it impossible to relate to her baby because her own needs are too great. A single mother, still in her teens, who had a distressing experience of birth and whose body had been mutilated by an episiotomy that did not heal well, performed in spite of her saying that she did not want one, said:

> I hated him [the baby] for ruining my body and I hated John [her boyfriend] for letting them do it. On the second day my mum was visiting me when one of the other mothers told me Alexander was crying. My mum and John said they would go. I was so upset that when I went into the ward, I pulled the curtain and I shook him very hard. I can't believe I did it, but I hated him. I just wanted him to die.[9]

In all this a woman's relationship with her partner is important. If she is getting loving support the task of coping with a difficult baby is made simpler, and as she learns to handle that relationship her mothering skills develop. But if the relationship with her partner is poor or there is no one else who will accept responsibility, she can reach breaking point quickly.

Severe depression can lead to an inability to feel love for a baby. But equally, failure to love a baby can result in depression, because a woman then feels a failure and may seek a quality in the baby, a rewarding warmth coming from the baby to her, which manifestly is not there. She may feel as if bereaved of the baby of her dreams, the child she hoped for and whom she sheltered in her body, and encounters instead a complete stranger who appears in its place.

Although we may think of mothers who use physical violence against their babies as monsters, in fact they are often sad, pathetic and terribly vulnerable. One depressed mother told me: 'The baby's cry makes no sense to me. Nothing is passing between us. We are not exchanging. There was a time, after the birth, when we were offering things, but I have turned full circle. I have done some awful things.' When I asked what things, she confessed, quietly and with shame, that she had 'thrown the children on the floor', and added that she was aware that her husband, a solicitor, was afraid of what he might discover when

202

he returned from work at the end of each day. In this case he desperately wanted things to 'work out' and 'come right somehow', without him having to do anything about it or their problem being made public. Like so many partners, he was colluding in the violence. The distress which both of them were feeling was itself a product of an unhappy relationship: 'All we do with each other is to look at each other to see how we are. We have had three conversations that I can think of ever since we were married. We seem to be paralysed with each other,' the wife said.

When a mother or father actually uses violence against a baby there is always a specific crisis which acts as a trigger. To anyone else it may seem minor, but it comes at the end of a long road of frustration and irritation. The washing machine breaks down, a mother-in-law comes to visit, there is no heat, or no food, or a partner loses his job.

Parents who are specially at risk of battering their children were often themselves maltreated as children, and come from families in which there is a history of violence. They tend to be people who are facing a multitude of other problems besides those involved in bringing up a family. For unhappy families often perpetuate themselves through the generations. This does not mean that individual men and women do not bravely break free. There is nothing pre-ordained about unhappy relationships. But those brought up with violence are at risk of resorting to violence themselves. A distorted relationship may be partly the result of an internal model which does not fit the real situation. A mother may see almost everything that goes on between herself and her six-week-old baby as a power struggle, for instance. Or she may see herself as the baby's victim, helplessly suffering the child's manipulative ploys and vicious attacks. A woman who is struggling to control a baby whom she sees as threatening her all the time is the one most likely to break down in a violent outburst against the child. The one who passively endures whatever her baby does tends to neglect the child, unable to love, unable to hate, simply withdrawing from emotion because everything hurts too much.[10]

Although there may exist a few mothers who get relief from their own tensions by deliberately inflicting pain on others, the vast majority are vulnerable women under stress, women who are also often the victims of violent men in their lives. They deeply regret the injuries they have inflicted and say things like 'When

I hit him I then pick him up and cuddle him.'

There is little social support for a mother who is in danger of physically abusing her child, and a great deal of depression amongst new mothers goes unnoticed and neglected. In some areas there are mother and baby units where mothers, and fathers too, if they can, are able to come in with their babies, so that not only can the staff learn more about the problems facing the woman and observe her behaviour with the child, but there is also an opportunity for the mother to learn in a facilitating environment which cares not only for the baby but for her. It may be that these unhappy women will only be able to mother when they have been mothered themselves. Yet attempts at therapy in general have not been very successful. Up to two-thirds of babies who have been physically abused are abused again within a few years.[11]

Being able to mother is something which is learned. Most cultures seem to manage this education extraordinarily effectively. We are only just beginning to be aware of the diffuse but important skills which our post-industrial society has neglected. Each woman brings a unique combination of skills and experience to motherhood. There is no such thing as the 'perfect' mother, if only because the role only achieves meaning when it is part of a growing and dyadic relationship with a child, and if there are other children in the family, the relationship between each of them and their mother, and between each and every combination of them. The mother sees herself in their eyes, as she must do also in the eyes of her partner. What she is and the way she conceptualizes her own role is the outcome of all these images of the self, which every day and every hour of the day go through kaleidoscopic changes, depending on the situation and the actors. Learning to be a mother is never completed. It is a multi-dimensional process. And it entails nothing less than the transmutation of self.

12

Working Mothers

Indian women breaking up stones to build a road or working in the fields, their babies tucked inside their saris, African women carrying fuel on their heads while their babies are strapped to their backs or astride a hip, Turkish women picking cotton, their babies suspended from the apex of three vertical poles stuck in the ground in a make-shift swing, South American women crouched to weed between subsistence crops on eroded land, their babies hidden under a *ruana* or other strip of cloth – everywhere in the world women labour from first light to dusk, either with their babies nestled against their bodies or close to them, or left in the care of grandmothers, other female relatives, or older children.

One common stereotype of a mother is of a woman who spends most of her time caring for children. This is accurate only for the small proportion of women in the world who live in affluent areas, and who have enough economic support not to have to be in paid employment. Ninety per cent of the women in the Third World must work on the land for survival. They grow crops, tend animals, and carry water and firewood, bowed under loads weighing up to thirty-five kilos, over distances as much as four miles from their homes. The cutting and carrying of wood may take four or five hours each day.[1] When crops are poor and the land is arid, they have to bring in cash from somewhere. A study in Tanzania revealed that women worked more than a third again as long as men.[2] In the dry season in Ghana women contribute 80 per cent of the household cash income.[3] The United

Nations summed it up with this statement: 'Although women represent half of the world's population and one third of the official labour force, they receive only one per cent of the world income and own less than one per cent of the world's property.'[4]

How Women Worked

In the West, too, throughout history it has been for the majority of women unthinkable that they could be 'just' a mother or 'only' a housewife. Home-making and childbearing and -care have always been part of a wider network of responsibilities to support the extended family economically and to keep it functioning. Women had jobs to do as well as homes to run and families to care for. In rural areas these jobs were done in the home and on land near it. The household itself was a productive unit, and every capable member of it had to work in order to keep it running. In wealthy families women had to run great households and estates. Women cottagers also often laboured in workshops for the production of goods which could be sold or bartered.

In England before the nineteenth century, poor women worked at rag-sorting and cutting in paper mills, cinder-sifting and collecting refuse. They laboured in brickyards and foundries, carried loads to and from market and worked alongside brick-layers and masons. When they worked at home they often laboured to produce woven cloth. The woollen industry was based on cottage labour, and for the members of many rural households their whole life-style was dictated by all the tasks to do with the dyeing, spinning and weaving of wool, and its transformation from a raw state into bales of cloth. It had to be sorted, cleaned and dyed in large vats in the dyeing sheds. It was combed and carded, spun, woven, fulled (beaten, to clean or thicken it), washed, tentered (stretched), bleached, dressed and sheared.[5] Mothers working with their children at home performed the early stages of this process, with the final operations done by men in the mill. Textile production entailed intricate organization, co-operation and unremitting labour from everyone in the community.

The making of clothing involved fewer people and could often take place entirely in the home. Most garments were made up by mothers helped by their older daughters. Some areas were famous for specific products: beaver hats in London, felt hats in Stockport and Manchester, straw hats in Bedfordshire, Buckinghamshire and Hertfordshire, and knitted stockings in Scotland and Wales. The manufacture of goods like these boomed in Stuart and Hanoverian England, and then suddenly declined in the closing years of the eighteenth century, as machines were invented which could only be used in factories.

Yet the earliest machines were set up in cottages. Framework knitting was an important part of Elizabethan cottage industry, and by the middle of the eighteenth century some Midland hosiers had 100 stocking frames working in different cottages. Mothers had to organize their home and everything that went on in it around this industry, which dictated a timetable in line with which the activities of each member of the family were set.

On farms the mother ran not only the house but also the dairy, the calves, the pigs and cows and the orchards. Where there was little help it was she who milked the cows at three or four in the morning and again in the evening, made the butter and cheese (often late into the night), and went to market to sell dairy products. She had to fetch heavy pails of water from the pump or well, carry stacks of firewood or peat to keep the range or open fire going, and was busy from before dawn till after dark.

On the smaller farms she also helped with hay-making and harvesting, and often drove the plough. The woman living in a cottage tilled the garden on which the family depended for its vegetables, and might also tend a goat and a few chickens, while her husband worked as a wage labourer. Her economic contribution to the household was often equivalent in cash terms to that of her husband. The children were depended on to work too, as soon as they could run errands, carry tools, help with the laundry, cook, brew ale or cider, feed livestock, take their father's dinner out to him in the fields, and care for still younger children.

Each farm and cottage was a hive of industry. Only on Sunday did the male members of the household have a break from ceaseless toil, and the mother could not stop even then. In winter, when work in the fields was difficult because the ground was hard and the days short, home industry increased, and the women and children dressed cloth, made and altered clothes to hand down to the little ones, sewed patchwork bedspreads and rag rugs, and made candles.

When the industrial revolution began at the end of the eighteenth century, whole families moved into the new factories. At the beginning they laboured together in much the same way as they had done in cottage industry. Women and children were employed for long hours in strenuous, exhausting and often killing work. Yet although at first the family worked as a unit under the supervision of the father, this system soon broke up. Family members were put to work as operatives in different parts of the factory, or even in different factories. Their daily lives were controlled by strangers and by foremen to whom the family was an irrelevance.

As more and more factories were built and towns grew, there was a complete physical separation between the home and the work-place. The man's work took him out of the house for longer periods than ever before, and new laws were passed to reduce the exploitation of women and children in the factories. The father was responsible for supporting the family economically, and the mother for running the home and rearing the children.

Cottage industries based on female labour continued in the textile industry for some time, alongside production of cloth in the mills. Power-driven machinery took over in the factories, producing cloth in quantities and at a speed with which cottage industry could not compete. So the men went off to learn the new techniques of cotton-spinning, using the steam engine and the mule, while women made cambric, calico and muslin on the old spinning jennys set up at home.

In the new urban industrial economy of the nineteenth century, however, people skilled in working on the land came to the factories unskilled, and could sell only their physical strength and hard labour. Women were seen as weaker, less reliable, less intelligent and less practical than men, so men were hired in preference, except for the lowest paid jobs of all. With no land on which to keep animals and grow vegetables, a woman could not earn enough to maintain herself and her children, and was completely dependent on her husband. Yet he could not earn enough to keep a family. Unable to get work, she was expected to concentrate exclusively on child care and running the home.

The division between male and female roles was complete.

Mothers on a Pedestal

There was a striking contrast between the Victorian working-class woman's life and that of the married woman in the rising and increasingly important middle class. A middle-class woman could leave all hardship and household drudgery to the servants below stairs while she concentrated on the moral development of her children.

Not only did middle-class women have no work outside the home, they did not work inside it, either. A middle-class household employed at least three domestic servants: a cook, a parlour-maid and a housemaid, or a cook, parlour-maid and nursemaid. The mother's new vocation was to cultivate and discipline her children, 'as the skilful gardener suits the seed to the soil'.[6] She was to be a 'constant directress of her children' and, even though she had to part with her sons when they were sent away to school, she should keep her daughters 'within the sacred precincts of home' so that they could 'drink in the refinement and courtesy' for which she must be the model.[7] Motherhood was idealized. Women were told that it was 'a crown of blessing . . . The best women are those who love children the most, and delight in their sweet caresses, reverently watch their opening minds, and who find their being drawn out and perfected in that of the little creature.'[8] The tenderness of the mother-child relationship was emphasized, and with it the mother's responsibility to nurture a child's psyche and to train the developing personality as a gardener might tend a delicate plant.

The ideas of Jean-Jacques Rousseau were incorporated into a new romanticism, and a child came trailing clouds of glory. Motherhood became almost a religion, and what were seen as the 'feminine virtues' of sensibility, compassion, temperance, self-sacrifice, chastity, gentleness, devotion and high morality all came to focus on the image of the Mother. Women were no longer so important as household managers, but had become the 'moral fiber in the family diet. They were responsible for making the home peaceful, harmonious, and uplifting for their husbands and children',[9] a refuge from the corruption of work, a place of sweetness and light.

A woman was told that her 'destiny' was to be 'the keystone of the family circle',[10] 'the administratrix, mainspring, guiding star of the home'.[11] Yet because her sphere was narrowed by maternity, 'an element fixed imperatively by nature',[12] she was warned that in concentrating on her role as a mother she ran the risk of losing her husband's love, and of becoming 'so utterly indifferent to anything outside the range of her maternal administrations, that she voluntarily lays aside all the accomplishments in which as a young woman she has rejoiced and which had formed no small item in the attractions by which she had gained the object of her maidenly ambition – a good husband.'[13] The late nineteenth century saw the first of the multitude of articles in women's magazines that advise mothers to be careful not to let themselves 'go' in case they lose their man.

As the wealth of the middle classes increased mothers, while remaining the symbolic focus of the household, had less and less to do with child-rearing. They came in for criticism from doctors for leaving their babies to the wet-nurse, neglecting their duties, and letting others mould their children's impressionable minds while they spent their time in frivolous pastimes.[14] When women attempted to invade male preserves and to aspire to higher education and entering the professions, they were sternly censured. Professor J. Stuart Blackie, for instance, in a book written for the guidance of women, pronounced that 'in the face of so many manifest differences, both physical and moral, it seems difficult for an impartial mind to believe absolutely in the cerebral equality of the sexes.'[15] It was acceptable, however, for middle- and upper-class women to do charitable work. Women represented the conscience of the nation, and they improved conditions in workhouses, prisons and schools, and among prostitutes, orphans and the poor.

Simultaneously there was a movement towards the training of mothers through a new pedagogical-psychological literature. Women were told that they should, above all, be consistently firm and unemotional with their children. Experts believed that women were incapable of mothering well unless they were guided in how to do it, and even higher education was subordinated to this purpose. The President of Bryn Mawr College in the USA defended women's colleges, stating that: 'Women cannot conceivably be given an education too broad, too high or too deep to fit them to become the educated mothers of the future race of men and women born of educated parents. The pity is that we only have the four years of the college course to impart such knowledge to women who are to be the mothers.'[16] In the USA, the new cult of motherhood found expression in the setting up of the Society for the Study of Child Nature (1888) and the National Congress of Mothers in 1897, organizations which merged in 1910 into the National Congress of Parents and Teachers.

By the 1930s the teachings of Sigmund Freud were being popularized and disseminated in women's magazines and in instructional books for mothers. Women now had to study the skills of 'mothercraft', and with this came the awesome responsibility not only to rear perfectly healthy children, but also to prevent neurosis, psychosis and other psychological illnesses, and to ensure, by the consistent and enlightened care they gave, a child's future psychic health. For middle-class women, motherhood had become a full-time occupation.

It was not until the Second World War, when they were called on to fill the jobs of men who had gone to war, and when British children were evacuated in large numbers to rural areas and put in the care of strangers, that middle-class mothers could with a clear conscience again work outside the home. This soon came to an end once the war was over. Peace brought with it a new emphasis on domesticity. Though it was accepted that women were in the market for employment, 'Women as mothers were taken to be wholly different beings, assumed to be always outside production, pursuing a distinct "creative" task of childbearing'.[17] There was a great deal of popular psychology written to and about 'the Mother', which depicted her as the disembodied incarnation of love, who never had to earn a living and had no interests and concerns other than her children.

Working Mothers Today

Today, two out of five British women with children below school age are employed outside the home, with more than twice as many working part time as full time.[18] This part-time work tends to be low-status, badly paid, non-pensionable, and denies women career opportunities. Yet it is for many women the only option, because child care arrangements are incredibly complicated and they are forced to rely on other people's good-will. As one woman doctor comments: 'The female job-sharing brain surgeon remains the futuristic fantasy of retainer scheme GPs in wart removal clinics.'[19]

The issues concerning working mothers raise questions about the education of girls, job opportunities for women, and the gap that exists almost everywhere between men's and women's wages. In Britain, in spite of sixteen years of laws against sex discrimination, women's pay is still only two thirds that of men, and jobs in which women workers predominate, such as speech therapy and nursery school teaching, consistently pay less than does comparable work for men. Britain's record on leave and benefits for working mothers is among the worst in Europe, and in 1991 Britain condemned a proposal by the European Commission that pregnant women should be entitled to at least fourteen weeks' leave on full pay with no loss of pension or promotion prospects.

Women are seeking opportunities for retraining and up-dating their skills after taking time off to have babies, and would like options such as home-based employment, job-sharing, flexi-time, and, yes, when it is their choice, part-time work. Many institutions have such uncompromising management structures and autocratic hierarchies that women find it impossible to continue working if they have children. In the National Health Service, for example, one in seven student nurses do not finish their basic training, and half the rest never return from honeymoon or maternity leave.[20] All the questions about who is going to look after the children must be tackled. Even if job prospects are good and women have managed to iron out everything else, many of them confront insurmountable obstacles in trying to find reliable, high quality child care. On top of this, unless women live in urban areas there is often no low-cost public transport to enable them to get to work, or their children to a nursery.

The debate about returning to work outside the home is a spurious one when there is no quality child care available, and when child care workers are themselves, as at present, among the lowest paid of all workers. Care of different kinds must be provided to suit children of different ages. Until about the age of two most children seem to need the security and continuity of a one-to-one relationship with not more than two or three loving primary care-givers, and it is vital that this nurturing closeness is offered. Yet even babies enjoy meeting different people. Their social capacities are often underestimated.[21] They are interested

213

in adults, older children and other babies long before they can say 'hello', and even before they can smile. A newborn baby will respond to and gaze at an older sibling. When babies who are only a few weeks old are in the right mood for social contact, and someone enters their visual field, their eyes open wide in concentration, and they watch and listen intently. Several weeks later they gaze steadily at an older child playing near them. They often respond with sympathetic awareness when another baby is distressed, and a one-year-old may reach out to comfort a crying child.

In the past, babies grew up in a social world from the beginning. Modern Western culture has stressed the mother-child bond to the detriment of these other bonds that may be an important element in the development of a child's social skills and sense of social responsibility. There has been a great deal of emphasis on the child's need for its mother, far less about what may also be a need for interaction with other children.

The two-year-old relishes an expanding social world, one in which there are other people, too, who are fun and can be trusted. In traditional societies there is often a lively community of children, ranging from babies to seven- or eight-year-olds, watched and tended by one or two mothers who are either taking time off from other chores or working nearby with an eye on the children. In these societies, as we have seen, there has never been any question of mothers being able to give their children uninterrupted personal attention. They have to get on with their work or the family will starve. The striking difference between technological and traditional cultures, however, is that traditionally women were able to take their babies to work with them, and that co-mothering, and sometimes even substitute mothering, from sisters, sisters-in-law, aunts, grannies and neighbours, was taken for granted. In traditional societies, too, there exists a common culture of mothering, so that child care is undertaken unselfconsciously and easily, based on the same values, and in the same style, whether it is the child's own mother or another woman acting in her place.

In technological culture, in contrast, co-mothers are hard to find, and there is virtually complete separation between home and work-place. Many mothers are socially isolated. The feminist barrister, Helena Kennedy, writes about how women with children have to compartmentalize their domestic and public lives:

The unspoken rule is never to mix the two, or evoke one in aid of the other. The image of the capable woman must never be tainted by the smell of baby powder; efficient women have that side of their lives well under control. Motherhood is like some skeleton kept in the cupboard and most of us collaborate in keeping our children invisible. We have the terrible fear that to concede that there are emotional pulls or practical complications will be used against us. In the legal profession, it is certainly more acceptable for a male counsel to explain his late arrival because of a car breakdown than it is for a woman counsel to evoke the illness of her children's nanny. Most judges are men of an older generation who feel that mothers of young children should not leave them anyway. Women therefore disguise the occasional hiccup in their domestic arrangements with the same broken-down car excuse as their male colleagues.

Recently, in a case in the Coroner's Court, one barrister asked the Court to rise early so that he could keep a pre-arranged appointment in connection with his legal practice. The Coroner was happy to oblige, but asked us all if we would sit at 8.30 a.m. the following day to catch up on lost time. I explained that as the mother of two young children, I could not easily re-arrange my childcare at such short notice. The Court sat at the usual time, but not without a lot of sighing and asides from Court staff about working mothers and our part in the degeneration of society.[22]

Helena Kennedy has a prestigious job and can buy the help she needs. There are many women who cannot afford paid help with their children, who are socially isolated, and even if they can call on help with child care from other women, confront the dissonance in mothering styles between women of different generations, social classes and cultural groups. When you hand over your child to someone else's care you cannot be at all sure that their values are the same as yours and that they will care for the child as you would.

In some Western societies, as in Britain, there is also a common assumption that for a woman with a young child to go back to work is self-indulgence. It reflects John Bowlby's teaching about 'maternal deprivation'. When his book *Child Care and the Growth of Love* was published in 1953 women were no longer needed in munitions factories, the land army and the armed forces, and they returned to their homes while men took over their jobs and provided financially for them and their children. Theories about the primacy of mother love were part of a larger social policy into which John Bowlby's ideas fitted neatly. In the fifties women were told that they were doing the right thing if they concentrated on domesticity and gave their children their continuing, comforting presence. Yet these beliefs represented a value system that was essentially middle-class, and could really only be implemented in families where there were two parents who were comfortably off so that the mother did not have to seek paid work outside the home, and also where violence and child abuse were unknown. It implied the security of a Janet and John existence.

Theories about maternal deprivation as the cause, and often the sole cause, of childhood psychological trauma cast a long shadow forward, so that even today women often believe that they must be all in all to their children, and that to let someone else care for them is to fail in the fundamental duty of a mother. That is to be close, loving and all-giving all the time.

These often passionately held beliefs are possible only because motherhood has been romanticized. The love, tenderness and deep satisfaction of motherhood has been focused on while the ambivalence, and emotions such as resentment, rage, a sense of being trapped, depression, and feelings of self-doubt and failure were ignored. Mothers dared not confess, even to themselves, that they did not fit the rosy picture of motherhood which was being promoted as the norm not only by the media, but by professional care-givers and psychological experts, and often also by other women. The romanticization and idealization of mothers persists today, and imposes on women a heavy burden.

Almost all mothers, in fact, are working mothers. The only exceptions are those who are so wealthy that they can hand over their children completely to the care of nannies, and can follow this up with boarding school, and that is a very small percentage of the population. The term 'working mother' is really a misnomer. It is used within the context of men's work patterns, with reference to their career goals, and as a way of dismissing and trivializing the work women do in the home. As

216

one woman protested: 'During the thirty-five years of my working life I have worked part-time, half-time and full-time, but when my three children were small, I worked all-the-bloody-time . . . !'[23]

One result of the romanticization of motherhood is that not only do women with children face enormous obstacles in getting employment, but that even when they succeed in overcoming difficulties, they often feel guilty about returning to work. The media investigate the harm that is caused to 'latch-key' children, a Prime Minister declares on the radio that 'we don't want a generation of crèche children', and salt is rubbed further into the wounds. At the same time, the British Government tentatively embarks on a policy to encourage women back into the work-force, but states that it is the responsibility of employers to provide child care – and then counters this by announcing that women should work part-time and get together with other women to organize child care. Then it changes tack and there is an announcement that mothers should be at home with their children for the first three or four years. No wonder women feel confused as well as guilty.

Not that all women *want* to work outside the home. To be forced to do so when you have young children can be just as bad as being denied work. In every country, including the wealthy nations of the West, where there is poverty women are among the poorest, especially women with children. They work because they must for their families to survive. It is often the birth of the first child that plunges a family into poverty. Income is slashed just as costs go up. In Britain today poverty is greatest among families with children, and above all in single-parent households.

In Communist countries, women have had to be in employment, and there has been no alternative to putting eighteen-month-old babies in a nursery unless a grandmother was available to provide child care. With the collapse of the Communist system in Eastern Europe, women celebrate the possibility of being able to stay at home and look after their children, and having the well-stocked shops, modern services and labour-saving equipment that make life easier for women in the West. Yet, even when this is not what women seek, in Czechoslovakia, Hungary and Poland, hundreds of thousands of women are being forced back to the kitchen sink because of the major economic problems their countries are facing and the rising unemployment that has been the result.[24] With the reunification of Germany women in what was East Germany, who for forty years have had 90 per cent employment and a free system of child care, lost many of their rights, with the result that female unemployment is soaring. It is also next to impossible to get an abortion, which, before 'restructuring', was freely available.

There are many mothers in the West, too, who feel under pressure to work outside the home when this is really not what they want when their children are young. They enjoy being full-time mothers at home, see bringing up children as a rewarding and stimulating task, and protest, as did one correspondent to a national newspaper, that 'the hardest thing I have to contend with is the lack of status and the derogatory attitudes of other people.'[25] We are constantly presented in women's magazines with the image of a high-flying career mother who, as one mother put it, 'takes a day off from the boardroom to produce, and as soon as the placenta hits the pedal bin she slides off the delivery table into her business suit, clips on her earrings, tosses the baby into the briefcase and drives the company car back to the office.'[26]

Some societies are organized so that women have a genuine choice. Sweden is an egalitarian society in which there are no very poor people and social services are good, especially so for single mothers and for all parents of young children. Either parent can choose to take fifteen months off work after a child is born. Fathers have the right to two weeks' fully paid leave following the birth, and two out of five take the whole fifteen months to care for their child. Each parent can take a number of paid days' absence from work each year to look after a child who is ill. Swedish couples now share equally in the task of caring for their sick children. The roles of men and women are undergoing dramatic changes to suit modern life-styles and goals, and institutions are changing to accommodate them. Couples are seeking employment which gives each of them 50 per cent time at work and 50 per cent at home.

In Swedish universities this has become a normal and accepted part of life. Employment possibilities of such a kind are still limited, and are largely in education, but gradually the system is spreading to other parts of Swedish society. At Stockholm University I was struck by the number of men wheeling buggies or with baby carriers on their backs as they did research or taught students. This happens because when parenthood is shared not only do fathers come into the home, but babies go out of it more and mobility becomes essential. The gulf between home and work-place disappears. This must have been more like it was for the hunter who carved arrowheads as his toddler watched, or the fisherman who mended nets as the children played beside him. Children can gain much from participating in the world outside the home, not only in planned play groups and carefully controlled child-centred environments, but in the hurly burly of adult activities. After all, they are going to grow up to become adults themselves.

In Britain the code-word for working women with children has to be 'gratitude'. Women are generally the lowest paid workers. When the value of a woman's life was estimated for the 1971 Roskill Inquiry into building a third London airport, it was revealed that average female incomes were so low that calculations 'suggested a net benefit to the economy if an aircraft crashed on a woman'.[27] Women with children do worse still. A mother has to be grateful to employers who allow her to shorten her working hours (reducing her pay in the process), grateful to employers who keep her on but delay promotion, or even demote her, so that she has the flexibility to care for a young child, and grateful also to her partner who 'will help if he's really needed', but who is merely an occasional helper when the going gets tough.[28]

Men's Work Patterns

Child care is not simply a women's issue. If we are to change employment patterns so that men can get to know their children, be active fathers and take their full share in family life, employers and governments will no longer be able to demand that men commit themselves to work as if their families did not exist, or were just a pleasant backdrop to real life. This will mean flexible working hours, job-share schemes, part-time work available for men and not just women, paternity as well as maternity leave, the recognition that parents of young children should be free to take time off work when children are ill or they have crises in family life, and the opportunity for men and women to have breaks from work, to work from home, and to vary their career patterns. Change in the home can occur only when there are radical changes in the work-place.

For those men who have been brought up according to a work ethic that forces them to ignore human needs – their own as well as other people's – and to value themselves only in terms of achievement in the world outside the home, this demands a rethinking of priorities. Most men have been reared this way in Western culture. They are trained to see home as the place to which they return that is free of the complex demands of the work-place, where they expect to find peace, and where they will be nurtured.

Yet the family – any family – also makes complex demands on each of its members, and human relationships in the family are no less demanding than in any other institution. Men often give family matters short shrift, and any help they offer with housework and child care is an optional extra, because they see the really important issues only in the world outside the home. This is one reason why mothers, including those working full-time with young children in the home, often feel so isolated.

Father Figures

Twenty or thirty years ago psychoanalysts wrote about how the father, 'free from all the noise and smell and responsibility of child care . . . provides a space in which the mother has elbow-room',[29] as if this were a God-ordained system, because only a mother can rear a child. John Bowlby introduced his theme of attachment between mother and baby with a passing reference to the father: 'While continual reference will be made to the mother-child relation, little will be said of the father-child relation: his value as the economic and social support of a mother will be assumed.'[30]

Many men now resist this stereotype of the father as the provider who offers only money and a strong shoulder. One father of a four-month-old daughter told me, 'I mind leaving her to go to work. I felt so close to her immediately she was born. We had a home birth and I spent ages just looking at her in the days that followed. She changed almost from hour to hour. I'm glad I didn't miss that unfolding of her as a person. But now Anna's taken over, she is the main person in her life because she is with her all the time.'

Another father thought it was inevitable that his partner

should be the one to care for their seven-month-old baby. 'I felt it was a woman's job – maternal instincts and all that. Her mother came to stay after the baby was born, and it was easier for me to be out of the house because I don't really get on with her. So I left them to it. But now I am wondering whether I've missed something. She isn't just a baby. She's got a tremendous personality. But I'm only just getting to know her.'

For fathers to become engaged with their children it is not simply a matter of emotional sensitivity to their needs. It entails new skills in the management of time, the learning of domestic crafts which for many men turn out to be much more complicated than they first appeared, the slow and painful acquisition of the art of being able to concentrate on several things at the same time, and full sharing in all the mess, dirt, muddle and anxiety of parenthood, as well as its pleasures.

The image of the new father first burst on the media scene in the late eighties, with pop-stars, princes and footballers who were sensitive and caring, and who got home in time to bath the children and read them a bed-time story. With the onset of the nineties a run of Hollywood films about the family in which fatherhood was centre-stage proved to be box-office draws. They were either tear-jerkers or comedies in which the man was left holding the baby and which projected the reassuring message that 'families are fun'.

It is sometimes assumed that because a man has not been pregnant and given birth and because he cannot breastfeed he cannot possibly meet a baby's needs. This is as if to say that a mother who is bottle-feeding, or an adoptive mother, is not qualified to care for her baby. It is not biology that produces a human being capable of nurturing. As we have seen, mothering is learned, and it is learned best in an environment where the mother herself is nurtured and where she is supported by other adults. An important challenge we confront as a society is whether we allow men the chance to learn to be fathers, and whether they can become fathers not only in the biological but in the fully social sense.

For some women, especially those for whom any power they have is restricted to the home, this means that men are invading the last female territory. A woman may feel as if a man is usurping her role; and she feels deprived. Her self-esteem is tied up with her domestic skills and her control of that small territory

221

within the four walls of home. This is how it was for one woman, furious with her husband, who said, 'Alan was on an oil rig the first time round and it was great. I just got on with it, asking for his help when he was around, but enjoying my mothering. Of course, I was tired but I felt this was something I was doing, and he admired me for it, was envious and a little in awe of me. This time round he is out of work and really keen on being this new father. I hate it. He is always barging in and telling me what to do. He still doesn't wash the sick off the Babygro, of course, but he thinks he is so great.'[31]

But in this case it was not just that the only role in which this woman felt she was functioning efficiently, and from which she derived personal satisfaction, was being eroded. Men are used to wielding power, to being in charge, and they often find it difficult to share and to help. Instead, they take over. They prefer to give directions, to manage, rather than to learn how to work in harmony in a partnership in which there is no boss.

Men also sometimes see the pursuit of empathy as an end in itself, and one for which they must be rewarded. Groups in which they learn to express their emotions, to touch, and to rid themselves of male machismo and toughness are an off-shoot of sixties' human potential psychology. 'I feel, I touch, I cry. Therefore I am a New Man.' There is nothing more irritating for a woman than a male who thinks he is a New Man, even claiming to be a 'feminist', and who cannot understand why women do not see him this way.

There is the man, for example, who spends hours with his ears resting against a woman's abdominal wall as he talks to his unborn child, delighted that in the last few months of pregnancy the baby will respond to his voice and even his touch. He can even buy an 'empathy belly', strapping on a belt to constrict his lungs, with a weighted pouch protruding beneath it with lead balls that roll around inside it to mimic foetal movements, and with special uncomfortable pressure over his bladder. The ultimate 'togetherness' for him is when a man can experience pregnancy!

As I wrote this last sentence, a male journalist who was writing a feature about reproductive technology rang me and invited me to comment on the prospects of male pregnancy. The technology is now so far advanced in Australia, his own country, that it is possible for men to be treated with a cocktail

222

of hormones and to have an embryo implanted and fixed against their gut or abdominal wall. He told me that fifteen men had already applied to an IVF research team wanting to have this done. I suspect that few men are going to want to put up with the discomforts of pregnancy, perhaps with an artificial placenta strapped to them like a growbag, or to endure the Caesarean section that will be necessary in order for the baby to be born. But the point is that it is not necessary for men to imitate female biology in order to be good fathers, and if men do decide that they want to take over pregnancy and childbirth many women will suspect that they are really saying, 'Anything you can do, I can do better.'

Being able to tune in to pregnancy, and the realization that it is not just an inanimate object inside the uterus but a living being, can be as important for a prospective father as it is for a mother, but to treat a man's fascination with pregnancy as if it were an exotic bloom is to set up an act which it is almost impossible to sustain in the evolving relationship with his partner and with his child over the months and years that follow. There is a risk that pregnancy and birth are treated as the high points of fatherhood, and that means that there is nowhere afterwards but downhill.

The Invisible New Man

As Mia Farrow says in the film *The Purple Rose of Cairo*, 'I've just met this gorgeous man. He's fictional – but then you can't have everything!'

The fictional New Father is tender, caring, sharing, changes dirty nappies without demur and accepts responsibility for domestic work and for child care without fuss. He is right there in the cologne advertisements showing that fatherhood is fragrant and in those for fast cars demonstrating how parenthood, too, is exciting. Here he is in his pinstripe suit, a banker or stockbroker, with a baby in a sling on his back instead of a briefcase in his hand. It looks as if a baby is the best accessory.

The New Father appears in TV comedies about family life reassuring us that all the problems connected with children are solvable and that it is just a matter of being easy and relaxed like he is and making friends with your kids. He is there, too, in newspaper and magazine profiles of successful men who take time off to be with their families. There he is, baby in his arms, kicking a ball around with a toddler, flying kites with the older children, rustling up a meal in the kitchen. There is the economist with triplets. If the nanny is off-duty in the evening 'he is presented with a series of clean, hungry boys to bottle-feed which he tries to do while watching television,' his wife says. 'I remove one baby and replace him with another as the first becomes noisy, smelly or sleepy.'[32]

Many men do not want to take on the New Father role. They protest that since they are providing well for their families it is demanding too much of them. They spend long hours in the work-place and, in Britain especially, often rely on overtime to bring in enough money. The European Commission reveals that one in three British fathers works more than 50 hours a week, and that approximately 46,000 fathers with children under nine are putting in 98 hours or more at the office.[33]

When he is at home a man tends to select a symbolic household or child care task which provides justification for opting out of other jobs. He may empty the kitchen wastebins, clean the family car, exercise the dog, make mayonnaise or bake bread while his female partner continues to do most of the other household chores, even when she has a full-time job outside the home. It is for her a second shift, but one that she is usually expected to do because she is a woman. Arlie Hochschild, in her study of dual-working parents, says that, 'Men converted a single act into a substitute for a multitude of chores in the second shift – a token.' On average, American women in the past two decades have 'worked roughly fifteen hours longer each week than men. In a year that adds up to an extra month of twenty-four hour days.'[34]

Hochschild found that in describing a typical day 97 per cent of women talked about the house, but only 54 per cent of their male partners did so. Ninety-seven per cent of mothers mentioned their children, but only 69 per cent of fathers. Women did 75 per cent of the housework. Only 18 per cent of men shared housework equally with their partners, and 61 per cent of men did little or none. Only those women who earned more than their partners did less than half the household tasks. Contrary to expectations, working-class men did rather more housework than the middle-class professionals, who were more likely to express liberal views about women working.

224

Women do around 70 per cent of all unpaid work. An Australian study revealed that, on average, a woman clocks up approximately thirty-six hours of unpaid work a week, while a man does less than half that.[35] However many hours of paid work a woman does, her husband's contribution to work at home remains the same. Microwaves, dishwashers, washing machines and freezers have not made much difference. The average woman still spends as much time in the kitchen and doing laundry as she did thirteen years ago, when there were far fewer automatic machines. In fact, shopping, child care and other housework take longer than they used to, while gardening, a job often done by men, is one of the few tasks that is actually taking less time now than it used to. The result is that women have less leisure time than they had back in the seventies.

When a woman marries she automatically increases her unpaid work by nearly 60 per cent. She spends almost twice the time cooking, clearing up and doing laundry than she did when she was single. Statistics show that laundry is one of the jobs that men are eager to hand over as soon as they can find a woman to do it, since a married woman spends nine times as long washing, drying and ironing as her male partner.

As soon as she has a child her unpaid work shoots up again by 91 per cent, to close on fifty-six hours a week, whereas a new father does no more unpaid work than before the baby was born. As they grow up, children contribute proportionately very little to housework and cooking. For every hour of unpaid work done by a son of fifteen, a daughter does 1 hour 20 minutes, a father 2 hours 45 minutes, and a mother 6 hours 30 minutes, and other members of the family contribute very little extra even when the mother is employed outside the home as well.

A psychological study of first-time mothers, which included them keeping diaries of their working day, disclosed that fathers were very reluctant to help, except on their own terms, and when they did so it had 'the status of the gift to the mother'.[36] The man usually spent around 20 minutes alone with his child during the 24 hours, compared with the mother's 6 hours.

It is very difficult for a woman to negotiate the help she needs from her partner when she has just had a baby, because it is a time when she is vulnerable and when, because there are few alternative sources of support for her, she is thrown back on to the relationship with him. It is also a time when, because she may no longer be employed, or is earning much less than before, she is economically dependent on him. The man can always choose which tasks he performs. These rarely include changing a dirty nappy, and much more often turn out to be playing with or tucking the child up in bed at night. When a man does help, it usually releases the woman so that she can get on with other jobs, rather than giving her any free time.

Sometimes women get so exhausted and depressed, and so caught up in conflict between ideals of equality and sharing parenthood on the one hand and the reality of a situation in which men expect women to get on with it, that the only answer, if they could afford it, is to get paid help. But that does not really resolve the issue of inequality. It simply means having another woman to do the work.

Women often believe that the difficulties they meet are unique to them, and that when they feel angry, frustrated and despairing, it is because there is something wrong with them. But 'the problem lies not in a mother's individual circumstances, but in the role of motherhood itself, which entails an exploitation of women's love for their children and for their partners, thus inducing them to accept working conditions which would not be tolerated in the male workplace.'[37]

A feminist writer, Pat Mainardi, wrote a monologue in the seventies that may still be familiar to many women twenty years on:

> — *I don't mind sharing the housework, but I don't do it very well. We should each do the things we're best at.*
> **Meaning**: *Unfortunately I'm no good at things like washing dishes or cooking. What I do best is a little light carpentry, changing light bulbs, moving furniture . . .*
> **Also meaning**: *Historically, the lower classes . . . have had hundreds of years' experience doing menial jobs. It would be a waste of manpower to train someone else to do them now.*
> **Also meaning**: *I don't like the dull stupid boring jobs, so you should do them.*
> — *I don't mind sharing the work, but you'll have to show me how to do it.*

Meaning: *I ask a lot of questions and you'll have to show me everything every time I do it . . . Also don't try to sit down and read while I'm doing my jobs because I'm going to annoy the hell out of you until it's easier to do them yourself.*[38]

And so on. The New Father must be out there somewhere, but he is a rare and endangered species.

Yet even when a man is happy to spend time with his children and to take on responsibility for child care there may be problems. There is no easy answer, nor one that is right for all couples and for all children. Many women want men to share their lives and to involve themselves with their children, but they are trapped in a double bind because they know that children are often sexually abused by fathers and other men in the family.

When a woman leaves a child with her male partner who turns out to have used the opportunity for a sexual assault on the child, it is she who is always blamed. It is implied that the child has been abused because she was not doing her duty as a mother, and was frittering her time away shopping or fulfilling herself in a career at the expense of her child. In one American court case the lawyer declared that 'this woman repeatedly went to the grocery store leaving this child alone with her father.' In one widely reported British case a father who was a house-husband killed his child, and a psychiatrist commented that he could have foretold that this was likely to happen because it was a 'highly unnatural' arrangement.

Much of the discussion about child abuse refers evasively to 'parents' or to 'adults' and the damage they can do to children. Yet it is almost always men who are the abusers. They are uncles, grandfathers, fathers and stepfathers, and the abused child is usually a girl. The abusers look perfectly ordinary, they are men with respected careers, and are from all social classes.

When I started studying social anthropology I soon realized that social systems are all about male power and the way in which men organize themselves so as to own, exploit and exchange women and children. Men are valued in terms of their work and achievements. Women have an identity merely because of their relationship with men. Women service men, women keep them sweet, and try to teach their daughters how to service and keep them sweet. In any family system where women and children are treated as a man's property, making use of them sexually is the logical outcome of possessing them. The Victorian ideals of the family are the lid on a cesspit. If you look underneath you find abuse of both women and children.

Today we still have a social system that sets children up not only for sexual exploitation but for abuse of all kinds. We must look at the ways in which men wield power and treat children as if they were their property. For we do not own our children.

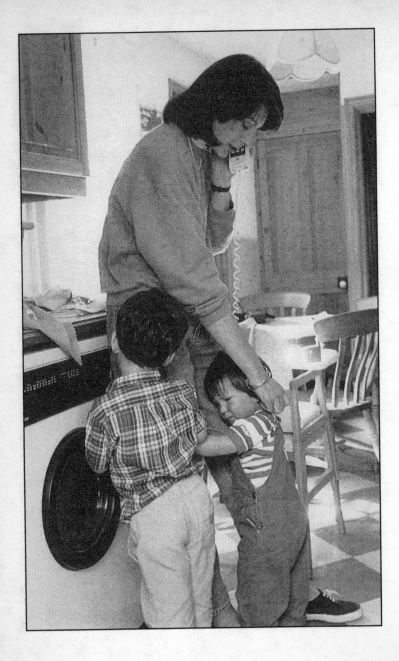

13

Is There A Future For Motherhood?

Looking at how it is to be a mother in other societies can give us a new perspective on our own culture. By studying other cultures we see more clearly both the benefits and the difficulties of being mothers in the industrialized West. We see, too, how stresses in our lives which we may have put down to flaws in personality, to our personal inability to cope, are caused by the ways in which the motherhood role is moulded by social forces. The pressures imposed on women can be changed only at a social and political level, and by women joining together to improve conditions for mothers, children and families.

Societies which we think of as 'simple', 'underdeveloped', 'primitive' or at least 'unsophisticated' may in fact have something to teach those of us who live in the West. We become aware of the living substance of women's experiences as they pass through the transformations of pregnancy and birth and go on to nurture their children. We see the support that women give each other through life crises, the closeness of mother and baby during the first months, and the power of women's shared lives together. And perhaps we take a fresh look at our own culture.

While technology has given us a much higher standard of living, and saved women from the backbreaking work of carrying fuel, drawing water and washing clothes in the river, our industrial, technological culture has stripped motherhood of many of its traditional multi-dimensional aspects. The responsibilities women had historically for healing, education and birthing, for example, have all been requisitioned by the professions. The result is that

231

women as mothers have been dispossessed and the motherhood role impoverished.

Yet the skills of mothering in other cultures cannot be simply transplanted piecemeal to our own. It is not a question of imitating aspects of behaviour that appeal to us, but rather of creating the social conditions in our own society in which women can find loving support from other women and from men, are free to be flexible in their mothering styles, can share their experiences with each other and can grow in confidence.

Women as mothers are denied positive social recognition, although much lip-service is paid to it, because in an industrial culture success is measured by performance in the world outside the home, rather than by everything that goes on inside it. There is a complete split between the two worlds of the public and the private, between on the one hand the world of important social activities – business and government, wheeling and dealing, the negotiations, fraternizations, alliances and the making and breaking of male systems of power – and on the other the concealed world of the home.

This is not just a domestic issue. Whole societies are organized to keep women as property to be handed down between men and exchanged between groups in which fathers rule. And indeed, today there is a pendulum swing back to values that reinforce the subordination of women. In the West welfare spending is slashed and there are cutbacks on social services and an increasing romanticization of babies and family life. In many parts of the world there is a rise in the religious fundamentalism that keeps women captive in the home, shrouds them in black, hides their faces behind veils, and, at best, treats them like domestic pets.

Housework and motherhood are political issues. They challenge us to political action, both at the national and international level, to eradicate discriminatory practices which ensure that women's work is either lower paid than men's or has to be done voluntarily, and that it must be concentrated in caring for the needs of the young and the elderly. This is not to undervalue the work that women do in these spheres, but it is not the only work of which they are capable. When women have no opportunity to have successful careers in business, science and the arts, it is a tremendous waste of their talents. At present, female employment is mainly in the service sector – in hospitals, schools and offices. Even there, a cleaner gets paid more than a child-minder. Yet in introducing job opportunities and retraining schemes, and ensuring that there is good child care so that women are free to fulfil their potential, men also need to change. They will have to accept responsibility for many of the things now done by women, because otherwise there will be no one to do them. This means that men must be willing to take on equal responsibility for housework.

Mothers are, above all, those who nurture. They are also those who plan, who manage, who work much longer hours than men, and who make life possible for other people.

In adverse circumstances, in war and famine, in tents in the desert in North Africa, in shacks like rotten teeth clinging to the mudscape of shanty towns in South America, dispossessed of their land in concrete block rows in South African townships, in highrise inner-city flats in Britain where public walkways are scrawled with obscene graffiti, crouching behind wire fences in refugee camps in the Middle East, with babies finding comfort from their shrivelled breasts, and reaching out bowls for food to stem their children's hunger – these are the mothers of the world, linked in sisterhood because they each know how to tend the flame of new life, to rear a child for the people. Each grieves over her children who die, worries about them when they are ill, comforts them in distress, encourages them to walk even though they stumble, to discover the precious gift of language, to explore the world around them, and to learn about their culture.

We are not extraordinary women. Yet we know how to nurture. We are mothers.

References

Chapter 1

1 Sana Al Khayyat, *Honour and Shame: Women in Modern Iraq*, London: Saqi, 1990

2 S.A. Morsy, 'Childbirth in an Egyptian Village', in Margaret Artschwager Kay (ed.), *Anthropology of Human Birth*, Philadelphia: F.A. Davis, 1982

3 *Oxford Times*, 8 February 1991

4 B. Bernstein, 'Theoretical studies towards a sociology of language', *Class, Codes and Control*, vol. 1, London: Routledge, 1973; B. Bernstein (ed.), 'Applied studies towards a sociology of language', *Class, Codes and Control*, vol. 2, London: Routledge, 1973; E. and J. Newson, *Infant Care in an Urban Community*, London: Allen and Unwin, 1963; E. and J. Newson, *Four Year Olds in an Urban Community*, London: Allen & Unwin, 1968

5 J. Brannen and P. Moss, *Managing Mothers: Dual Earner Households After Maternity Leave*, London: Unwin Hyman, 1990

6 Sheila Kitzinger, *The Crying Baby*, Harmondsworth: Penguin, 1989

7 D.W. Winnicott, *The Maturational Processes and the Facilitating Environment*, London: Hogarth Press, 1965

8 H.Z. Lopata, *Occupation: Housewife*, Oxford: Oxford University Press, 1971

9 Ann Oakley, 'Towards a sociology of childbirth', *Women Confined*, Oxford: Martin Robinson, 1980

Chapter 2

1 Daniel H.H. Ingalls (trans.), *Sanskrit Poetry from Vidyadara's Treasury*, Cambridge, MA: Harvard University Press, 1968

2 I. Schapera, *Married Life in an African Tribe*, Harmondsworth: Pelican, 1971

3 Lois Paul, 'Work and Sex in a Guatemalan Village', in Michelle Zimbalist

Rosaldo and Louise Lamphere (eds.), *Woman, Culture and Society*, Palo Alto, CA: Stanford University Press, 1974

4 G.R. Leslie, *The Family in Social Context*, New York: Oxford University Press, 2nd edition, 1973

5 D.P. Moynihan, *The Negro Family: The Case for National Action*, Washington, DC: Office of Policy Planning and Research, Department of Labor, 1965

6 V. Uchendu, quoted by Nancy Towner in Michelle Zimbalist Rosaldo and Louise Lamphere (eds.), *Woman, Culture and Society*, Palo Alto, CA: Stanford University Press, 1974

7 G.P. Murdock, *Social Structure*, New York: Macmillan, 1949

8 Helene Deutsch, *Psychology of Women*, vol. I, New York: Grune & Stratton, 1944

9 Sheila Kitzinger, 'When Im Seem Bellyful Im Burps and Stops: Breastfeeding Contrasts', *Health Visitor*, 49, 1976; 'Communicating with Immigrant Mothers', in N.L. Kellmer-Pringle (ed.), *Caring for Children*, London: Longman, 1969

10 L. Kohlberg, 'A cognitive-developmental analysis of children's sex-role concepts and attitudes', in Eleanor E. Macavey (ed.), *The Development of Sex Differences*, Palo Alto, CA: Stanford University Press, 1966

11 Leslie, op. cit.

Chapter 3

1 A Kharia chant, quoted in Verrier Elwin, *Folk Songs of Chattisgarh*, Oxford: Oxford University Press, 1946

2 A Hottentot song, translated by and quoted in Willard R. Trask, *The Unwritten Song: Poetry of the Traditional and Primitive Peoples of the World*, vol. 1, New York: Macmillan, 1966

3 A Didinga mother's song, translated by and quoted in Jack Driberg, *Initiation: Translations from the Poems of the Didinga and Lango Tribes*, London: Golden Cockerel Press, 1932

4 I. Schapera, *Married Life in an African Tribe*, Harmondsworth: Pelican, 1971

5 F.N. Clive Wood and Beryl Suiters, *The Fight For Acceptance: A History of Contraception*, London: Medical and Technical Publishing Company, 1970

6 Jean Medawar and David Pyke (eds.), *Family Planning*, Harmondsworth: Pelican, 1971

7 Ibid.

8 Ibid.

9 E.A. Wrigley, 'Family Limitation in the Past', in Medawar and Pyke, op. cit.

10 Medawar and Pyke, op. cit.

11 Ibid.

12 S.A. Morsy, 'Childbirth in an Egyptian Village', in Margaret Artschwager Kay (ed.), *Anthropology of Human Birth*, Philadelphia: F.A. Davis, 1982

13 Ibid.

14 C. Steven, 'The unnatural selection of suitable parents', *Independent*, 23 October 1987

15 M.B. Rosental, 'Psychological Implications of New Reproductive Technology', in Eylard van Hall and Walter Everard (eds.), *The Free Woman: Women's Health in the 1990s*, Cornforth: Parthenon Publishing, 1989

16 E. Freeman, M. Freeman et al., 'Psychological Evaluation and Support in Programs of *in vitro* Fertilization and Embryo Transfer', *Fertility and Sterility*, 43(1), 1985, pp.48–53

17 I. Craft, P. Brinsden, P. Lewis et al., 'Multiple Pregnancy, Selective Reduction and Flexible Treatment', *Lancet*, ii, 1988, p.1087

18 *Observer*, 30 June 1991

19 F. Price, *Three, Four or More: A Study of Triplet and Higher Order Births*, Her Majesty's Stationery Office, 1990

20 *The Australian*, 15 September 1989

21 D. Roher, personal communication

22 Ibid.

Chapter 4

1 Richard Lannoy, *The Speaking Tree: A Study of Indian Culture and Society*, Oxford: Oxford University Press, 1971. I am drawing particularly on Lannoy's material in this chapter

2 A. Ross, *The Hindu Family in its Urban Setting*, Toronto: Toronto University Press, 1961

3 K. Shridharani, *My India, My America*, New York: Duel, Sloan and Perce, 1941, quoted in Lannoy, op. cit.

4 L. Minturn and J.T. Hitchcock, *The Rhajputs of Khalapur, India*, New York: Wiley, 1966

5 Lannoy, op. cit.

6 H. Hubert and M. Mauss, *Essay on the Nature and Function of Sacrifice*, London: Cohen & West, 1965

7 The Athar-Veda, quoted in Lannoy, op. cit.

8 Lannoy, op. cit.

9 Chaim Bermant, *The Walled Garden: The Saga of Jewish Family Life and Tradition*, London: Weidenfeld & Nicolson, 1974. I am particularly indebted to this work for the information contained in this section

10 Quoted in Bermant, op. cit.

11 Bermant, op. cit.

12 Quoted in Bermant, op. cit.

13 Leviticus 20:18

14 Bermant, op. cit.

15 Quoted in Bermant, op. cit.

16 Bermant, op. cit.

17 Ibid.

18 J. De Boulay, *Portrait of a Greek Mountain Village*, Oxford: Oxford University Press, 1974. I am indebted to this book for much of the information in this section

19 De Boulay, op. cit.

20 J.K. Campbell, *Honour, Family and Patronage: A Study of Institutions and Values in a Greek Mountain Community*, London: Clarendon Press, 1964

21 Campbell, op. cit.

22 De Boulay, op. cit.

23 Ibid.

24 Ibid.

Chapter 5

1 J.M. Whitworth, *God's Blueprints: A Sociological Study of Three Utopian Sects*, London: Routledge, 1975

2 C. Nordhoff, *The Communistic Societies of the United States*, New York: Dover, 1966 (this edition is a reprint of the original work, which was first published by Harper & Row in 1875)

3 Pierrpont Noyes, 'A Goodly Heritage', quoted in Nordhoff, op. cit.

4 René Spitz, 'Anaclitic Depression', in *A Psychoanalytic Study of the Child*, vol. 2, London: International Universities Press, 1946; John Bowlby, *Attachment and Loss*, Harmondsworth: Penguin, 1971

5 Nordhoff, op. cit.

6 D. Davin, *Woman-work: Women and the Party in Revolutionary China*, Oxford: Oxford University Press, 1976. I am grateful for material from this book used in this section

7 M. Wolf, 'Chinese women: old skills in a new context', in *Women and the Family in Rural Taiwan*, Palo Alto, CA: Stanford University Press, 1972

8 Lyn Durward, 'One Happiness', *Maternity Action* 45, 1990, pp.6–7

9 Chaim Bermant, *The Walled Garden: The Saga of Jewish Family Life and Tradition*, London: Weidenfeld & Nicolson, 1974

Chapter 6

1 Nancy Towner, 'Matrifocality in Indonesia and Africa and Among Black Americans', in Michelle Zimbalist Rosaldo and Louise Lamphere (eds.), *Woman, Culture and Society*, Palo Alto, CA: Stanford University Press, 1974

2 E.P. Skinner, 'Christianity and Islam Among the Mossi', in John Middleton (ed.), *Gods and Rituals*, Austin: University of Texas Press, 1976

3 M. Douglas, *Purity and Danger*, Harmondsworth: Penguin, 1970

4 Ibid.

5 Lois Paul, 'Work and Sex in a Guatemalan Village', in Michelle Zimbalist Rosaldo and Louise Lamphere (eds.), *Woman, Culture and Society*, Palo Alto, CA: Stanford University Press, 1974

6 Carolyn Niethammer, *Daughters of the Earth: The Lives and Legends of American Indian Women*, London: Collier Macmillan, 1977

7 C. Turnbull, *Wayward Servants*, London: Eyre and Spottiswoode, 1966

8 Veronic Evaneshko, 'Tonawanda Seneca childbearing culture', in Margaret Artschwager Kay (ed.), *Anthropology of Human Birth*, Philadelphia: F.A. Davis, 1982

9 S.A. Morsy, 'Childbirth in an Egyptian Village', in Kay, op. cit.

10 D. Sich, 'Conflict between modern obstetrics and East Asian traditional birthing systems: The Korean Case', in O. Teizo, (ed.), *History of Obstetrics*, Osaka: Taniguchi Foundation, 1982

11 J. Hendry, *Marriage in Changing Japan*, Beckenham: Croom-Helm, 1981, p.200

12 B. Thompson, 'Infant Feeding and Child Care in a West African Village', *Journal of Tropical Pediatrics*, 13, 3, 1967

13 Sheila Kitzinger, *Change in Antenatal Care*, London: National Childbirth Trust, 1980; Jo Garcia, 'Women's Views of Antenatal Care', in M. Enkim and I. Chalmers (eds.), *Effectiveness and Satisfaction in Antenatal Care*, London: Spastics International Medical Publications and Heinemann, 1982

14 Sheila Kitzinger, *Some Women's Experiences of Induced Labour*, London: National Childbirth Trust, 2nd edition, 1978 (out of print)

15 N.J. Eastman and E. Jackson, 'Weight Relationships in Pregnancy', *Obstetric and Gynaecological Survey*, 23, 1968, pp. 1003–10; J.E. Westphal and M. and K. Niswander, 'Relationship of weight gain during pregnancy to birthweight and infant growth in first years of life', Report from collaborative study of cerebral palsy, *Obstetrics and Gynecology*, 31, 1968, pp.417–22; E.F. Hytten, 'Weight gain in pregnancy – 30 years of research', *South African Medical Journal*, 60, 1981, pp.15–19

16 L.M. Dunlop Furness, 'Maternal haemoglobin concentration, haematocrit and renal handling of urate in pregnancies ending in the birth of small-for-dates infants', *British Journal of Obstetrics and Gynaecology*, 85, 1978, pp.938–40; G. Maw, 'Haemoglobin changes during pregnancy and growth disturbances in the neonate', *Journal of Perinatal Medicine*, 5, 1977, pp.172–7; O. Koller et al. 'Fetal growth retardation associated with inadequate haemodilution in otherwise uncomplicated pregnancy', *Acta Obstetrica Gynecologica*, Scandinavia, 82, 1979, pp.656–61

17 D.E. Soper, C.G. Marshall and H.P. Dalton, 'Risk factors for intra-amniotic infection: A prospective epidemiological study', *American Journal of Obstetrics and Gynecology*, 161, 3, 1989, pp.562–8

18 J. Kitzinger, 'Strategies of the early childbirth movement: A case study of the NCT', in Jo Garcia, Robert Kilpatrick and Martin Richards (eds.), *The Politics of Maternity Care*, London: Clarendon, 1990

19 I. Velvovsky et al., *Painless Childbirth Through Psychoprophylaxis*, Moscow: Foreign Languages Publishing House, 1960

20 P. Briance, *Natural Childbirth Association Newsletter*, 2 March 1957

21 J. Kitzinger, in Garcia, Kilpatrick and Richards, op. cit., p.99

22 *New Generation*, April 1968

23 E. Bing and R. Ramel, *A Practical Training Course for the Psychoprophylactic Method of Painless Childbirth*, New York: Bantam, 1961

24 J. Kitzinger, 'Minutes of Area Organisers' Meetings (1960)', in Garcia, Kilpatrick and Richards, op. cit.

Chapter 7

1 V.W. Turner, 'Ritual as communication and potency: a Ndembu case study', *Proceedings of the Southern Anthropology Society*, 9, 1, 1975

2 *Safe Motherhood Newsletter* 1, November 1989–February 1990, p.7

3 A.W.O. Hassall, *How They Lived 55 BC–1458*, Oxford: Blackwell, 1962

4 R.M. Berndt, *Three Faces of Love*, Melbourne: Nelson, 1976

5 Margaret Mead, *Male and Female: A Study of the Sexes*, New York: Morrow, 1949

6 P.A. Rajadhon, *Some Traditions of the Thai*, Bangkok: Thai Inter-Religious Commission for Development and Sathirakoses Nagapradipa Foundation, 1987

7 Jane Richardson Hanks, 'Maternity and Its Rituals in Bang Chan', Data Paper No. 51, Southeast Asian Program, Dept. of Asian Studies, Cornell University, 1963, quoted in Judith Goldsmith, *Childbirth Wisdom from the World's Oldest Societies*, New York: East-West Health Books, 1990

8 Mead, op. cit.

9 J. Donnison, *Midwives and Medical Men*, London: Heinemann, 1977

10 Ritsuko Toda (ed.), *Childbirth in Japan*, Tokyo: Birth International, 1990

11 N.S. Dye, 'The Medicalization of Birth', in Pamela S. Eakins (ed.), *The American Way of Birth*, Philadelphia: Temple University Press, 1986

12 J.W. Leavitt, *Brought to Bed: Child-Bearing in America, 1750–1950*, New York: Oxford University Press, 1986

13 Dr. J.H. Guinn, quoted in Leavitt, op. cit. p.61

14 C. Dew, 'A child is born', *She*, Christmas 1988

15 K.E. Laman, *The Kongo*, Uppsala: Oxford University Press, 1957

16 Mary Beck Moser, 'Seri: From conception through infancy', in Margaret Artschwager Kay (ed.), *Anthropology of Human Birth*, Philadelphia: F.A. Davis, 1982

17 Kathleen West, in a traditional birth attendant case study for *Sierra Leone*, a report prepared for the World Health Organization, 1979

18 D.B. McGilvray, 'Sexual Power and Fertility in Sri Lanka: Batticaloa Tamils and Moors', in C.P. MacCormack (ed.), *Ethnography of Fertility and Birth*, London: Academic Press, 1982

19 A.J. Koopman, 'Prepared childbirth in native American culture', *ICEA Sharing*, VI, 3, 1979, pp.5–7

20 T. Ishihara, 'Development of Obstetrics and Gynecology in Japan and Resemblances to Western Counterparts', in O. Teizo (ed.), *History of Obstetrics*, Osaka: Taniguchi Foundation, 1982

21 Claude Levi-Strauss, *Structural Anthropology*, New York: Anchor Books, 1967

22 C. Laderman, *Wives and Midwives: Childbirth and Nutrition in Rural Malaysia*, Berkeley: University of California Press, 1983

23 Ibid.

241

24 D. Meltzer (ed.), *Birth*, New York: Ballantine Books, 1973

25 P.M. Dunn, 'Obstetric Delivery Today', *Lancet*, 10 April 1976

26 Ritsuko Toda, op. cit.

27 Mead, op. cit.

28 Ibid.

29 B. Thompson, 'Infant Feeding and Child Care in a West African Village', *Journal of Tropical Pediatrics*, 13, 3, 1967

30 J.G.B. Russell, 'The rationale of primitive delivery positions', *British Journal of Obstetrics and Gynaecology*, 89, 1982, pp.712–15

31 Dew, op. cit.

32 M. Flint, 'Lockmi: An Indian Midwife', in Kay, op. cit.

33 B. Jordan, *Birth in Four Cultures*, Montreal: Eden Press Women's Publications, 1978, p.25

34 Laderman, op. cit., p.151

35 F. Boas, *Ethnology of the Kwakiutl*, US Bureau of Ethnology, 35th Annual Report, 1913–14

36 J. Goodale, *Kiwi Wives: A Study of Women of Melville Island, Northern Australia*, Seattle: University of Washington Press, 1971

37 T. Szasz, *The Manufacture of Madness*, London: Routledge & Kegan Paul, 1971

38 Barbara Ehrenreich and Deirdre English, *Witches, Midwives and Nurses, A History of Women Healers*, New York: Glass Mountain Pamphlets, 1973

39 Ibid.

40 Mary Douglas, 'The Lele of the Kasai', in Daryll Forde (ed.), *African Worlds*, Oxford: Oxford University Press, 1954

41 Donnison, op. cit.

42 E. Nihell, *A Treatise on the Art of Midwifery: Setting Forth Various Abuses Therein, Especially as to the Practice with Instruments*, London: (publisher's name not available), 1758

43 T. Dawkes, quoted in Donnison, op. cit.

44 H. Graham, *Eternal Eve*, London: Hutchinson, 1950

45 *Lancet*, i, 1879, pp.746–7, quoted in J. Carter and T. Duriez, *With Child: Birth Through the Ages*, Edinburgh: Mainstream Publishing, 1986

46 I. Loudon, 'Obstetric care, social class, and maternal mortality', *British*

Medical Journal, 293, 1986, pp.606–8

47 J.P. Fairbairn, 'The medical and psychological aspects of gynaecology', *Lancet*, ii, 1931, pp.999–1004, quoted in Loudon, op. cit.

48 Carter and Duriez, op. cit.

49 Henry Jellet, *Causes and Prevention of Maternal Mortality*, London: (publisher's name not available), 1929, p.238, quoted in Carter and Duriez, op. cit.

Chapter 8

1 J. Waterman, 'The functions of the isthmus uteri', *Caribbean Medical Journal*, XIV, 1952, pp.3–4

2 D. Adams, D. Magnus and C. Seaforth, *Poisonous Plants in Jamaica*, Kingston: University of the West Indies, 1963

3 Vasamazulu Credo Mutwa (a Zulu witchdoctor), personal communication

4 Ibid.

Chapter 9

1 J.R. Wilson, C.T. Beecham and E.R. Carrington, *Obstetrics and Gynecology*, St Louis, MO: Mosby, 4th edition, 1971

2 E. Goffman, *Relations in Public: Microstudies of the Public Order*, Harmondsworth: Penguin, 1971

3 R.E. Davis-Floyd, 'The Role of Obstetrical Rituals in the Resolution of Cultural Anomaly', *Social Science and Medicine*, 31, 2, 1990, pp.175–89

4 E. Goffman, *Interaction Ritual – Essays on Face-to-face Behaviour*, Harmondsworth: Penguin, 1972

5 Ibid.

6 H. Kantor et al., 'Value of shaving the pudendal-perineal area in delivery preparation', *Obstetrics and Gynecology*, 25, 1965, pp.509–12

7 G.W. Theobald, 'The Induction of Labour', in D.F. Hawkins (ed.), *Obstetric Therapeutics*, London: Balliere-Tindall, 1974

8 Ibid.

9 J.F. Pearson, in R. Beard, M. Brudenell, P. Dunn and D. Fairweather (eds.), *The Management of Labour*, London: Royal College of Obstetricians and Gynaecologists, 1975

10 J. Selwyn-Crawford, in R. Beard et al., op. cit.

11 C.R. Whitfield, in R. Beard et al., op. cit.

12 S. Simmons, 'Induction of Labour', in R. Beard et al., op. cit.

13 K.K. Shy, D.A. Luthy, F.C. Bennett et al. (Department of Obstetrics and Gynecology, University of Washington, Seattle, WA), 'Effects of electronic fetal-heart-rate monitoring, as compared with periodic auscultation, on the neurologic development of premature infants', *New England Journal of Medicine*, 1 March 1990

14 Sheila Kitzinger, *Some Women's Experiences of Induced Labour*, London: National Childbirth Trust, 2nd edition, 1978

15 M.G. Elder and C.A. Hakim, 'The puerperium', in D.F. Hawkins, op. cit.

16 D.D. Moir, 'Drugs used in labour: analgesics, anaesthetics and sedatives', in D.F. Hawkins, op. cit.

17 D.H. Jones, 'Epidural analgesia in obstetrics', *Midwives Chronicle*, November 1975

18 J. Roth, 'Ritual and magic in the control of contagion', *American Social Review*, 22, 1957

19 J.F.R. Barrett et al., 'Inconsistencies in clinical decisions in obstetrics', *Lancet*, 336, 1990, pp.549–51

20 Sheila Kitzinger, *Woman's Experience of Sex*, Harmondsworth: Penguin, 1990

21 G.M. Bassell, S.G. Humayun and G.F. Marx, 'Maternal bearing-down efforts – another fetal risk?', *Obstetrics and Gynecology*, 56, 1980, pp.39–41; E. Noble, 'Controversies in maternal effort during labor and delivery', *Journal of Nurse-Midwifery*, 26, 1981, pp.13–22; C.S. Mahan and S. McKay, 'Are we overmanaging second-stage labor?', *Obstetrics and Gynecology*, December 1984

22 M. Harrison, *A Woman in Residence*, New York: Random House, 1982

23 D. Llewelyn Jones, *Fundamentals of Obstetrics and Gynaecology*, vol. 1, 'Obstetrics', London: Faber & Faber, 1973

24 Sheila Kitzinger and R. Walters, *Some Women's Experiences of Episiotomy*, London: National Childbirth Trust, 1981; Sheila Kitzinger, 'Episiotomy, body image and sex', in S. Kitzinger and P. Simkin (eds.), *Episiotomy and the Second Stage of Labor*, Seattle, WA: Penny Press, 1984

25 Ian Suttie, *The Origins of Love and Hate*, London: Routledge & Kegan Paul, 1935

26 A.D. Jones and C. Dougherty, 'Childbirth in a scientific and industrial society', in C.P. MacCormack (ed.), *Ethnography of Fertility and Birth*, London: Academic Press, 1982

27 Sheila Kitzinger, *The New Good Birth Guide*, London: Fontana, 1989

28 'Laughter's Medicine', *The Sunday Times*, 12 February 1989

29 E. Martin, *The Woman in the Body: A Cultural Analysis of Reproduction*, Boston, MA: Beacon Press, 1987

30 Franca Pizzini, 'The woman patient in an obstetrical situation: communicative hierarchies in humour', paper presented at the Third International Interdisciplinary Congress on Women, held in Dublin, July 1987

31 Ibid.

32 Claude Levi-Strauss, *The Savage Mind*, London: Weidenfeld & Nicolson, 1966

Chapter 10

1 A. Montagu, *Touching: The Human Significance of the Skin*, New York: Harper and Row, 1972

2 John Bowlby, *Attachment*, Harmondsworth: Penguin, 1965

3 K. Lorenz, *Methods of Approach to the Problems of Behavior*, New York: Academic Press (date not available)

4 Lorenz, op. cit.

5 Montagu, op. cit.

6 Ibid.

7 A. Gesell, 'The ontogenesis of infant behaviour', in L. Carmichael (ed.), *Manual of Child Psychology*, New York: Wiley, 1954

8 A. Ambrose, 'The Comparative Approach to Early Child Development: the data of ethology', in E. Miller (ed.), *Foundation of Child Psychiatry*, Oxford: Pergamon, 1968

9 Ambrose, op. cit.

10 H.F. Harlow, 'Development of affection in primates', in E.L. Bliss (ed.), *Roots of Behavior*, New York: Harper, 1962

11 D.S. Lehoman, R.A. Hinde, and W. Shaw (eds.), 'Problems of behavioral studies in the newborn', *Advances in the Study of Behavior*, New York: Academic Press, 1965

12 Aiden MacFarlane, *The Psychology of Childbirth*, London: Fontana/Open Books, 1977

13 Ambrose, op. cit.

14 N. Newton, D. Peeler, and C. Rawlins, 'Effect of lactation on maternal behavior in mice with comparative data on humans', *Journal of Reproductive Medicine*, 1, 1968

15 M.H. Klaus, J.H. Kennell, N. Plumb and S. Zuehlke, 'Human maternal behavior at the first contact with her young', *Pediatrics*, 46, 1970

16 MacFarlane, op. cit.

17 H.F. Harlow, 'The maternal affectional system', in B.F. Foss (ed.), *Determinants of Infant Behaviour*, London: Methuen, 1963

18 N. Tinbergen, 'Social releasers and the experimental method required for their study', *Wilson Bulletin*, 60, 1948

19 P.H. Wolff, 'Observations on the early development of smiling', in B.F. Foss, op. cit.

20 William N. Stephens, *The Family in Cross-cultural Perspective*, New York: Holt, Reinhart and Winston, 1963

21 Joan Raphael-Leff, *Psychological Processes of Childbearing*, London: Chapman and Hall, 1991

22 A.M. Lucas, *Women in the Middle Ages*, New York: Harvester Press, 1983

23 Laurel Thatcher Ulrich, *A Midwife's Tale: The Life of Martha Ballard*, New York: Knopf, 1990

24 Ibid.

25 R.R. Williams, 'Cultural Structuring of Tactile Experience in a Borneo Society', *American Anthropologist*, 68, 1966

26 Carolyn Niethammer, *Daughters of the Earth: The Lives and Legends of American Indian Women*, London: Collier Macmillan, 1977

27 J. Oakley, 'Gypsy women: Models in conflict', in S. Ardener (ed.), *Perceiving Women*, London: J.M. Dent, 1975

28 Ritsuko Toda (ed.), *Childbirth in Japan*, Tokyo: Birth International, 1990

29 G.L. Hundt, 'Ethnicity, class and gender in post-partum health care to Negev Bedouin Arab women and children in Israel', doctoral thesis, 1989

30 C. Laderman, *Wives and Midwives: Childbirth and Nutrition in Rural Malaysia*, Berkeley: University of California Press, 1983

31 S. Cosminsky, 'Childbirth and change: A Guatemalan study', in C.P. MacCormack (ed.), *Ethnography of Fertility and Birth*, London: Academic Press, 1982

32 N. Fuller and B. Jordan, 'Maya women and the end of the birthing period: post-partum massage and binding in Yucatan, Mexico', paper presented at Conference on Women in Anthropology, California State University, Sacramento, 1979

33 P.A. Rajadhon, *Some Traditions of the Thai*, Bangkok: Thai Inter-Religious Commission for Development and Sathirakoses Nagapradipa Foundation, 1987

34 Cosminsky, op. cit.

35 Laderman, op. cit., pp.178–9

36 C. Laderman, 'Taming the wind of desire', *Asia*, 2(5), 1980, pp.34–9; C. Laderman, *Wives and Midwives: Childbirth and Nutrition in Rural Malaysia*, Berkeley: University of California Press, 1983

37 Clare Claydon, personal communication

38 Klaus et al., op. cit.

39 W.H. Liston and H.J. Campbell, 'Dangers of oxytocin-induced labour to fetuses', *British Medical Journal*, 3, 1974, pp.606–7

40 Ibid.

41 M. Richards, 'The one-day-old deprived child', *New Scientist*, 61, 1974

42 Sheila Kitzinger, *Some Women's Experiences of Induced Labour*, London: National Childbirth Trust, 2nd edition, 1978

43 T. Berry Brazelton, 'The effects of prenatal drugs on the behavior of the neonate', *American Journal of Psychiatry*, 126, 1973, pp.1261–6

44 C. Laderman et al., 'Maternal, psychological and physiological correlates of fetal newborn health status', *American Journal of Obstetrics and Gynecology*, 139, 8, 1981, p.956

Chapter 11

1 Nawal El Saadawi, *The Hidden Face of Eve*, London: Zed Books, 1980

2 Alex Comfort, *The Joy of Sex*, New York: Simon and Schuster, 1972

3 Sara Maitland, in Stephanie Dowrick and Sybil Grundberg (eds.), *Why Children?*, London: Women's Press, 1980

4 K.S. Robson and H.A. Moss, 'Patterns and determinants of maternal attachment', *Journal of Pediatrics*, 77, 1970, pp.85–97

5 Joan Raphael-Leff, *Psychological Processes of Childbearing*, London: Chapman and Hall, 1991

6 H. Feldman, 'Development of the Husband-Wife Relationship: A Research Report', Ithaca, NY: Cornell University mimeograph, 1964

7 R. Firth, J. Hubert and A. Forge, *Families and Their Relatives: Kinship in a Middle-Class Sector of London*, London: Routledge & Kegan Paul, 1970

8 Colin M. Turnbull, *The Mountain People*, New York: Simon & Schuster, 1973

9 Sheila Kitzinger, *The Crying Baby*, Harmondsworth: Penguin, 1989

10 P.M. Crittenden, 'Distorted patterns of relationships in maltreating families: the role of internal representational models', *Journal of Reproductive and Infant Psychology*, 6, 1988, pp.183–200

11 F.P. Rivara, 'Physical abuse in children under two: a study of therapeutic outcome', *Child Abuse and Neglect*, 9, 1985, pp.81–7

Chapter 12

1 D. Nagbrahman and Sambrani Shreekant, 'Women's drudgery in firewood collection', *Economic and Political Weekly*, 1–8 January 1983

2 D. Taylor, 'Women: A World Report', *New Internationalist*, London: Methuen, 1985

3 Irene Dankelman and Joan Davidson, *Women and Environment in the Third World: Alliance for the Future*, London: Earthscan Publications, with the International Union for Conservation of Nature and Natural Resources, 1988

4 Patrick C. Fleuret and Anne Fleuret, 'Fuelwood use in a peasant community: A Tanzanian Case Study', *Journal of Development Areas*, April 1978

5 T.S. Ashton, *The Industrial Revolution*, Oxford: Oxford University Press, 1968

6 L.M.S., 'Economy', *The British Mothers' Magazine*, April 1855

7 E. Clark, 'Woman's Life – Childhood and Girlhood', *Cassell's Family Magazine*, 1887

8 Anonymous, 'Phases of a woman's life – wifehood and motherhood', *Cassell's Family Magazine*, 1887

9 Sandra Scarr, *Mother Care/Other Care*, New York: Basic Books, 1984

10 J. Stuart Blackie, 'A man's thoughts about women', *Cassell's Family Magazine*, May 1887

11 Mrs Caddy, *Household Organisation*, London: (publisher's name not available), 1877

12 Stuart Blackie, op. cit.

13 Ibid.

14 Mrs Baines, letter to *British Medical Journal*, 2 February 1861; G. Greaves, 'Observations on some of the causes of infanticide', *Transactions of the Manchester Statistical Society* 1862–3; Leader, *British Medical Journal*, 19 June 1869

15 Stuart Blackie; op. cit.

16 Sandra Scarr, op. cit.

17 D. Riley, *War in the Nursery: Theories of the Child and Mother*, London: Virago, 1983

18 Her Majesty's Stationery Office, *Social Trends*, 21, 1991

19 T. Greenhalgh, 'The collapse of the conventional career', *British Medical Journal*, 302, 1990, p.491

20 Ibid.

21 Marion Kozak, (ed.), *Daycare for Kids: A Parents' Survival Guide*, London: Daycare Trust, 1990. A copy of this paper can be obtained by sending an s.a.e. to Daycare Trust, Wesley House, 4 Wide Court, London, WC2B 5AU

22 Helena Kennedy, in Katherine Gieve (ed.), *Balancing Acts: On Being a Mother*, London: Virago, 1989

23 Jean Hampton, letter to *Observer*, 19 August 1990

24 P. Clough, 'Dreaming of a Return to the Kitchen Sink', *Independent*, 2 July 1990

25 L. Rimmer (from the Family Policy Studies Centre), 'Poverty – A Crisis for Babies', speech given at the Maternity Alliance Conference, April 1985

26 C. Bois, 'I'm a domestic engineer dear – what are you?', *New Generation*, June 1990

27 J. McLoughlin, 'Life: Is the price right?', *The Financial Times*, 1990

28 J. Brannen and P. Moss, *Managing Mothers: Dual Earner Households After Maternity Leave*, London: Unwin Hyman, 1990

29 D.W. Winnicott, *The Child, the Family and the Outside World*, Harmondsworth: Penguin, 1964

30 John Bowlby, *Child Care and the Growth of Love*, Harmondsworth: Penguin, 1953

31 Y. Alibhai, 'Trouble and strife', *New Statesman and Society*, 1, 24, 1988

32 C. Wiseman, 'A Day in the Life of . . . ', *The Sunday Times Colour Supplement*, 1991

33 *Independent*, 9 April 1990

34 Arlie Hochschild, *The Second Shift*, London: Viking, 1989

35 Office of the Status of Women, *Juggling Time: How Australian Families Use Time*, Department of the Prime Minister and Cabinet, Commonwealth of Australia, 1991

36 Rosaleen Croghan, 'First Time Mothers' Accounts of Inequality in the Division of Labour', *Feminism and Psychology*, 1(2), 1991, pp.221–46

37 Ibid.

38 Pat Mainardi, 'The Politics of Housework', in R. Morgan (ed.), *Sisterhood is Powerful*, New York: Vintage, 1970

Photographic Credits

The photographs which appear in this book are copyrighted as follows:

page x: © Roz Laurie
page 14: © Marcia May
page 16: © Nancy Durrell McKenna
page 32: © Marcia May
page 46: © Marcia May
page 58: © Marcia May
page 62: © Sally and Richard Greenhill
page 72: © Marcia May
page 90: © Nancy Durrell McKenna
page 120: © Rachel Hirsch
page 134: © Sally and Richard Greenhill
page 158: © Uwe Kitzinger
page 184: © Nancy Durrell McKenna
page 206: © Klaus-Otto Hundt
page 229: © Försakringskasseförbundet
page 230: © Sally and Richard Greenhill

Index

251

252

255